DAY HIKER'S GUIDE
TO SOUTHERN CALIFORNIA II

Cover photo: San Rafael Wilderness, by David Muench

Book design and cartography by Susan Kuromiya

ACKNOWLEDGMENTS

For their expertise in trails, natural history, history and eco-politics, I'd like to thank Ruth Kilday of the Santa Monica Mountains Conservancy, master trail builder Ron Webster, Glen Owens and the Big Santa Anita Historical Society, John Bailey and Harold Johnson of the U.S. Bureau of Land Management, Ernie Max well. guardian of the San Jacinto Mountains, Sheila Ortega of the Los Angeles County Department of Parks and Recreation. A tip of the hat also to the rangers of Los Padres, San Bernardino and Angeles National Forests; the rangers of Point Mugu, Leo Carrillo, Malibu Creek, Topanga, Mount San Jacinto, Torrey Pines, Mitchell Caverns State Parks. Thanks also to Noel Young, Capra Press editor-in-chief, who guided me over the perilous paths of publishing and whose skill and enthusiasm made possible the first edition of this book.

Cristine Agyrakis, pp. 181; Avalon Chamber of Commerce, pp. 180; Brand Library, p. 110 ; Calif. Dept. of Parks and Recreation, pp. 248; David Crane / Los Angeles Daily News, pp. 90; First American Title Insurance Company, pp. 186,191, 197, 199; Jon Foster, pp. 168; Susan L. Goldman / Ojai Valley News, pp. 43; Linda M. Hardie-Scott, pp. 77; James Kenney, pp. 74, 87; Bob LeRoy, pp. 46, 61; Living Desert Reserve, pp. 267; Ernie Maxwell, pp. 233; John McKinney, pp. 25, 28, 33, 35, 49, 55, 62, 67, 72, 83, 85, 104, 107, 117, 123, 126, 129, 130, 132, 134, 153, 160, 164, 183, 189, 223, 240, 243, 247, 250, 253, 256, 260, 265; Roy Murphy, pp. 8, 140, 158, 166, 206, 226; Orange County Dept. of Parks and Recreation, pp. 200, 205; Palm Springs Aerial Tramway, pp. 234; Ramona Pageant Association, pp. 239; San Bernardino County Museum, pp. 212; Santa Barbara County Parks Department, pp. 51; United States Bureau of Land Management, pp. 18, 255; United States Forest Service, pp. 31, 143, 149; David M. Werk, pp. 114, 218

Published by
Olympus Press
P.O. Box 2397
Santa Barbara, CA 93120

DAY HIKER'S GUIDE
TO SOUTHERN CALIFORNIA II

John McKinney

Olympus Press
SANTA BARBARA, CALIFORNIA

CONTENTS

A Word About Volume II

More *Day Hikes? Son of Day Hiker's Guide? Bride of Volume I?*
I must confess that when I completed *Day Hiker's Guide to Southern California*, I had no thought of compiling a second volume. Readers of the first book and my *Los Angeles Times* "Day Hike" column, as well as park rangers throughout the Southland, convinced me otherwise.

The first book was the author's choice of hikes and destinations. In a way, this second volume represents your choice. Volume II visits many of the same geographical areas as Volume I, but takes different trails to different destinations.

Experienced hikers will recognize some familiar terrain—Mounts Baldy, Gorgonio and San Jacinto—but will find some new trails to travel. Newcomers to the Southland, and less-experienced hikers will find helpful introductions to the land—the major mountain ranges, the desert and the coastline.

Particular to this volume are chapters covering the parks and preserves of the San Fernando Valley, Orange County and the East Mojave Desert.

I hope that in some small way this book, like its predecessor, besides suggesting some enjoyable hikes, contributes to a better understanding of the unique and fragile ecology of Southern California.

—J.M.

As Their Land Is

After all anybody is as their land and air is.
Anybody is as the sky is low or high,
the air heavy or clear
and anybody is as there is wind or no wind there.
Is that which makes them and the arts they make
and the work they do and the way they eat
and the way they drink
and the way they learn and everything.

— Gertrude Stein

Chapter 1

UNDERSTANDING DAY HIKING
IN SOUTHERN CALIFORNIA

THE LAND WE CALL SOUTHERN CALIFORNIA is an island, ecologically isolated from the rest of the continent by a combination of geographic and climatic factors. Helen Hunt Jackson once said of Southern California: "It's an island on the land." Carey McWilliams popularized the phrase in his definitive history of the region, *Southern California: An Island on the Land*. The land's island nature is apparent when you enter it from the north or east. When you round Point Conception and the north-south orientation of California becomes east-west, it is obvious that you have entered a unique geographical province. If you come to Southern California from the east through Cajon Pass or San Gorgonio Pass, the change is immediately evident. Light is softer, the climate more temperate.

The land includes seven counties: Santa Barbara, Ventura, Los Angeles, Orange, Riverside and San Diego. Usually, only those parts of San Bernardino, Riverside and San Diego Counties "west of the mountains" are in Southern California, but a case can be made for including all of them and adding Imperial County as well. Some boosters insist Southern California's northern boundary is San Luis Obispo or even the Monterey County line, but geographically and ecologically it's at Point Conception. Southern California is the land south of the Transverse Range, which knifes across California toward the Pacific, just north of Santa Barbara.

Southern California is protected from the Mojave Desert by the San Bernardino and San Gabriel Mountain Ranges on the east and walled off from the San Joaquin Valley by other Transverse Ranges. The lowlands are covered with alluvial fans formed by earth washed down from the mountains. The coastal plain is "watered" by some of the driest rivers in the west: the Los Angeles, Mojave, San Gabriel and Santa Ana. Mark Twain may have been joking about them when he said he'd fallen into a California river and "come out all dusty."

Compass directions can be confusing to both newcomers and oldtimers. "Up the coast" in other parts of the world is usually taken to mean north, but it's not north in Southern California. To travel north from L.A., you head directly into the Mojave Desert, crossing out east-west trending mountains in the process. If you traveled a straight line, as the crow flies, from San Bernardino to Santa Barbara, you would travel 137 miles west and only 27 miles north.

Carey McWilliams has suggested that "The analyst of California is like a navigator who is trying to chart a course in a storm: the instruments will not work; the landmarks are lost; and the maps make little sense." California may be geographically cockeyed and Southern California even more so, but we day hikers before heading for the hills, ought to get our bearings. We need to find a few landmarks and consult a map. Orienting yourself to Southern California isn't *that* difficult. Try this:

SOUTHERN CALIFORNIA GEOGRAPHY MADE EASY

Get yourself an Auto Club map of California or one of those that gas stations used to give out free. Spread it on the floor. (This is hands-on learning, so if you have small hands, you might want to borrow a friend with larger ones.) Put your thumb on Santa Barbara, your right pinkie on San Diego and spread your fingers in as wide a fan as you can manage. One of the first things you may notice is that your palm covers the L.A. Basin. Keep your palm firmly pressed down on L.A. to keep it from spreading into the wilderness. Look at your thumb. Above it is Point Conception, the northernmost point of Southern California. Above Santa Barbara are the Santa Ynez Mountains and beyond are those parts of the Los Padres National Forest we call the Santa Barbara Backcountry. Along your index finger are the San Gabriel Mountains and the Angeles National Forest. (Careful! Don't get your finger pinched in the San Andreas Fault.) Your middle finger is in the San Bernardino Mountains. Near the eastern terminus of this range is Mount San Gorgonio, the highest peak in Southern California. Between your middle and ring fingers, paralleling the coast in Orange Country are the Santa Ana Mountains, protected by the Cleveland National Forest. At the tip of your ring finger at the north end of Anza-Borrego Desert State Park lie the Santa Rosa Mountains. Take note of the Colorado Desert and farther to the north, the vast Mojave Desert. Due east from your pinkie is the southern part of the the Cleveland National Forest, as well as the Palomar and Cuyamaca Mountain Ranges. Now that you're oriented, raise that right hand of yours and pledge to preserve, protect, and enjoy these places.

12

HOW TO USE THIS BOOK

First decide where you want to hike. A palm oasis? An alpine meadow? A deserted beach? Consult our Southland map. Pick a trail number in your geographical area of interest. Once you've selected a number, turn to the corresponding hike description in the main body of the book. Unsure of what to expect in the Santa Monica, San Bernardino or San Gabriel Mountains? Read the appropriate chapter introductions.

There are 80 trails in this guide. Add the suggested options and you can design about 200 different hikes. Beneath the name of the trail is the trailhead and one or more destinations. Every day hike in this book has a soul and a goal. You provide the soul; this guide will provide the goals. Let's face it, we're a goal-oriented society and we hikers are no exception. We hike for majestic views or for the best fishing spot, not just to be out there. Some day hikers collect peaks the way motorhome drivers collect decals.

MILEAGE, expressed in **ROUNDTRIP** figures, follows each destination. The hikes in this guide range from 2 to 20 miles, with the majority in the 5 to 10 mile range. **GAIN** or **LOSS** in elevation follows the mileage. In matching a hike to your ability, you'll want to consider both mileage and elevation as well as condition of the trail, terrain, and season. Hot, exposed chaparral or miles of boulder-hopping can make a short hike seem long. I haven't graded the *Day Hiker's Guide* as to difficulty because I believe day hikers vary too much in physical condition to make such an evaluation. However, you may wish to use the following guideline: A hike suitable for beginners and children would be less than 5 miles with an elevation gain of less than 700-800'. A moderate hike is considered a hike in the 5 to 10 mile range, with under a 2,000' elevation gain. You should be reasonably fit for these. Preteens sometimes find the going difficult. Hike over 10 miles and those with more than a 2,000' gain are for experienced hikers in top form.

SEASON is the next item to consider. Although Southern California is one of the few places in the country that offers four-season hiking. You can hike some of the trails in this guide all of the time, all of the trails some of the time, but not all of the trails all of the time. Season recommendations are based partly on hiker comfort and partly on legal restrictions. Those recommendations based on comfort can sometimes be disregarded by intrepid mountaineers. You can, if you so desire, hike to the top of Mount San Jacinto in the dead of winter, but you better bring snowshoes. It's possible to hike in the California Desert in the middle of summer, but you'd better bring a water truck or a camel. Seasonal recommendations based on legal restrictions must not be disregarded. Closure for fire season is the chief restriction in certain state park and national forest areas. Length of

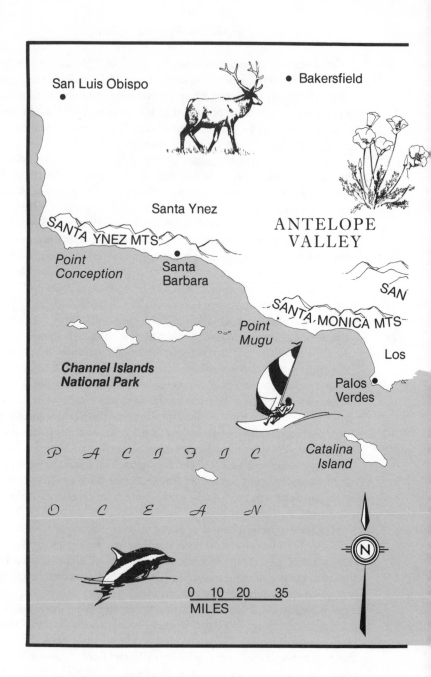

San Luis Obispo

Bakersfield

Santa Ynez

ANTELOPE
VALLEY

SANTA YNEZ MTS

Point
Conception

Santa
Barbara

SAN

SANTA MONICA MTS

Point
Mugu

Los

Channel Islands
National Park

Palos
Verdes

PACIFIC

Catalina
Island

OCEAN

N

0 10 20   35
MILES

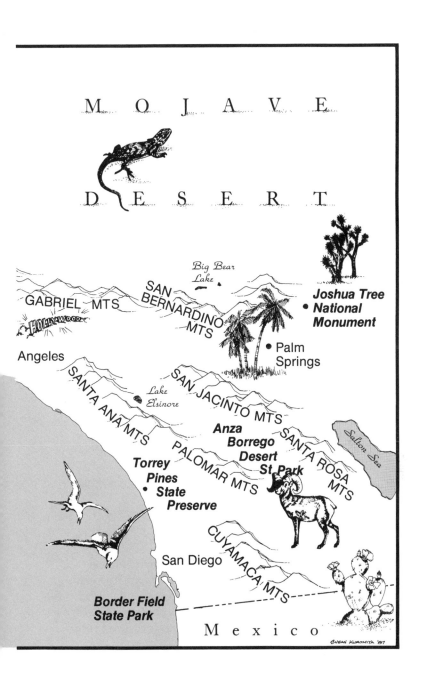

MOJAVE

DESERT

GABRIEL MTS

HOLLYWOOD

Angeles

SAN BERNARDINO MTS

Big Bear Lake

Joshua Tree
• National
Monument

• Palm
Springs

SANTA ANA MTS

Lake Elsinore

SAN JACINTO MTS

Anza
Borrego
Desert
St Park

SANTA ROSA MTS

Salton Sea

Torrey
Pines
• State
Preserve

PALOMAR MTS

San Diego

CUYAMACA MTS

Border Field
State Park

Mexico

SUSAN KUROMIYA '87

15

closure varies from area to area, depending on the year's rainfall. Some sections of national forest close automatically on July 1, and do not open up again until after the first heavy rain of winter. Others restrict entry for only a few weeks at the end of summer. A few trails in this guide may be impassable in winter and spring due to high water. Relevant fire and flood information has been noted below the season recommendation.

An introduction to each hike will describe what you'll see along the trail: plants, animals, panoramic views. You'll also learn about the geologic and human history of the region. This section will also tell you to "bring your fishing pole" or "check a tide table."

DIRECTIONS TO TRAILHEAD take you from the nearest major highway to trailhead parking. Alternative transportation, via bus or train where practical, has been suggested. For trails having two desirable trailheads, directions to each are given. A few trails can be hiked one way, with the possibility of a car shuttle. Suggested car shuttle points are noted. You may notice a slight L.A. bias to the directions when you proceed "up" to Santa Barbara or "down" to San Diego. For the sake of clarity and orientation, I've chosen downtown L.A. as a reference point. It seems to me; L.A. is as good a place to leave from as any. My apologies to Chula Vista, Pomona and Oxnard.

After the directions to the trailhead, you'll read a description of **THE HIKE**. Important junctions and major sights are pointed out, but I've left you to discover the multitude of little things that make a hike an adventure.

It's not important that you follow the trail exactly as I've described it. Whether you hike the length of a trail and every one of its options, or snooze under the first sycamore you find, is your decision and no one else's. There's enough regimentation in your life without me telling you where you must hike. This guide is for you to plan your day in the backcountry. Don't stick your nose in this guide; stick it in some of the wildflowers.

ON THE TRAIL

Choose the pace that's best for you. Rest once an hour for a few minutes. To keep your momentum and to avoid stiffness, several shorter rest periods are better than one long one. Set a steady pace, one you can keep up all day. Wear a watch, not because you have an appointment with a waterfall and you have to be punctual, but because a watch gives you some idea of pace and helps you get back to the trailhead before dark.

Hiking uphill takes energy. Hiking 2 miles an hour up a 10 percent grade requires as much energy as hiking 4 miles an hour on level trail. Climbing can be especially difficult in high altitude. Altitude sickness affects some hikers at about 8,000 feet. Only a few hikes in this guide are above this elevation. Altitude can cause discomfort—shortness of breath, headache and nausea above 5,000 feet.

Hiking alone or with company is strictly a matter of personal preference. Most rangers warn you never to hike alone, primarily because they think most hikers are inexperienced, uncoordinated or both, and they hate to make rescues. Having two or three in your party is a definite advantage if something goes wrong; someone can go for help. Hiking with a group is a good idea for first-time hikers. Most inexperienced hikers are uncomfortable going solo. Alas, backcountry travelers are not always immune from urban attitudes, stresses and crimes. While most of our Southland parks and preserves are far safer than our urban environment, hikers—particularly women hikers—must be aware that unsavory characters are not unknown on the trail.

Your "street smarts" coupled with your trail sense are two keys to avoiding trouble.

Sometimes, after a few hikes, a craving for solitude develops—by which time you should be able to take care of yourself on the trail. There's a lot to be said for solitary hiking, as the writings of Thoreau, Whitman and Muir would seem to indicate.

DAY HIKING THROUGH THE SEASONS

Many have sung praises of Southern California's Mediterranean climate. Relentless sunshine, winter and summer, is how the climate is usually stereotyped. But the semi-tropical stereotype holds true only in coastal regions and only at certain times of the year. There is nothing Mediterranean about the climate of the Mojave Desert or the San Jacinto high country. In Southern California's backcountry, seasons arrive with clarity and distinction. Day hikers can find trails that are "in season" in every month of the year.

WINTER brings snow to mountains in the Angeles, San Bernardino and Los Padres National Forests. Rain visits the coastal lowlands. Deciduous trees and shrubs lose their leaves. Some animals hibernate or become torpid. But winter doesn't mean an end to all of nature's activities in Southern California, particularly in the lowland valleys and deserts. January is a fine time to take a beach hike, to visit shores laid bare by minus tides, or to see what treasure winter storms have cast ashore. In February, the desert begins to bloom. February and March, last of the winter months, are often looked upon by many Southern Californians as the first months of spring. Day hikers are guaranteed solitude in these months. High country trails are covered with snow and those on the lower slopes are muddy going.

Wildflowers, East Mojave National Scenic Area

SPRING comes early to Southern California. Even the chaparral, so dull gray in other seasons, looks inviting. Ceanothus covers the lower slopes of the Santa Barbara Backcountry, the Santa Monica Mountains and San Gabriel Mountains with its dainty white and blue blossoms. Yellow violets and wild peony bloom amidst the chaparral. In March, the giant coreopsis on Anacapa Island grows wild. As spring temperatures increase, flowers in the hotter Colorado Desert diminish, but those in the higher Mojave Desert arrive with a flourish. In June, the flower show moves to the high country of the Transverse Ranges. Lemon lilies appear streamside and lupine everywhere. Flocks of birds go about the business of building nests, laying eggs, raising young.

In SUMMER, snowmelt-swollen creeks water emerald-green meadows. Scarlet-stemmed snow plant emerges in the pine forests. By August, even the highest peaks have lost their mantle of snow and day hikers can stand atop their summits and sign the hiker's register. A beach hike in the middle of summer is a pleasure. With the sun on your back, the surf at your feet and miles of beach in front of you, summer seems endless.

AUTUMN has its critics and its fans. Some say there's little use for a day that begins with frost, becomes hot enough to sunburn your nose by noon, and has you shivering by sunset. Wiser heads, those attached to day hikers no doubt, believe autumn is the best of all seasons. The high country is crisp, but still inviting and desert washes have cooled. Autumn colors oaks, dogwoods, willows and sycamores. There's enough color change to satisfy even the most homesick New Englander.

DAY HIKING HINTS

Many day hikes require little more equipment than comfortable shoes, yet hikers often overburden themselves with such nonessentials as hunting knives, hatchets, and propane stoves. The idea with equipment is to take only what you need. You want to get so comfortable with your equipment that you don't think about it; what little you need is on your back and what you don't need is far away.

FOOTWEAR: Day hiking begins and ends with the feet. You've no doubt seen hikers wearing everything from old sneakers to World War II combat boots. For the last two decades, lug-soled boots have been considered mandatory, but if you're carrying a day pack over easy terrain you don't need a heavy pair of boots. Running shoes can serve to get you started. But if you do much hiking over rough terrain, a good pair of boots is necessary and well worth the money. A lightweight pair with a Vibram sole will do nicely. Don't buy more boot than you need. Blisters can ruin any hike, so be sure to break-in your boots before you hit the trail. Walk around town and be sure your feet develop a callous indifference to your boots.

A number of fine walking shoes and running shoe/hiking boot combinations on the market will give you miles of comfortable walking.

CLOTHING: You have most of what you need lying around the house.

- A T-shirt with a cotton shirt that buttons gives you lots of temperature regulating possibilities. Add a wool shirt and a windbreaker with a hood and you'll be protected against sudden changes in temperatures.

- Shorts are useful much of the year in Southern California. Test your shorts to make sure they're not too tight. Step up on a chair and if they pull around the groin, butt or thigh, they're too tight.

- For cooler days or walking through brush, a sturdy pair of long pants is necessary.

- Hats prevent the brain from frying and protect from heat loss when it is cold.

19

- Sunglasses are a big help when walking over snow or on hot, exposed slopes. Make sure you buy a pair that provides UV protection.

- Ponchos—a cheap vinyl one is okay unless you walk through brush. The Boy Scout ones aren't too bad. Some of the new breathable, high-tech fabric laminates are superb, but expensive.

FOOD: On a day hike, weight is no problem, so you can pack whatever you wish. Remember to pack out what you pack in. The day you hike is not the day to diet. There's a lot of calorie burning on a hike and quite an energy cost. You'll need all your strength, particularly on steep grades. Gorp, or trail mix, with fruit, nuts, raisins, and M&M's is good high-octane fuel. A sandwich, fruit and cookies make a good lunch. Sourdough bread, a fine cheese and a bottle of chablis is also nice. Avoid a big lunch. Exertion after a big lunch sets up a competition between your stomach and your legs and your legs lose, leading to weakness and indigestion.

WATER: It's still possible to drink from some backcountry streams and springs without ill effect, but each individual water source should be carefully scrutinized. Many hikers assume water is pure and 48 hours later have a queasy feeling that tells them that their assumption was wrong. Water may harbor the organism *Giardia Lamblia*, one of the causes of "traveler's diarrhea." When you approach that stream, Sierra cup in hand, think about what may be upstream. A campground? Cows? High rushing mountain streams are usually safer than stagnant ponds. Bring purification tablets or a filter purification system and use them if you have the slightest doubt about water quality.

FIRST AID KIT: A standard kit supplement with an ace bandage in the event of hiker's knee or a sprained ankle. Take moleskin for blisters. Insect repellant won't stop mosquitos from buzzing around but it will inhibit their biting.

DAY PACK or "Summit Pack": A day pack is a soft frameless pack that attaches to your shoulders and sometimes includes a hip band or waist belt for support. A good one will last a lifetime. Those thin cotton or nylon bike bags or book bags won't hold up well. Shoulder pads are a nice feature in a day pack. You'll only be carrying five or ten pounds, but the pads are comfortable on a long hike. Get one with a tough covered zipper. Double-O rings slip and aren't the greatest shoulder strap adjusters. Get tabler buckles; they don't slip and they adjust quickly.

PRECAUTIONS

We still react in instinctive ways when we feel threatened by some aspect of the natural world. Don't let the few biters, stingers, and hazards mentioned make you apprehensive about going into the backcountry.

BLISTERS: There's nothing worse than walking on feet that burn like hot coals. To avoid blisters, make sure your boots fit properly. Keep pulling up your socks and see to it that they don't bunch up. Act quickly if you feel a blister develop. Cut a hole in moleskin a little larger than your red spot and stick it in place with the blister poking through the hole. The idea is to surround it so the boot can't get at it. (If you covered it you could irritate it further and you'd have to peel the tape off the blister. Ouch!) Some hikers put a double layer of tissue paper over the blister and tape the tissue in place with surgical tape. If you get a full grown blister, pop it with a clean needle inserted under the edge and apply antiseptic, put moleskin over the area.

Poison Oak

Effects of Poison Oak

POISON OAK: This infamous plant grows abundantly throughout Southern California mountains up to an elevation of 5,000 feet. It's a sneaky devil. It may lurk under other shrubs or take the form of a vine and climb up an oak tree. The leaves are one to four inches long and glossy, as if waxed.

All parts of the plant at all times of the year contain poisonous sap that can severely blister skin and mucous membranes. Its sap is most toxic during spring and summer. In fall, poison oak is particularly conspicuous; its leaves turn to flaming crimson or orange. However, its color change is more a response to heat and dryness than season; its "fall color" can occur anytime in Southern California. Leaves on some plants can be turning yellow or red while plants in most spots are putting out green leaves. In winter, poison oak is naked, its stalks blending into the dull hue of the forest.

21

Contrary to popular belief, you can't catch it from someone else's rash, nor from oozing blisters, but petting an animal or handling a piece of clothing that carries it can make you a victim.

There are a multitude of remedies. Perhaps most common is the regular application of calamine lotion or cortisone cream. If you're particularly sensitive to poison oak, always wash down thoroughly immediately after a hike with cold water and a basic soap such as laundry detergent. Launder your hiking clothing separately as soon as possible. A dip in the ocean can help; a few tablespoons of baking soda added to a tub of lukewarm water calms the itchies as well. You organic types will probably want to pick some mugwort, an effective panacea. Its fresh juice applied directly to the pained area relieves itching.

RATTLESNAKES: Like typical Southern Californians, rattlesnakes take to the trail to enjoy the sunshine, so keep an eye out. Despite the common fear of rattlers, few people see them and rarely is anyone bitten. An estimated 300 yearly snake envenomations occur in the Southland. Only a small percentage of these bites cause serious injury.

The red diamond rattlesnake is found in coastal, hill and desert regions, the sidewinder and Western Diamondback in the desert, and the Southern Pacific rattler lives in coastal regions between Malibu and San Juan Capistrano and in inland areas like remote sections of Griffith Park.

If you've been bitten, remain calm. Check to be sure you've actually been envenomated. Look for swelling around the wound within five minutes. If it doesn't swell, you've probably escaped and may not require hospital treatment. If swelling and other symptoms occur—numbness around the lips or hairline, a metallic taste in the mouth or twitching facial muscles, it got you and you need immediate treatment.

Getting to a hospital emergency room is more important than any other first aid. Keep the site of the wounds as immobilized as possible and relax. Cutting and suction treatments are now medically out of vogue and advised only as a last resort if you're absolutely sure you can't get to a hospital within four hours.

BEES: More fatalities occur from allergic reaction to insect stings than from rattlesnake bites. People allergic to bee stings can get a desensitization shot and a specially equipped bee kit from an allergist.

TICKS: They're 1/4 to 1/2 inch long and about the same color as the ground, so they're hard to see. Ticks are usually picked up by brushing against low vegetation. When hiking in a tick area it's best to sit on rocks rather than fallen logs. Check your skin and clothing occasionally. You and your loved one can groom each other like monkeys at the zoo. If one is attached to the skin, it should be lifted off with a slow gentle pull. Before bathing, look for ticks on the body, particularly in the hair and pubic region.

GETTING LOST AND FOUND

No one expects to get lost in the Southern California backcountry. "After all," say novices, "the mountains aren't big and icy like the High Sierra and we're only out of the day and..." Even the experienced can get lost. Getting lost is usually the result of taking a "short cut" off an established trail. Danger is magnified if a hiker ventures out alone or fails to tell anyone locale and return time.

Try to avoid getting lost in the first place. Know your physical condition and don't overtax yourself. Check your boots and clothing. Be prepared for bad weather. Inquire about trail conditions. Allow plenty of time for your hike and allow even more for your return to the trailhead.

When you're on the trail, keep your eyes open. If you're hiking so fast that all you see is your boots, you're not attentive to passing terrain—its charms or its layout. STOP once in a while. Sniff wildflowers, splash your face in a spring. LISTEN. Maybe the trail is paralleling a stream. Listen to the sound of mountain water. On your left? On your right? Look up at that fire lookout on the nearby ridge. Are you heading toward it or away from it? LOOK AROUND. That's the best insurance against getting lost.

So you're *really* lost? Stay calm. Don't worry about food. It takes weeks to to starve to death. Besides, you've got that candy bar in your day pack. You have a canteen. And you have a poncho in case of rain. You're in no immediate danger, so don't run around in circles like a mindless chicken.

LOOK AROUND some more. Is there any familiar landmark in sight? Have you been gaining elevation or losing it? Where has the sun been shining? On your right cheek? Your back? Retrace your steps, if you can. Look for other footprints. If you're totally disoriented, keep walking laterally. Don't go deeper into the brush or woods. Go up slope to get a good view, but don't trek aimlessly here and there.

If it's near dark, get ready to spend the night. Don't try to find your way out in the dark. Don't worry. If you left your itinerary, your rescuers will begin looking for you in the morning. Try to stay warm by huddling against a tree or wrapping yourself in branches, pine needles or leaves. The universal distress signal is three visible or audible signals—three shouts or whistles, three shiny objects placed on a bare summit. Don't start a fire! You could start a major conflagration.

Relax and think of your next hike. Think of the most beautiful place you know—that creek of snowmelt gushing down from that stony mountain, a place where the fish bite and the mosquitos don't...You'll make it, don't worry.

TRAILS THEN AND NOW

The first Southern California trailmakers were wild animals, breaking down the brush as they journeyed to and from water. Indians used these ready-made trails and fashioned new ones for trade and travel. Indian trails rarely climbed via switchbacks; instead, they took the steepest and most direct route. The Spaniards blazed few new trails, contenting themselves with Indian paths.

The restless Americans were tireless trailmakers. They hurried into the mountains to dig for metals, to graze their cattle, to cut timber. They needed trails and they needed them right away. Trees were felled and brush was cleared. Gunpowder was rammed in holes drilled into rock and the most immoveable granite was blown to smithereens.

Fortunately for Southern California backcountry, mountaineering became popular before the backcountry was wrecked. Day hikers can thank nineteenth-century Englishmen for the "invention" of hiking. Between 1850 and 1870, Englishmen assaulted every Alp and established the lodge, the resort, and the picture postcard. Alpinism is what the English called their new sport. Americans on the East Coast imported alpinism, then brought it with them when they traveled west to Southern California. During the latter part of the nineteenth century, great tracts of land, stretching from San Bernardino to San Luis Obispo, were set aside as Timberland Reserves by the federal government. A flood of immigrants to Southern California and the few natives all headed into the timberland to enjoy the mountain life.

"Our Italy" and "Little Switzerland" are what tourist brochures called Southern California. Bragged one brochure of that era: "The Santa Monica Mountains provide the hiker a paradise. Incomparable scenic panoramas are to be had by those willing to spend the effort. The combination of mountains, oceans and valleys, provide awe-inspiring landscapes when viewed from the promontories."

The years between 1890 and 1930 were a wonderful time to be a Southern California day hiker. "The Great Hiking Era," historians would later call it. Residents of the L.A. Basin could take the electric red cars to the base of the San Gabriel Mountains and then hike trails up Arroyo Seco or Mount Wilson. The San Bernardino Mountains, the San Jacinto Mountains and the Santa Barbara Backcountry also experienced the clomp-clomp of hobnailed boots. Trail camps, fishing camps, and resorts were

Los Angeles Conservation Corps trail crew, La Tuna Canyon Trail

established in local mountains. Soon Southern California was crisscrossed with trails leading to these resorts and camps, and to the best fishing spots and the highest peaks.

But, alas, by 1930, Southern California took to wheels. As Southlanders learned to drive, they forgot how to hike. During the Depression, the CCC boys built a number of car campgrounds and highways into the mountains. Soon drive-in campgrounds and paved roads replaced trail camps and trails.

In the 1950s Southern California, perhaps realizing how auto-bound they had become, began rediscovering the joys of the local mountains. In the last three decades, hundreds of miles of trail have been overhauled and many more miles of new trail constructed. Today, thanks to local mountaineers, conservation organizations, and state and federal rangers, Southern California has more miles of trail than most states. There's a trail waiting to take you wherever you want to go.

MAPS

About one-half the hikes in this guide take place in one of the four Southern California national forests: Los Padres, Angeles, San Bernardino and Cleveland. Forest Service maps are available at ranger stations for a small fee. They're general maps, showing roads, rivers, trails and little else. You'll learn where the trailheads are located and where entry is restricted during the fire season. The Forest Service keeps its maps fairly up-to-date, so they're useful for checking out-of-date topographic maps.

25

Each route and trail in the national forest system has a route number. A route number might look like this: 2S21. Wooden signs, inscribed with the route number, are placed at some trailheads and at the intersection of trails to supplement other directional signs. The route numbers on your map usually correspond to the route numbers on the trail, but be careful because the Forest Service periodically changes the numbers.

Trails on Forest Service maps are drawn in red and black. Red trails are usually maintained and are in good shape. Black trails are infrequently maintained and their condition ranges from okay to faint.

Some hikers have a love affair with topographic maps. Those blue rivers, green woods and labyrinthine contour lines are...well, artistic. Topos show terrain in great detail and are the best way to prevent getting lost. If, for example, you know absolutely there's a road one mile to the west that runs north and south, it can be quite a comfort. Topos show trails, elevations, waterways, brush cover and improvements. Along with a compass, they're indispensable for cross-country travel.

Topos come in two scales: the 15' quadrangle and the 7 1/2' quadrangle. The 15' series is approximately 1 inch to 1 mile, and the contour interval (the gap between contour lines) is 80 feet. 7 1/2' series maps have a scale of 2 1/2 inches to a mile with a contour interval of 40 feet. For the day hiker, the 7 1/2' series is preferable. Most of the hikes in this guide utilize 7 1/2' topos. Topos can be bought at many sporting goods and mountaineering or camping stores.

BACKCOUNTRY COURTESY

• Leave your radio and tape player at home.

• Dogs, depending on the personality of the individual pooch, can be a disruption to hikers and native wildlife. Be warned, many state and county parks don't allow dogs, either on or off a leash.

• No smoking on trails

• Resist the urge to collect flowers, rocks or animals. It disrupts nature's balance and lessens the wilderness experience for future hikers.

• Litter detracts from even the most beautiful backcountry setting. If you packed it in, you can pack it out.

• You have a moral obligation to help a hiker in need. Give whatever first aid or comfort you can, and then hurry for help.

• Don't cut switchbacks.

DAY HIKING TO A NEW LAND ETHIC

In the Santa Ana Mountains, 200-year-old oaks are uprooted to make room for a suburb. The toppled oaks, their roots drying in the sun, provide mute testimony against a culture that is still searching for meaningful land ethic. Santa Ynez Canyon in the Santa Monica Mountains is suffering a similar fate. The canyon's sandstone walls have been blasted away and terraced for hundreds of luxury homes. What was to be the jewel of Topanga State Park is now a tract of asphalt and stucco.

Environmentally unsound construction is evident all over Southern California. The forces of *Cut & Fill and Grade & Pave* each year engulf more and more open space. There are still places that remain inviolate from the earthmover and the cement mixer, but these places grow fewer each year. As the late twentieth-century version of the good life creeps into Southern California's backcounty, it may be time to ask ourselves, "What color is paradise?"

I think it's green.

A change in our land ethic begins with a change in perception and a change in perception begins with you. It's not a difficult change to make; in fact, day hiking can provoke it. The change I'm suggesting requires only that you open your eyes a little wider and see the natural world from a different perspective.

Perception is a funny thing. Did you ever notice the change in pitch of a train whistle as it goes away from you? A nineteenth-century Austrian physicist, Christian Doppler, figured that sound waves varied with the relative velocity of the source and the observer. He applied his Doppler effect to light waves, as well. He saw that as the position of observer and light source change, the colors of light will shift. Day hikers can notice a Doppler effect of their own. Looking up at Mount San Gorgonio from the L.A. Basin, the hiker sees a snowy peak rising above the smog. Atop the mountain, the hiker looks down on a thick brown inversion layer blanketing the Southland. Quite a difference in views between the bottom of the Basin and the top of the mountain!

To day hike is to alter your perceptions, to see things in a new light. You see where you are and what you left behind, and you realize that the two are closer together than you had imagined. The distinction between "out there" and "right here" blurs; when that happens, you've become a conservationist. As a conservationist, you'll perceive that our boulevards, our wilderness, and we ourselves, are part of a fragile island. The future of the island depends on your perceptions.

Chapter 2

LOS PADRES NATIONAL FOREST
(Santa Barbara/ Ojai Backcountry)

That anybody should undertake a jaunt of hundred and fifty miles or so on foot for the pleasure of walking was unthinkable by the conventional Western mind; but I was already familiar with the strong points of tripping afoot and the lure of that splendid chain of mountains back of Santa Barbara...To motor there seemed out of key with such a land, though thousands do it; and besides, motoring is expensive. No, for me "The footpath way" with kodak over my shoulder, a pocketful of dried figs, and freedom from care.

—Charles Francis Saunders
Under the Sky in California (1913)

Santa Barbara Backcountry

WILDERNESS-BOUND TRAVELERS have a difficult task in deciding what to call the rugged mountain terrain arranged in a wide semi-circle around Santa Barbara. The padres left behind many names, but none of them fit. Elsewhere in Southern California, wilderness areas were named for the dominant mountain range in the vicinity. But there isn't a dominant mountain range behind Santa Barbara. Instead, there are a number of smaller ones with names like Pine and Topatopa, Sierra Madre and Santa Ynez. So when we go, where do we say we're going? Hikers sometimes say they're "going up to the Los Padres," an imprecise term at best, because the Los Padres National Forest includes lands as far north as Big Sur. Geologists aren't much help either. They call the land the "Transverse Ranges Geomorphic Province." Until popular use gives mapmakers new inspiration, the best name we have is the Santa Barbara Backcountry. Anyway, whatever this land of great gorges, sandstone cliffs and wide blue sky is called, it's guaranteed to please.

Most of the Santa Barbara Backcountry is in the Los Padres National Forest. Together, Santa Barbara and Ventura Counties have more than a million acres of national forest land. The backcountry is under the jurisdiction of three forest districts. The Ojai District includes Sespe and Piru Creeks as well as the Sespe Condor Sanctuary. The Santa Barbara District includes the Santa Ynez and San Rafael Mountain ranges. Mount Pinos District protects high conifer forest and includes the backcountry's highest peak, Mount Pinos (8,831 feet).

Archeological work in the backcountry has been extensive and has contributed much to our understanding of Chumash Indian culture. Several thousand years before the arrival of the Spanish, an estimated 10,000 to 18,000 Chumash lived in the coastal mountains from Malibu Canyon north to San Luis Obispo. Early Spanish explorers admired Chumash craftsmen, their fine houses and wood plank canoes. But the padres and soldiers of Spain who followed the explorers forced the Chumash to give up their ancient ways. Mission life broke the spirit of the Chumash and destroyed their culture. Living conditions were so desperate at the missions that a brief revolt took place at the Santa Barbara, Santa Ynez and La Purisima Missions in 1834. However, most Chumash were forcibly returned to the missions and suffered further enslavement.

Gold and grass brougl⋅ Americans to the Santa Barbara Backcountry. From the time of the early padres, rumors of the lost Los Padres Mine lured prospectors. There was enough gold in the hills and streams to keep prospectors prospecting until well into the twentieth century, but no one ever found a big bonanza or the lost mine. Other mining endeavors were

30

more profitable. Near the turn of the century, U.S. Borax Company mined borax from Lockwood Valley. Lush grass on the San Joaquin side of the backcountry provided grazing for thousands of cattle. Cattle have grazed these hills since the era of the Spanish land grants, and the hiker will often surprise a few cows.

Wildfire was a major problem in the late nineteenth and early twentieth centuries. Within a twenty-year period, much of the backcountry burned, prompting the federal government to realize that the land needed protection. For fire prevention and and watershed management purposes, large backcountry sections were set aside in the Pine Mountain and Zaca Lake Forest Reserve and the Santa Ynez Forest Reserve by decree of President Theodore Roosevelt. Two years later, the area became known as the Santa Barbara National Forest. In later years, acreage was added and subtracted, with the backcountry finally coming under the jurisdiction of the Los Padres National Forest in 1938.

More than 1,600 miles of trail range through the various districts of Los Padres National Forest. Nearly half of this trail system winds through the area we call the Santa Barbara Backcountry. Many of these trails have been used for centuries. Follow a trail to its end and you might be surprised at what you find. Remains of Indian camps may be found in the farthest reaches of the forest, and in remote meadows are remnants of early homesteads. Backcountry trails take you over some rough terrain—slopes are unstable and steep. Geologists classify more than half the land as "extremely sensitive" or "highly sensitive" to slippage. But what is agony for the homeowner is a delight for the hiker. As you day hike through this folded and fractured land, you might conclude that the backcountry was made for hiking, not settling.

1

Davy Brown Trail

Davy Brown Camp to Harry Roberts Cabin
   3 1/2 miles round trip; 900-foot elevation gain
Davy Brown Camp to Figueroa Mt. Rd.
   6 1/4 miles round trip; 1,700-foot elevation gain
Davy Brown Camp to Figueroa Mt. Lookout
   7 1/2 miles round trip; 2,400-foot elevation gain

Figueroa Mountain, located in Los Padres National Forest 25 air miles behind Santa Barbara, is one of the most botanically intriguing areas in Southern California. The mountain's upper slopes are forested with Coulter pine, yellow pine and big cone spruce. Spring wildflower displays on the lower slopes are often exceptional. Among the more common roadside and trailside flowers are fiddleneck, Johnny jump-ups, shooting stars, lupine and cream cups.

Tree-lovers will find a variety of arboreal companions, including large specimens of California bay laurel and big leaf maple, and picturesque coastal, valley and blue oaks. At lower elevations are abundant digger pine. Its distinguishing features are long needles in bunches of three and the forking broom-like appearance of its trunk. The pines are named for a tribe of Indians in California's gold country, who were disparagingly called "diggers" by the Forty-Niners.

On higher slopes grows another three-needled pine—the yellow pine. It's a tall, regal tree with a reddish bark that looks fashioned of rectangular mosaic tiles. And yet another three-needled pine is the Coulter, which produces huge cones, the largest and heaviest of any native conifer.

One good way to explore the mountain's flora and colorful history is to take a hike on Davy Brown Trail, which acends cool, moist Fir Canyon, climbs to the headwaters of Davy Brown Creek and visits the Forest Service fire lookout atop 4,528-foot Figueroa Mountain. The mountain honors Jose Figueroa, Mexican governor of California from 1833 to 1835. Anyone who climbs to the mountain's lookout, where there are grand views of the San Rafael Wilderness, Santa Ynez Valley, Point Conception and the Channel Islands, will agree that having such a mountain take your name is indeed an honor.

The trail, as well as a camp and a creek, is named for William S. (Davy) Brown who kept a cabin here during his retirement years, 1880 to 1895. Born in Ireland in 1800, Brown was 80 years old by the time he arrived in the Santa Barbara Backcountry with his two white mules, Jinks and

Tommy. If even half of the accounts of his early years are true, he certainly had an adventurous life. He was reportedly an African slave trader, Indian fighter, hunter with Kit Carson and meat supplier for California '49ers. Though he was considered a recluse, many said that he welcomed visitors into his humble cabin. Davy Brown died in the sleepy Santa Barbara County town of Guadalupe in 1898, having fully experienced the 19th Century. His 16 by 20- foot cabin burned in a 1930 fire and is now the site of Davy Brown Camp.

Directions to trailhead: From Highway 101 in Santa Barbara, exit on Highway 154 and proceed 14 miles over Cachuma Pass and past Lake Cachuma to Armour Ranch Road. Turn right and drive 1.3 miles to Happy Canyon Road. Make a right and wind 14 pleasant miles to Cachuma Saddle Station. To reach the lower Davy Brown trailhead, you'll bear right at the saddle onto Sunset Valley Road and proceed 5 miles to Davy Brown Campground. To reach upper Davy Brown trailhead, bear left at Cachuma Saddle Station onto Figueroa Mountain Road and drive 5 miles to a turnout and signed Davy Brown Trail on your right.

You can also gain access to both trailheads by exiting Highway 101 north of the Buellton turnoff on Highway 154, turning left on Figueroa Mountain Road and driving 15 miles to the upper trailhead. During wildflower season consider a drive up Figueroa Mountain Road and down Happy Canyon Road—or vice-versa—to make a scenic loop through the Santa Barbara Backcountry.

The Hike: From the northwest end of Davy Brown Camp, you'll pass a green gate and a vehicle barrier and join the unsigned trail. You'll head west through forested Munch Canyon, cross Davy Brown Creek a couple of times, then begin angling southwest up Fir Canyon. Actually, no firs grow in Fir Canyon but its cousin, the big cone spruce, is plentiful here.

About 1 3/4 miles from the trailhead, you'll descend into a blue oak-shaded draw and arrive at the ruins of chrome miner Harry Robert's cabin, built in the 1920s. A large big-leaf maple shades the cabin, which is a good lunch stop or turnaround point if you're not feeling too energetic.

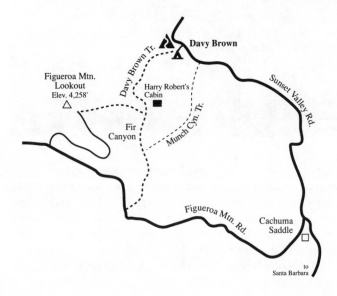

Among the ruins of Harry Roberts Cabin

Beyond the cabin, maple-shaded Davy Brown Trail crosses and re-crosses the creek. Keep a sharp lookout right for the unsigned side trail leading to Figueroa Mountain Lookout. (If you see Munch Canyon Spur Trail on your left, you overshot the trail; double back a hundred yards.)

Those wishing to follow Davy Brown Trail to its end will continue ascending along Davy Brown Creek through a wet world of mushrooms and banana slugs under the shade of oaks and laurel. A half-mile from the top of the trail you'll step carefully over a splintered white Monterey shale outcropping at a point where the canyon makes a sharp turn. Old-timers called this bend the Devil's Elbow.

Davy Brown Trail climbs to the headwaters of Davy Brown Creek, then out onto a grassy slope dotted with digger pine and buttercups. You might encounter a herd of bovine forest users on this grassy slope. Trail's end is Figueroa Mountain Road.

Figueroa Mountain Lookout-bound hikers will head right at the above-mentioned junction. The path gains elevation rapidly as it climbs out onto a drier slope cloaked in chaparral—toyon, ceanothus, black sage, scrub oak and mountain mahogany.

The trail descends for a short distance to a tiny meadow then immediately climbs steeply again. As the trail nears the top, notice the progression of pines from digger to Coulter to yellow.

The trail intersects a road to Figueroa Peak. Bear left on the road a half-mile to the lookout. Enjoy the far-reaching views of the major peaks of Los Padres National Forest and of the coast and Channel Islands.

2

Manzana Creek Trail

Davy Brown Camp to Potrero Canyon Camp
 2 1/2 miles round trip; 100-foot elevation loss
Davy Brown Camp to Coldwater Camp
 5 miles round trip; 200-foot elevation loss
Davy Brown Camp to Dabney Cabin
 14 miles round trip; 500-foot elevation loss
Davy Brown Camp to Manzana School House Camp
 17 miles round trip; 700-foot elevation loss

Manzana Creek forms the southern boundary of the San Rafael Wilderness, the first Wilderness Area in California set aside under the Federal Wilderness Act of 1964.

"San Rafael is rocky, rugged, wooded and lonely," President Lyndon B. Johnson remarked when he signed the San Rafael Wilderness bill on March 21, 1968. "I believe it will enrich the spirit of America."

Enriching the day hiker's spirit is plucky Manzana Creek, one of the delights of this part of Los Padres National Forest. Up-creek is Manzana Narrows, a narrow canyon where there are some fine pools for fishing and cooling off. Down-creek are some pleasant trail camps and a storied land that has attracted more than its share of eccentric settlers.

The lower stretch of the Manzana Creek Trail begins near a camp and creek named for William S. (Davy) Brown who kept a cabin here during his retirement years, 1880 to 1895.

The trail ends at the confluence of Manzana Creek and the Sisquoc River, where Hiram Preserved Wheat and his cult of religious fundamentalists from Kansas settled in. Wheat, it was said, had the power to heal with his hands. Hostile Indians were so impressed by the spiritual power of this white man that they inscribed his wagon with a sign indicating he was to be granted protection. Wheat and his followers stayed until almost two decades, but a number of drought years and restrictions on homesteading brought about by the creation of the Santa Barbara National Forest combined to end the settlement.

As you hike Manzana Creek Trail, don't be surprised to come across stone foundations and chimneys, or perhaps an old bottle or bit of barbed wire, all that remain of a rough life in a rough land.

Manzana means "apple" in Spanish, and it's guessed that apple orchards once grew in the area. On second guess, it takes its name from manzanita, "little apple" in Spanish.

36

A mellow day hike would be a journey down-creek to Potrero Canyon Camp or Coldwater Camp. Intrepid hikers in good condition will enjoy the much longer treks to the Dabney Cabin or historic Manzana School House; this would be a lot of ground to cover in one day but there's little elevation loss or gain to slow you down. Use caution at the many creek crossings and expect to get your feet wet if the creek is high.

Directions to trailhead: From U.S. 101 in Santa Barbara, exit on California 154 and follow the latter highway over San Marcos Pass. Beyond Lake Cachuma, turn right on Armour Road and proceed 2 1/2 miles to Happy Canyon Road. Make another right and continue 16 miles (Happy Canyon Road becomes Sunset Valley Road after passing an intersection at Figeroa Mountain Road.) Just past the turnoff to Davy Brown Campground, the road crosses Davy Brown Creek; park just after the crossing.

The Hike: A San Rafael Wilderness sign marks the beginning of the Manzana Creek Trail. The path heads down-creek. Keep the creek on your right. A bit more than a mile's easy travel brings you to Potrero Canyon Camp in an oak woodland near the creek.

From the camp, you can push down-creek via either a high or low trail. The low trail crosses the creek many times as it winds to Coldwater Camp; the higher—and drier—high trail contours over digger pine- and chaparral-covered canyon walls. Coldwater Camp, set amongst pine and oak, is a fine place for a picnic. Even during dry years, water bubbles up from the creek bedrock, hence the camp's name.

Beyond the camp, the trail crosses Manzana Creek several more times before arriving at Dabney Cabin. The cabin, built by Charles Dabney in 1914, is leased by Santa Barbara's Sierra Club.

More creek crossings follow until you reach Manzana School House Camp, located near the confluence of Manzana Creek and the Sisquoc River. One-room Manzana School House, built at the turn of the century and now a County Historical Landmark, still stands.

3

Reyes Peak Trail

Reyes Peak Roadhead to Potrero John Overlook
    3 1/2 miles round trip; 300-foot elevation gain
Reyes Peak Roadhead to Haddock Peak
    7 1/2 miles round trip; 600-foot elevation gain
Reyes Peak Roadhead to Haddock Trail Camp
    11 miles round trip; 800-foot elevation loss

The invigorating scent of pine, great views, and a dramatic ridgetop trail are some of the highlights of a hike atop Pine Mountain. The mountain, which straddles the Mount Pinos and Ojai Ranger Districts in Los Padres National Forest, is made up of several 7,000-foot-plus peaks, each offering a different backcountry panorama.

Wilderness-bound travelers have always had a difficult task in deciding what to call the rugged mountain terrain arranged in a very wide semi-circle around Ojai and Santa Barbara. The padres left behind many names, but none of them took. Geologists aren't much help either. They call the land the "Transverse Ranges Geomorphic Province." Unlike other areas of Southern California, there isn't a single dominant mountain range, but number of smaller ones with names like Sierra Madre and Santa Ynez, Pine and Topatopa.

Anyway, whatever this land of great gorges, sandstone cliffs and wide blue sky is called, it's guaranteed to please.

Reyes Peak and Reyes Peak Trail, as well as a nearby camp and creek, are named for an early California family that began ranching in the Cuyama Valley in the 1850s. One descendant, Jacinto Reyes, was among the first forest rangers of the Santa Barbara (later Los Padres) National Forest.

For most of its length, Reyes Peak Trail stays atop, or contours just below the ridgetop connecting Reyes to its sister peaks. The well-constructed footpath is shaded the whole way by white fir, Jeffrey, ponderosa and sugar pine. Inspiring views are offered from uninspiringly-named Peaks 7091, 7114 and 7416, as well as from the saddles between the summits.

Directions to trailhead: From Highway 101 in Ventura, exit on Highway 33 and head north 47 miles (32 miles past Ojai) to the signed turnoff for Pine Mountain Recreation Area. Follow the narrow paved road past some campgrounds. After 6 miles the paved surface ends and you'll continue east one more mile on a dirt road (suitable for most passenger cars) to road's end, where there's a modest amount of parking.

The Hike: Follow the dirt road (closed to vehicles beyond the trailhead) about 150 yards. As the road curves southeast, join the unsigned eastbound trail that begins on the east side of the road. The trail descends slightly and soon passes below the pine and boulder-covered summit of Reyes Peak (7,510 feet), high point of the Pine Mountain massif. Pine and fir shade the trail, which alternately follows the ridgeline and contours just below it.

You'll look down to the northwest at the farms and ranches of Cuyama Valley, and beyond to the stark sandstone Cuyama Badlands. There are occasional pine-framed views of Mount Pinos (8,831 feet), highest peak in Los Padres National Forest. From the ridgetop, you'll be able to peer southwest into the Sespe River gorge.

After about 1 3/4 miles of travel, you'll be treated to a view of the canyon cut by Potrero John Creek. The eroded cliffs at the head of the canyon recall Utah's Bryce Canyon National Park or Cedar Breaks National Monument.

Reyes Peak Trail continues east through pine and fir forest. After two more miles of travel, you'll spot an orange, triangular-shaped metal Forest Service marker, drop into and switchback out of a hollow, and arrive at signed Haddock Peak. The peak offers good views to the south and west of the Ojai backcountry.

From the peak, the trail descends in earnest. Almost two miles of travel brings you to Haddock (pronounced Hay Dock) located on the banks of Piedra Blanca Creek.

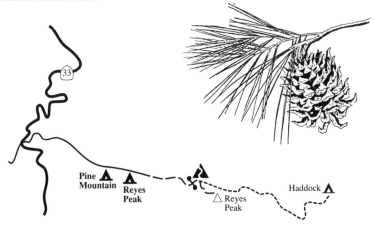

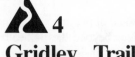 **4**

Gridley Trail

Gridley Road to Gridley Spring
    6 miles round trip; 1,400-foot elevation gain
Gridley Road to Nordhoff Peak
    12 miles round trip; 3,500-foot elevation gain

*"California...a mild climate, not enervating but healthful and
health-restoring; a wonderfully and variously productive soil, without
tropical malaria; the grandest scenery; strange customs, but neither
lawlessness nor semi-barbarism.'*

—Charles Nordhoff, 1872
California: for Health, Pleasure, and Residence

Prussian-born journalist Charles Nordhoff was one of the 19th Century's biggest boosters of California and the California way of life.
Nordhoff, an editor with the New York Evening Post, traveled extensively
throughout the Golden State in 1870-1871, and wrote *California: for
Health, Pleasure and Residence,* an enormously popular book that
prompted much visitation and settlement. The book had a profound effect
on the nation's attitude toward California. No longer would California be
regarded as the uncivilized far Western frontier, but as the perfect place in
the sun—one that offered the chance to build a home or business, to raise
crops or children in America's answer to the Mediterranean.

One of Nordhoff's favorite discoveries—quintessential Southern California as he saw it—was a beautiful valley located about 15 miles inland
from Ventura. Nordhoff wrote about this valley for several Eastern
magazines and newspapers, and as a result, the peaceful hamlet here
quickly grew into a town. Grateful townspeople named it Nordhoff in
1874. Nordhoff it remained until 1916 when the anti-German sentiment of
World War I prompted a change of name to Ojai.

Nordhoff's name remains on the 4,425-foot peak that forms a dramatic
backdrop for the town of Nordhoff, er...Ojai. The summit offers splendid
views of the Ojai Valley, the Ventura County coastline and the Channel
Islands.

Directions to trailhead: From the intersection of Highways 33 and 150
in Ojai, proceed on the latter road, known as Ojai Avenue. You'll pass
through town, and about 2 miles from the intersection, look for Los Padres
National Forest Ojai Ranger Station on the left at 1190 Ojai Avenue. This

is a good place to get the latest trail information. Proceed another half-mile and take the second left beyond the ranger station—Gridley Road. Follow Gridley 1.7 miles to its end. Signed Gridley Trail is on the left.

The Hike: Gridley Trail climbs a brushy draw, overhung with tall ceanothus. A half-mile's gentle ascent brings you to Gridley Fire Road (Forest Service Road 5N11). Turn right and follow this crumbling dirt road as it ascends above avocado groves planted on steep slopes. Leaving behind the "Guacamole Wilderness," the route enters Gridley Canyon, climbing to the northwest (and thankfully a bit cooler) side of the canyon.

Not much remains of Gridley Spring Camp, incinerated along with thousands of acres of the Ojai backcountry in the Wheeler Fire. Still, the vegetation in the area has made an astonishing recovery, and the spring named for an early homesteader, still flows.

Past Gridley Spring, peak-bound hikers will continue along the dirt road into an east fork of Gridley Canyon and join a switchbacking trail for the rigorous ascent. Notice the superb succession of sedimentary rocks displayed by the Topatopa mountains above you. Far below is the Pacific Ocean.

Two miles from the springs, you'll meet Nordhoff Fire Road (5N05). Turn left and follow this road a mile to Nordhoff Peak.

To the south is Ojai Valley, with Lake Casitas and the Pacific beyond. To the west rise the higher peaks of the Topatopa range, including the 6,210-foot signature peak, Topatopa. Also to the west is Sespe Condor Sanctuary, empty of the great birds, and a sad reminder of past puny efforts to save the last of the California condors. To the north is the Pine Mountain range and many more Los Padres National Forest peaks.

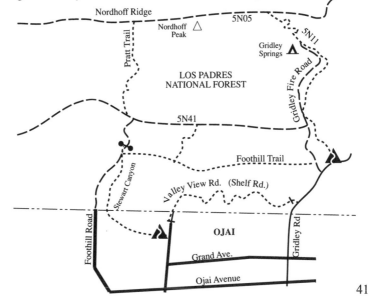

⚡ 5
Foothill Trail

Stewart Canyon to Gridley Road
Return via Shelf Road
5 1/2 miles round trip; 600-foot elevation gain

Ojai, nestled in a little valley backed by the Topatopa and Sulphur Mountains, has meant tranquility to several generations of settlers and citrus growers, artists, musicians and mystics. Ojai Valley was the setting for Shangri-La in the 1937 movie "Lost Horizon."

The 10-mile-long, 3-mile wide valley, surrounded by coastal mountain ranges has always had a sequestered feeling. Chumash Indians called this region Ojai, which means "nest." The meditative setting has spawned an artists colony, music festival and a number of health resorts. The environment has attracted the metaphysically minded too; the hiker can look down on the Krotona Institute of Theosophy on one side of town and the Krishnamurti Foundation on the other.

Foothill Trail offers the best view of the town and valley. From the path, hikers get great views of the harmonious Spanish architecture of Ojai, sweet-smelling citrus groves and the sometimes misty, sometimes mystical Ojai Valley.

Directions to trailhead: From the intersection of Highways 150 and 33, head east on the latter route one mile to North Signal Street in downtown Ojai. The post office and The Oaks resort are on this corner. Turn north on North Signal and drive 3/4 mile to a junction with an unsigned road on your left. A large water tower and a chain link fence are at this junction. Park along Signal.

The Hike: (See Trail 4 map.) Take a look up North Signal, which ends in another hundred yards at its meeting with Shelf Road, the dirt fire road that will be your return route. Now turn west on the paved road below the water tank. The road soon turns to gravel and you'll march past the Ventura County flood control works, the Stewart Canyon Debris Basin. Two hundred yards from the trailhead, just as your road turns north toward some residences, you'll spot a white pipe fence and a Forest Service trail sign. Join the trail which soon dips into brushy Stewart Canyon.

The trail zigzags under oaks and a tangled understory of native and nonnative shrubs. You'll cross two dirt roads then wind through a eucalyptus grove, which marks the site of the elegant Foothill Hotel, a casualty of fire just after the turn of the century. Foothill Trail turns north and ascends along the west wall of Stewart Canyon. The trail nears some private homes, crosses a paved road, then joins a dirt one and passes a water tank on your left. Shortly thereafter is a signed trail on your left for Foothill Trail 22W09 and Pratt Trail 23W09. Continue another 100 yards on the dirt road to another signed junction with the Foothill Trail; this path you'll take east.

Foothill Trail ascends up fire-scarred slopes and over meadowland seasonally dotted with wildflowers. Keep an eye out for abundant poison oak. Just as you're beginning to wonder if this trail will ever deliver its promised views, it tops a rise and offers a first glimpse of Ojai Valley.

The trail soon descends to an unsigned junction. A connector trail leads north to Forest Road 5N11; this road heads east to Gridley Road but offers no valley views. Stay with Foothill Trail, which descends to a little seasonal creek then climbs eastward out onto open slopes for great views of Ojai. From some vantage points you can see almost the whole Ojai Valley, Shangri-La indeed.

About a half-mile from Gridley Road, you'll spot dirt Shelf Road 200 yards or so below Foothill Trail. Experienced bushwhackers can blaze a trail down to the road, but think twice; it's probably more trouble than the little time/distance saved.

Foothill Trail, near its end, descends more steeply, its route stabilized by railroad ties. The trail emerges at a crumbling asphalt road, which you'll follow 50 yards to Gridley Road. Turn right on Gridley Road. Walk a hundred yards, cross a one-lane bridge, then descend another hundred yards to Shelf Road on your right.

Shelf Road, closed to vehicle traffic by a white pipe gate, heads east and ascends moderately into the hills. Skirting orange trees and avocado groves, Shelf Road serves up views that are just a little less dramatic than those offered by higher Foothill Trail.

Just after the road bends south, you'll reach a gate and Signal Road, which you'll follow the short distance back to the trailhead.

Foothill Trail offers great Ojai Valley views

6

Santa Paula Canyon Trail

Santa Paula Canyon to Big Cone Camp
6 miles round trip; 800-foot gain
Santa Paula Canyon to Cross Camp
8 miles round trip; 900-foot gain

Waterfalls, wading pools and swimmin' holes are some of the attractions of tranquil Santa Paula Canyon. A trail winds along the river bed through the canyon and visits some perfect-for-a-picnic trail camps.

The lovely trail begins at St. Thomas Aquinas College, and near a malodorous oil field once owned by infamous oilman and Southern California booster, Edward Lawrence Doheny. Doheny's black gold discoveries of 1892 made him an extremely wealthy man and began the first oil industry boom in Los Angeles. (Doheny's 30-room mansion is located behind iron gates just off Highway 150.)

During the Harding administration, Doheny received drilling rights on federal land in Elk Hills without undergoing the inconvenience of competitive bidding. A 1923 Senate investigation of the "Teapot Dome Scandal" uncovered Doheny's $100,000 loan to Secretary of the Interior Fall's conviction for accepting a bribe; Doheny, however, was acquitted of offering one.

Floods periodically sweep Santa Paula Canyon and wash out the trail. And Los Padres National Forest administrators periodically take the trail of the forest map. Mapped or not, Santa Paula Canyon Trail is a great walk.

Directions to the trailhead: From the junction of Highways 33 and 150 in Ojai, head east from town on the latter road about 9 1/2 miles to the bridge spanning Santa Paula Creek. The trailhead is located at the entrance to St. Thomas Aquinas/Ferndale Ranch on the north side of the road, but you continue on Highway 150 across the Santa Paula Creek bridge to a wide turnout on the south side of the highway. A sign informs you that the Santa Paula Canyon Trail begins across the highway 500 feet away.

The 1985 Ferndale fire burned a portion of Santa Paula Canyon; prior to 1985, the canyon was closed during fire season. Santa Paula Canyon is currently open year-round, but the Forest Service may again institute fire closure, so check with them before traveling there during the hot summer months.

The Hike: From the often-guarded Ferndale Ranch/college entrance, you'll ignore a road leading to the oil fields and follow the asphalt drive onto the college grounds. The road curves around wide green lawns and handsome classrooms. At a few junctions, signs keep you "Hikers" away from the route taken by "Oil Field Traffic." A bit more than a half-mile from the trailhead, you pass an orchard and some cows, pass through a pipe gate, and finally reach Santa Paula Creek and the true beginning of Santa Paula Canyon Trail.

The trail travels a short distance with Santa Paula Creek, crosses it, then joins a retiring dirt road—your route to Big Cone Camp. After crossing the creek again, the trail begins a moderate to stiff climb up a slope bearing the less-than-lyrical name of Hill 1989. The trail then descends to Big Cone Camp, perched on a terrace above Santa Paula Creek.

Just below the camp, the trail, now a narrow footpath, descends to the creek. As you descend, you'll look up-canyon and spot a waterfall and a swimming hole.

The trail crosses Santa Paula Creek and switchbacks up to an unsigned junction. A right at this junction leads above the east fork of Santa Paula Canyon 3 1/2 miles on poor, unmaintained trail to Cienega Camp. Hardy hikers will enjoy bushwhacking along to this camp set in a meadowland shaded by oak and big cone spruce.

A left at the above-mentioned junction leads north up Santa Paula Canyon past some inviting pools. The path, sometimes called Last Chance Trail, climbs a mile to Cross, another big cone spruce-shaded camp. Here Santa Paula Creek offers some nice falls and great swimming holes. Caution: The creek current can be quite strong on occasion.

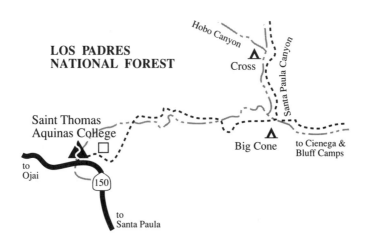

Chapter 3

SANTA YNEZ MOUNTAINS

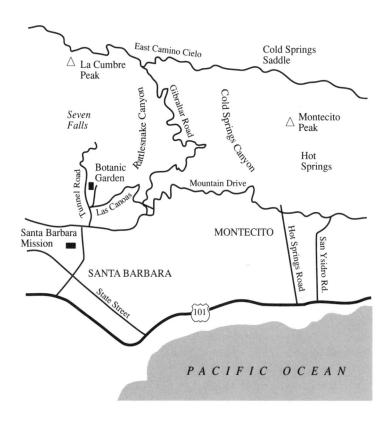

Santa Ynez Mountains

A few million years ago, the Santa Ynez Mountains rose slowly from the sea. The mountains are not secretive about their origin and display their oceanic heritage in a number of ways. Tilted blocks of sedimentary rock, which aggregated tens of thousands of feet in thickness, provide the first clue to the mountains' former undersea life. Fossils of sea animals give further testimony that the mountains were once many leagues under the sea. Even the vegetation betrays the mountains' origin. The mineral-poor sandstone slopes formed in the ocean deep can support little more than dense brush, so it's the chaparral community—buckthorn, mountain lilac and scrub oak—that predominates.

The Santa Ynez Mountains are part of a series of east/west trending ranges known as the Transverse Ranges, which encircle Southern California from San Diego to Point Conception. The backbone of the Transverse Range is the San Bernardino and San Gabriel Mountains, while the Santa Ynez Mountains form the uppermost or most westerly part of the Transverse Spine. The Santa Ynez extend almost fifty miles from Matilija Canyon on the east to Gaviota Canyon on the west. Compared to other ranges in the Transverse system, the Santa Ynez are quite small, ranging from 2,000 to 4,000 feet.

At first glance, the range seems smothered with a formless gray mass of tortured vegetation. On closer inspection, the Santa Ynez reveals more charm. Sycamores and bays line the canyons and a host of seasonal creeks wash the hillsides. In spring, the chaparral blooms and adds frosty whites and blues to the gray-green plants. The backcountry looks particularly inviting after the first winter rains. On upper peaks, rain sometimes turns to snow.

Santa Ynez Mountain trails mainly follow the canyons above Santa Barbara and Montecito. The network of trails generally follows streams to the top of the range. They start in lush canyon bottoms, zigzag up the hot, dry canyon walls, and follow rock ledges to the crest. Many of the trails intersect El Camino Cielo (the sky road), which follows the mountain crest. From the top, enjoy sweeping views of the Pacific, Channel Island and coastal plain. Northward, row after row of shar mountains spread toward the horizon. These mountains were born beneath the sea and may someday return to their birthplace. In the meantime, say for the next million years or so, the mountains will continue to provide splendid hiking.

Cachuma Lake, Santa Ynez Mountains

7

Tequepis Trail

Camp Cielo to West Camino Cielo
8 miles round trip; 2,300-foot elevation gain
Camp Cielo to Broadcast Peak
9 miles round trip; 2,800-foot elevation gain

Cachuma Lake, besides storing an important part of Santa Barbara County's water supply, is a popular weekend destination for Southland anglers, campers and bird-watchers. For the hiker, Tequepis Trail offers the best view of the lake, as well as a 360-degree panorama from the high peaks of Los Padres National Forest to the Channel Islands. It's one of the most beautiful, yet least-used, trails in the Santa Ynez Mountains.

Much of the trail is shaded with live oak and sycamore. Near the top, are two arboreal surprises—tan oak and madrone, trees more commonly found in the northern part of the state. In springtime, lupine, bush poppy and other wildflowers splash color along the trail.

Tequepis, possibly the most carefully pronounced trail name in Southern California, is the Chumash word for seed-gatherer. Indians beat the grasses on nearby slopes with a tennis racket-like tool to gather the seeds.

You can get an eagle's-eye-view of Cachuma Lake by taking Tequepis Trail and you can get an eagle's eye view of eagles on a two-hour boat cruise. More than a hundred bald eagles make the shores of Cachuma their winter home. Eagle Tours, conducted by the park's naturalist, offer a close-up look at the eagles, as well as dozens of other resident and migratory birds.

Directions to trailhead: From Highway 101 in Santa Barbara, exit on Highway 154 (San Marcos Pass Road) and drive 17 1/2 miles to a left turn lane and a road leading left signed "Cachuma Camp" and "Camp Cielo." Proceed with caution over the first half of this road, which is dirt and full of potholes. The second half of the 1.3-mile road is paved. Park in a dirt lot just outside the wooden gate of the

Campfire Girls' Camp Cielo. Walk, don't drive, up the asphalt service road into the camp.

The Hike: Walk up the paved camp road 75 yards, past a swimming pool, to the signed beginning of the trail. Tequepis Trail, actually the camp road for its first quarter mile, passes some tiny A-frame tent cabins. Leaving "Magic Forest Camp" behind, the dirt road crosses and recrosses a seasonal creek. Only after a good winter rain is there water in the creek.

One mile from the trailhead, the dirt road dead-ends. Signed Tequepis Trail, from this point forward a narrow path, veers left. The trail climbs moderately for a quarter-mile, then very steeply for another quarter-mile. After this strenuous stretch, the path ascends at a more accomodating pace via well-graded switchbacks.

About a mile from the top, you'll get a great view of the lake, then pass near a stand of cinnamon-colored madrone. In bloom, the small tree sprouts white urn-shaped flowers and clusters of red/orange berries. Farther along the trail, look for the tan oak, or tanbark oak, a handsome tree more often associated with redwood or Douglas fir forest.

The trail tops a ridge and ends at unpaved West Camino Cielo. From the ridgetop just above the road, you'll have commanding views to the north of the San Rafael and Sierra Madre Mountains. Just below is Cachuma Lake and the Santa Ynez Valley. Far to the east you might spot Mount Pinos, highest peak in Los Padres National Forest. To the south is a good view of Isla Vista and the University of California, Santa Barbara, and the state beaches of Refugio and El Capitan. Anacapa, Santa Cruz, Santa Rosa and San Miguel islands float upon the horizon.

If you're still feeling frisky and want to do a little bushwhacking, take the very rough and steep side trail from the ridgetop to Broadcast Peak. Thrash a half-mile through manzanita and yerba santa up to the 4,028-foot summit, which is crowned with the transmitting tower of Santa Barbara TV Station KEYT. The peak and its great views can also be reached by West Camino Cielo, a longer but much easier route. Ultra-energetic hikers can continue another mile west on West Camino Cielo to the lookout on 4,298-foot Santa Ynez Peak.

8

Santa Ynez River Trail

Season: All Year
Caution in times
of high water

Red Rock Trailhead to Gibraltar Dam Picnic Area
6 miles round trip; 400-foot elevation gain

Our State Water Resources Control Board suggests that one of the most beneficial uses of the upper Santa Ynez River is for "water contact recreation." Translated from bureaucratic jargon: "Go jump in the river!" Great swimming holes await hikers who venture to the attractive Santa Ynez Recreation Area, located in the mountains behind Santa Barbara.

During dry years, the river's swimming holes are filled by periodic releases from Gibraltar Reservoir, located up-river from the recreation area. Thanks to Santa Barbara's contribution of a small part of its municipal water supply, some of the pools maintain year-round depths of 6 to 18 feet.

Santa Ynez River Trail leads to several pleasant swimming holes and is an easy hike, suitable for the whole family. The most popular ol' swimmin' hole is Red Rock Pool, located only a short distance from the trailhead. The trail to the pools and to Gibraltar Dam Picnic Area follows the remains of an old mining road, built in the 1870s during a quicksilver mining boom. The road was later used by workers during the 1920 construction of Gibraltar Dam.

For more information about the Santa Ynez Recreation Area, stop by Los Padres National Forest Los Prietos Ranger Station, located about midway between Highway 154 and Red Rock Trailhead on Paradise Road.

Directions to trailhead: From Highway 101 in Santa Barbara, take the "Lake Cachuma, Highway 154" exit. Proceed east on Highway 154. At the top of San Marcos Pass, you'll spot the historic Cielo Store, featured as "Papadakis Tavern," in the remake of "The Postman Always Rings Twice." A short distance over the pass, just past a Vista Point (about 10 miles from Santa Barbara if you're watching your odometer), turn right on Paradise Road and drive to the end of the road—10.7 miles. Leave your car in the dirt parking lot adjacent to the trail, which begins at a locked gate.

If you're the kind of hiker who loves loop trips, note the presence of a second trail leading from the parking lot to Gibraltar Dam. The "high road," as its known by locals, makes a gentle traverse across the mountains above the river. Like the "low road,"—Santa Ynez River Trail—it's about three miles long. It's a good trail to keep in mind for times of high water.

The Hike: Wide, flat Santa Ynez River Trail passes a "No Nudity Allowed" sign and after 1/4 mile crosses the river. Near this crossing you might observe some scattered bricks, all that remains of a turn-of-the-century quicksilver furnace. Quicksilver ore, mined in the nearby hills, was crushed and heated in the furnace. The ore became gaseous at a low temperature and the gas condensed into liquid mercury. Mercury, a very heavy element, was transported in small, foot-long cylinders, each weighing about 75 pounds.

Soon after the first river crossing, you'll reach Red Rock, the most popular swimming hole. Geologically minded hikers will examine the red rock, metamorphosed volcanics of the Jurassic age. Other hikers will plunge into the river.

The trail passes through oak woodland and zigzags from bank to bank along the river. Alongside the river is a canopy of cottonwood, sycamore and willow.

Wildlife viewing opportunities, particularly during the early morning hours, are quite good near the Santa Ynez River because the area includes several different habitats: oak woodland, coastal sage scrub, grassland and freshwater marsh.

You might spot a deer, gray fox, striped skunk, lizard, cottontail rabbit or raccoon. Watch for pond turtles basking on the rocks, logs and banks of large pools.

The ecological diversity of the area also means a wide assortment of wildlife. In the woodland areas, birders might sight a mourning dove, warbling vireo, northern oriole or a woodpecker. Cliff swallows, flycatchers and belted kingfishers swoop over the river.

Several more dry river crossings and a couple of wet ones, and some travel beneath the boughs of some handsome coast live oaks, will bring you to Gibraltar Picnic Area, located a few hundred yards down-river from the dam. Oaks shade some picnic tables.

You may continue up the trail to Gibraltar Dam, named for the large rock here, which is said to resemble the great guardian rock of the Mediterranean. A second, shadeless picnic site is located at the southeast top edge of the dam. Observe the warning signs at the dam and stay out of restricted areas.

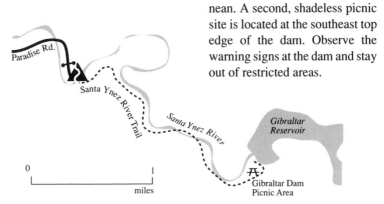

▲9

Snyder Trail

Paradise Road to Knapp's Castle
   6 1/2 miles round trip; 2,000-foot elevation gain
Camino Cielo to Knapp's Castle
   1 mile round trip

"This tract, at the edge of the grand canyon of the SantaYnez Mountains, is one of the most magnificent, in point of scenic glories, in California."

—the view from Knapp's Castle, as reported
by the *Santa Barbara Morning Press*, April 9, 1916

In 1916, George Owen Knapp's recurrent bouts of hay fever sent him high into the Santa Ynez Mountains behind Santa Barbara to seek relief. The wealthy former Chairman of the Board of Union Carbide found relief—and an ideal locale to build the mountain home of his dreams.

The high, huge, and presumably hypo-allergenic parcel belonged to Homer Snyder, once the chef at Santa Barbara's Arlington Hotel. Back in 1902, Snyder had built a rustic hostelry atop Camino Cielo, "the Sky Road." Visitors during the early 1900s included Theodore Roosevelt and William Howard Taft. Knapp bought the Snyder place, renamed it Laurel Springs Ranch, and charitably offered it as a weekend retreat for Santa Barbara's hardworking nurses and hospital workers.

Knapp's dream home, carved from thick sandstone blocks, took four years to complete. It was a magnificent residence, complete with illuminated waterfalls and a room housing one of Knapp's other passions—a huge pipe organ.

While Knapp was developing his private retreat, he was also helping to boost public access to the Santa Barbara Forest Reserve, as it was known in those days. Knapp and a couple of his wealthy friends were tireless promoters of roads and trails, in order to make the backcountry accessible to all. Knapp's enthusiasm and money helped extend trails west to the top of Refugio Canyon (now part-time rancher Ronald Reagan's spread) and east to Ojai.

The trail building efforts of Knapp and his buddies were much appreciated by the local populace. As a 1917 editorial in the *Santa Barbara Daily News* put it: "They are strong advocates of the great out-of-doors, and under their leadership places in the wild heretofore denied humans because of utter inaccessibility are being opened up to the hiker and horseback rider."

Knapp was 60-something when he threw himself into his castle-building and trail-building efforts. He spend most of the rest of his long, productive life in his castle in the sky. In 1940, he sold his retreat to Frances Holden, who nearly became the first and only person to lose money in the Santa Barbara real estate market when a forest fire destroyed the castle just five months after she bought it. Fortunately, she had insurance.

Stone walls, part of the foundation, and a couple of chimneys are all that remain of Knapp's Castle. But the view of the Santa Barbara Backcountry is still magnificent, particularly if you arrive at sunset and watch the purple shadows skim over the Santa Ynez and San Rafael Mountains.

Snyder Trail, which receives sporadic maintenance from the Santa Barbara Sierra Club and the U.S. Forest Service, leads to the castle ruins. The upper part of the trail, formerly Knapp's long driveway to his retreat, offers an easy walk down to the ruins from Camino Cielo. From Paradise Road, Snyder Trail takes you on a steep ascent to the castle. Quite an aerobic workout, if you're in the mood.

Ruins of George Knapp's Castle

Directions to Paradise Road trailhead: From Highway 101 in Santa Barbara, exit on Highway 154 and proceed 11 1/2 miles up and over San Marcos Pass to Paradise Road. Turn right and proceed 4.4 miles to a turnout on the right side of the road. (If you spot the road leading to Sage Hill Campground, you went a little too far on Paradise Road.) The trail begins at a dirt road that's closed to vehicles.

Directions to Camino Cielo trailhead: From Highway 101 in Santa Barbara, exit on Highway 154 and proceed 8 miles to East Camino Cielo. Turn right and drive 2 1/2 miles to a saddle, where you'll spot a parking area and a locked Forest Service gate.

The Hike (from Paradise Road): From the turnout, walk 50 yards up the dirt road to the signed beginning of the Snyder Trail, which is actually the road you're following. The road passes under some stately oaks and after 1/4 mile reaches a large green water tank.

The road narrows to a trail, passes some planted pines and a second water tank, then begins ascending a series of switchbacks. For the most part, you'll be climbing in shade. Behind and below are good views of the canyon cut by the Santa Ynez River.

About two miles from the trailhead, Snyder Trail joins an abandoned dirt road. The old road/trail crosses a cottonwood-lined seasonal creek and tunnels beneath the boughs of pungent bay laurel. Around a bend you'll get your first glimpse of Knapp's Castle, then ascend another 3/4 mile to the ruins.

The Hike (from Camino Cielo): It's a short half-mile descent on dirt road to the castle. Chamise, ceanothus, toyon and other members of the hardy chaparral family line the old road.

From the ruins of Knapp's Castle, enjoy the view of the Santa Ynez River, Cachuma Lake and the wide blue Pacific. And take in the panorama of peaks from Mount Pinos to Figueroa Mountains to the Casmalia Hills.

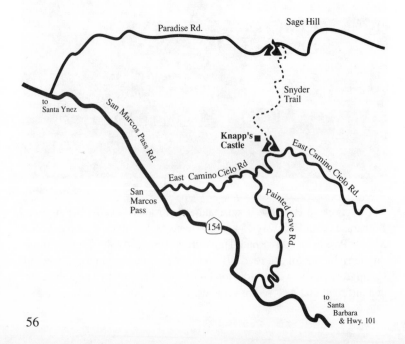

10
Hot Springs Trail

Hot Springs Road to Hot Springs Hotel ruins
   3 1/2 miles round trip; 700-foot elevation gain
Hot Springs Canyon/ Cold Springs Canyon Loop
   7 miles round trip; 1,100-foot elevation gain

One of our favorite resorts was the Sulphur or Hot Springs, situated some five or six miles from Santa Barbara, to the southward. The springs would make the fortune of any town in the United States, but here are left alone and deserted, visited only by the native sick or the American sojourner in Santa Barbara. They are remarkably, and very romantically, situated; sequestered from human habitation and almost inaccessible save to the pedestrian.

—Walter Murray,1847
"Narrative of a California Volunteer"

By the time the first New York Volunteers arrived in Santa Barbara in 1847, the "conquest of California" was complete. The war with Mexico was over. While garrisoned in Santa Barbara, one Army volunteer, Walter Murray, seemed to have spent most of his enlistment touring the Santa Barbara Backcountry and recording his enthusiastic descriptions in a journal. Particularly impressive to Murray was a pretty canyon aptly named Hot Springs for the sulfurous waters that gushed into inviting bath-size pools.

"I never yet came across a more picturesque sight, nor do I expect to in the future," Murray wrote.

A decade after Murray's bubbly report, Wilbur Curtiss made his way to Santa Barbara—for health reasons, as the story goes. Curtiss took the cure and left us a story chock-full of cliches: He was suffering from an incurable disease. His doctors gave him by six months to live. Then one day he met a 110-year-old Indian who attributed his longevity to some secret springs. Curtiss bathed in the springs and experienced a miracle cure.

Or so the story goes...

Fable or not, Curtiss soon felt well enough to file a homestead claim on Hot Springs Canyon and begin its commercial development.

By the early 1880s, the homestead became the property of wealthy Montecitans who built a three-story wooden hotel at the springs. Rates were $2 a day, $10 a week, including the baths. Guests enjoyed a library, a billiards room and a well-stocked wine cellar. Another attraction was hiking: Trails meandered around the hillsides and provided excellent panoramas of Santa Barbara and the Channel Islands.

By the turn of the century, the Hot Springs Hotel was more exclusive than Baden-Baden and other fine European resorts. It was said only those with seven-digit incomes felt at ease in the healing waters.

The hotel burned down in 1920, and a small but still quite posh clubhouse was built on the site. The new spa was even more exclusive: Membership was limited to 17 Montecito estate owners who also controlled the Montecito Water Co. Members would telephone the caretaker, tell him to draw a bath, then arrive a short while later by limousine. The club burned down in the 1964 Coyote Fire.

Since then, Hot Springs Canyon and its hot pools have been accessible to the less affluent. Hot Springs Trail—the old stagecoach road—leads to the ruins of the resort. Condition and temperature of the two hot pools vary, so hikers should use their best judgement when deciding whether to take the plunge.

Directions to trailhead: From U.S. 101 in Montecito, just down the coast from Santa Barbara, exit on Olive Mill Road, which, after intersecting Alston Drive, continues as Hot Springs Road. Three miles from U.S. 101, you'll reach Mountain Drive. Turn left and proceed a quarter of a mile to the trailhead, which is on the right side of the road and is marked by a Montecito Trails Foundation sign. Park in a safe manner alongside the road.

The Hike: The trail climbs moderately through a wooded area, skirting some baronial estates. The first few hundred yards of Hot Springs Trail might give you the impression you're on the wrong trail because it crosses and parallels some private driveways. However, keep following the path with the aid of some strategically placed Montecito Trails Foundation signs.

After a quarter-mile of travel, you'll leave the villas behind. The trail veers right, dips into the canyon, crosses Hot Springs Creek and joins a dirt road, The dirt road passes under the embrace of antiquarian oaks, then begins climbing moderately to steeply along the east side of Hot Springs Canyon. Notice the stone culverts and the handsome stone retaining walls as you walk up the old coach road.

A mile's travel along the old road brings you to a junction. A left at the junction puts you on a power-line road that climbs over to Cold Springs Canyon. Stay right, and another quarter-mile of hiking brings you to the ruins of the Montecito Hot Springs Club. Some stone steps and foundations are about all that's left of the exclusive club.

Nearby, some exotic flora thrive—bamboo, agave and geraniums, as well as palm, banana and avocado trees—remnants of the landscaped gardens that surrounded the spa during its glory days. Two hot pools, reconstructed by locals, offer an opportunity to take a soak. If they look inviting, drop in.

You can return the same way, or follow one of two routes to Cold Springs Canyon. You may double back to the above-mentioned road junction and ascend with the power-line road to the ridge separating Hot Springs Canyon from Cold Springs Canyon. Or you can follow the trail above the resort ruins and climb north, then steeply east over to that same ridge.

Once atop the ridge, marred by power-line towers, descend on the unsigned but well-maintained Cold Springs Trail 1 1/2 miles through Cold Springs Canyon—perhaps the prettiest in the Santa Ynez Mountains. The trail ends at Mountain Drive. You'll turn left and walk a mile along one of Santa Barbara's more bucolic byways back to your car and the Hot Springs trailhead.

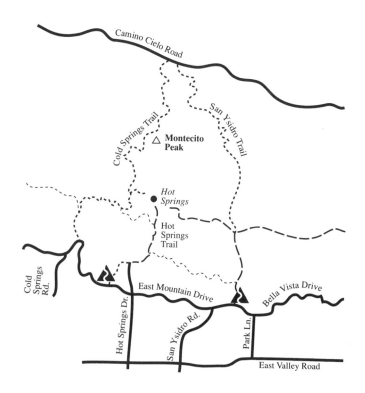

▲ 11
San Ysidro Trail

East Mountain Drive to pools
3 miles round trip; 70-foot elevation gain
Mountain Drive to East Camino Cielo
8 miles round trip; 2,900-foot elevation gain

San Ysidro Trail is attractive and typical of Santa Barbara's foothill trails. It is suitable for several levels of hiking ability. Families with small children will enjoy sauntering along is lower creekside stretches. The more serious hiker will enjoy sweating up the switchbacks to Camino Cielo, the Sky Road. Truly decadent hikers will make reservations for the sumptuous Sunday brunch at San Ysidro Ranch located very close to the trailhead.

Directions to trailhead: From Highway 101 in Montecito, take the San Ysidro Road offramp. Drive north on San Ysidro a mile to East Valley Road, turn right and drive a mile to Park Lane, which appears on the left just after crossing San Ysidro Creek. Turn left on Park Lane and in a half-mile veer left onto East Mountain Dive, which passes through a residential neighborhood to the trailhead. The signed trailhead is just opposite San Ysidro Stables. Parking is along East Mountain Drive.

The Hike: (See Trail 10 map.) The trail, lined with sea fig, bougainvillea, and other exotic plants, parallels a driveway for a short time, passes a couple houses, then becomes a dirt road. Continue up the dirt road and look up occasionally at the handsome Coldwater sandstone formations above you. To your left across the creek is "the gateway," a popular rock climbing area. After a half-mile's travel, you'll pass two signed connector trails, which lead to canyons on either side of San Ysidro. To the east is Old Pueblo Trail, to the west, Colonel McMenemy Trail.

San Ysidro Trail continues along the bottom of the narrow, snaky canyon. In the springtime, the path may be brightened with blossoms.

Along San Ysidro Creek you encounter beautiful oak woodlands. With mighty oaks in the foreground and impressive rock formations in the background, it is a striking scene. A number of quiet pools await in the creek. Hikers have stacked up rocks to make shallow swimming and wading pools. You'll spot a large pool on your left, just before the trail ascends into the upper canyon.

Those hikers heading for the upper stretches of San Ysidro Canyon will leave the creek behind and follow the steep rocky trail. Along one length of trail, pipes serve as handrails and you'll feel as though you've walked the precarious Angel's Landing in Zion National Park rather than this supposedly gentle path through the Santa Ynez Mountains. (The rails really aren't necessary.) The trail continues along a rocky ledge, finds more solid ground, then crosses over the west side of the canyon.

You'll continue marching through the chaparral up long, steep switchbacks. During the ascent, the geologically inclined will look up at the Matilija sandstone of the gray-white Coldwater sandstone formation, which has been wind-sculpted into striking cliffs and bluffs. When you reach East Camino Cielo you may return the way you came.

"The Gateway," popular rock-climbing area above San Ysidro Creek

Chapter 4

SANTA MONICA MOUNTAINS

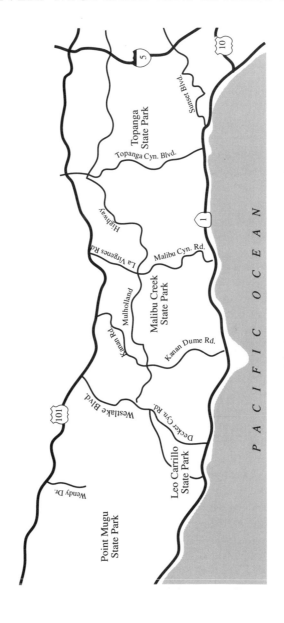

Santa Monica Mountains

The copper hued men who roamed these hills not so long ago were very likely better tenants than you and I will be. And when we are gone, as we will go, a few unnoticed centuries will wipe out out bravest scars, our most determined trails.

—John Russell McCarthy
Those Waiting Hills: The Santa Monicas, 1924

The Santa Monicas are the only relatively undeveloped mountain range in the U.S. that bisects a major metropolitan area. They are a near-wilderness within an hour's drive of six million people, and stretch all the way from Griffith Park in the heart of Los Angeles to Point Mugu, 50 miles away. The mountains, which include the civilized Hollywood Hills and the oh-so-civilized Beverly Hills, run westward to the steep wildlands above Malibu.

The range is 12 miles wide at its broadest point, and it reaches an elevation of a little over 3,000 feet. Large stretches are open and natural, covered with chaparral and oak trees, bright in spring with wildflowers. Water from winter rains runs down steep slopes and fosters a wide variety of life on canyon floors. Oak woodland and fern glens shade gentle seasonal streams. Within the mountains is a variety of animal life, from the most sociable of frogs to the most reclusive of mountain lions. The coyote, mule deer, raccoon, rabbit, rattlesnake, skunk and fox find shelter in the Santa Monicas. Bird-watching is excellent. The wrentit, the brown towhee, red-tailed hawk, quail, turkey vulture, and many, many more birds patrol the skies.

The hills and canyons used to be hiding places for bandits. The notorious highwayman Vasquez had a refuge here, but visited his sweetie once too often and fell into the sheriff's net. The fog-covered Santa Monicas, with few roads and trails, were a favorite haunt of the contrabandistas. Under Mexican rule, every sea trader had to land in San Francisco or Monterey and pay duty. To avoid the drastic customs, the contrabandistas slipped their cargo ashore by moonlight at secret coves, then trekked the goods over the mountains to Los Angeles.

In the nineteenth century, the Santa Monicas were controlled by a few large holdings including the Rancho Malibu and the Rancho Guadalasca, and used primarily for cattle raising. As the land holdings were broken up, ranchers supplemented their modest living by renting space to visiting horsemen and vacationers. At the turn of the century, eccentric oilman Colonel Griffith J. Griffith gave 3,000 acres of his ostrich farm to Los Angeles on the condition that it be forever maintained as a park. Thus

Early auto touring, Topanga Canyon

Griffith Park was formed on the eastern terminus of the Santa Monicas. Throughout the past three decades, conservationists have made inch-by-inch progress to secure park lands.

The largest areas of open space are in the western part of the mountains. Point Mugu State Park holds the finest native tall grass prairie and the best sycamore grove in the state. The gorge cut by Malibu Creek is an unforgettable sight.

In the eastern part of the mountains, open space is harder to come by, but those little pockets that do exist are all the more valuable for being so close to the metropolis. Canyons such as Los Liones, Caballero, and Franklin are precious resources for the park-poor Los Angeles Basin.

Southern California nature lovers put on their hiking boots and jumped for joy in 1978 when the bill creating the Santa Monica Mountains National Recreation Area was approved by Congress. Eventually a larger park will be formed, to be overseen by the National Park Service. Allocations are slowly being made by the state and federal government to fund purchase of private land to supplement the four major holdings: Will Rogers, Topanga, Malibu Creek and Point Mugu State Parks.

The National Recreation Area is not one large area, but a patchwork of state parks, county parks, and private property still to be acquired. The network of trails through the Santa Monicas is a rich pastiche of nature walks, scenic overlooks, fire roads and horse trails, leading through diverse ecosystems: meadowlands, savannas, yucca-covered slopes, handsome sandstone formations, and springs surrounded by lush ferns. The Backbone Trail, to run from Will Rogers State Historic Park to Point Mugu State Park, is slowly being completed and when finished, will literally and symbolically link the scattered beauties of the Santa Monicas.

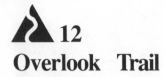 **12**

Overlook Trail

Loop from Sycamore Canyon Trailhead
10 miles round trip; 1,300-foot elevation gain

Overlook Trail is a fine way to explore the autumn delights of Point Mugu State Park, the largest preserved area in the Santa Monica Mountains. The trail offers fine views of the coast and Channel Islands and by returning via Sycamore Canyon you can see the park's handsome sycamores cloaked in their fall colors.

Fall is the season when millions of Monarch butterflies arrive in the coastal woodlands of Central and Southern California. The Monarch's awe-inspiring migration and formation of what entomologists call overwintering colonies are two of nature's most colorful autumn events.

All Monarch butterflies west of the Rockies head for California in the fall; one of the best places in Southern California to observe the arriving Monarchs is near the campground in Big Sycamore Canyon at Point Mugu State Park.

During October and November, Sycamore Canyon offers the twin delights of falling autumn leaves and fluttering butterflies. Ask park rangers where the butterflies cluster in large numbers.

Directions to trailhead: From Santa Monica, drive up-coast on Highway 1 for 32 miles to the Big Sycamore Canyon Campground in Point Mugu State Park. Outside the campground entrance, there's parking. Walk past the campground entrance through the campground to a locked gate. The trail (a fire road) begins on the other side of the gate.

The Hike: (See Trail 13 map.) Take the trail, up-canyon, following the all-but- dry creek. Underground water keeps much of the creekside vegetation green year-round.

One-half mile from the the campground, you'll spot the signed Overlook Trail. Bear left and follow the wide trail, which climbs steadily to the sharp ridge that separates Big Sycamore Canyon and La Jolla Canyon. From the ridge you can look down at the ocean and a sandy beach. Listen carefully and you can hear the distant booming of the surf.

The Overlook Trail turns north and continues climbing. To your right, you'll get an aviator's view of Big Sycamore Canyon. Three miles from the trailhead, you'll see La Jolla Canyon below and to the west of the ridge you've been following. Mugu Peak, Laguna Peak with its missile-tracking equipment, and La Jolla Peak tower above La Jolla Valley.

Overlook Trail ends at a signed junction and you will bear right on a dirt road, known as Pumphouse Trail, and descend somewhat steeply to Deer Camp Junction. Drinking water and picnic tables under the shade of oak trees, suggest a lunch stop here.

From Deer Camp Junction, you'll descend 3/4 mile on Wood Canyon Trail to Wood Canyon Junction, the hub of six trails leading to all corners of the park. If you have a trails map, this is a good place to orient yourself and perhaps plan future day hikes in the state park.

This day hike joins the signed Big Sycamore Canyon Trail and heads south (down-canyon) for four gentle miles through one of California's finest sycamore savannas back to the trailhead. Don't let the large and cranky blue jay population discourage you from dawdling under the magnificent sycamores.

View of Point Mugu from Overlook Trail

⛰13

Serrano Canyon Trail

8 1/2 mile loop through Point Mugu State Park
1,100-foot elevation gain

"When the trail had climbed to a height of fifteen hundred feet, there opened a still more striking landscape. Near by to the north rose the fine shape of Boney Mountain, its highest crags hidden in dragging mists...More to the west, blue with summer haze, the wide valley stretched away to the Pacific, and between lay the expanse of rough, brush hills through which I had to find a way."

—Joseph Smeaton Chase
California Coast Trails, 1913

Trail writer/rider Joseph Smeaton Chase had a tough time finding his way through the west end of the Santa Monica Mountains. The tumbled-up hills and valleys between Little Sycamore and Big Sycamore Canyons were crisscrossed with cattle paths, which threw him off track. Though a bit lost, the beauty of the land we now call Boney Mountain Wilderness launched the British-born author into paroxysms of purple prose.

Fortunately for Chase and Western literature, he spotted a small farm belonging to old Jesus Serrano and his son Francisco. The dirt-poor Serranos offered Chase all they had—a bed in their tiny cabin, one of their fine homemade Spanish cheeses and directions for getting back on the right trail. Francisco Serrano led Chase down the canyon that now bears his name and over to Big Sycamore Canyon, where there was a more distinct trail.

Steep-walled Serrano Canyon and aptly-named Big Sycamore Canyon are two wonderfully scenic destinations in Point Mugu State Park, the largest preserved area in the Santa Monica Mountains. The valley is a beauty, as quiet a place as you'll find in the Santa Monicas. A couple of Park Service trail markers keep you on the trail, which passes a solitary sumac and an abandoned aluminum and wood shed that houses an old pump.

The path cuts across the grasslands and reaches a signed junction. Serrano Valley Loop Trail veers right, but you contiue straight on the path signed "To Old Boney Trail" You'll reach an unsigned junction with Old Boney Trail, turn left and soon reach another unsigned trail that leads left. You can see Big Sycamore Canyon below. You'll join this trail, which plunges down the steep canyon wall.

The very steep trail drops to the floor of Big Sycamore Canyon. When you reach the fire road at the bottom of the canyon, you'll turn left. The fire road, Big Sycamore Canyon Trail, takes you through a peaceful wooded canyon, where a multitude of Monarchs dwell in the fall, and past some magnificent sycamores. It's a bit more than three miles down-canyon back to the trailhead.

The sycamores that shade the canyon are incomparable. The blue jay population will scold you, and lots of mountain bicyclists will whiz by, but don't let them stop you from enjoying what is perhaps California's finest sycamore savanna.

Autumn is a particularly good time to visit Big Sycamore Canyon because migrating Monarch butterflies arrive to form what entomologists call over-wintering colonies. During the fall months, Sycamore Canyon offers the twin delights of falling autumn leaves and fluttering butterflies.

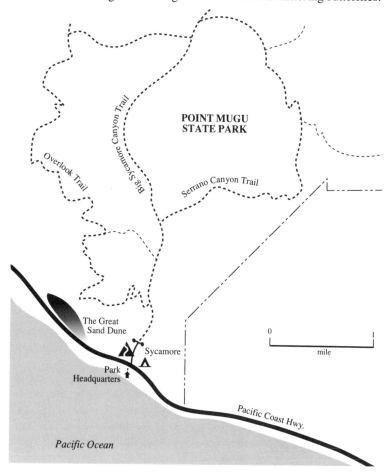

A warning: Autumn colors you might not be thrilled to see are the oranges, reds and crimsons of the poison oak bushes that line Serrano Canyon. As a precaution, wear long pants and a long-sleeved shirt when you hike through the canyon.

Directions to trailhead: From the end of the Santa Monica Freeway (10) in Santa Monica, continue up-coast on Pacific Coast Highway 35 miles to Big Sycamore Canyon Campground. It'll cost you a vehicle day-use fee to park in the new lot.

The Hike: Walk through the campground and join the fire road (closed to vehicular traffic) that leads into Big Sycamore Canyon. One-half mile from the campground you'll spot signed Overlook Trail, which switchbacks to the west up a ridge, and then heads north toward the native tall grass prairie in La Jolla Valley. Make a note of this fine trail for another day's hike.

Another mile of nearly level canyon walking brings you to a signed junction with Serrano Canyon Trail. Join this trail, which soon enters its namesake canyon, a dramatic, water-cut, high-walled gorge. The trail is narrow and lightly-traveled; it's also off-limits to horses and mountain bicyclists.

The trail climbs moderately through a coastal sage community and eventually works its way down to the creek at the bottom of the oak- and sycamore-lined canyon. First a footbridge, then some railroad tie-stair steps on the creek banks help you across the creek. The creek is sprightly, with pretty pools in winter and spring, while in summer and autumn it flows with far less enthusiasm. The footbridge is as good a place as any to wiggle into those long pants for your upcoming meeting with the abundant poison oak that grows creekside.

The trail continues for more than a mile through the fern-filled canyon bottom. Finally, the trail emerges from the canyon. (You'll miss the shade and luxuriant vegetation, but not the poison oak.) The trail ascends a canyon wall, then comes to an unsigned junction in a shallow gully. Take the right fork, uphill, about 50 yards to an old fence line separating the chaparral community from the sweeping grasslands of Serrano Valley. The valley is a beauty, as quiet a place as you'll find in the Santa Monicas.

A couple of Park Service markers keep you on the trail, which passes a solitary sumac and an abandoned aluminm and wood shed that houses an old pump.

The path cuts across the grasslands and reaches a signed junction. Serrano Valley Loop Trail veers right, but you continue straight on the path signed "To Old Boney Trail". You'll reach an unsigned junction with Old Boney Trail, turn left and soon reach another unsigned trail that leads left. You can see Big Sycamore Canyon below. You'll join this trail, which plunges down the steep canyon wall.

14

Mishe Mokwa Trail

5-mile circle tour of Circle X Ranch
1,100-foot elevation gain

Sandstone Peak, highest peak in the Santa Monica Mountains, is one of the highlights of a visit to Circle X Ranch, a park located on the border of Los Angeles and Ventura counties. The park has more than 30 miles of trail and a much-needed public campground.

The State Coastal Conservancy awarded funds to the Santa Monica Mountains Conservancy to purchase the 1,655-acre Circle X Ranch from the Boy Scouts of America. The National Park Service now administers the park.

Half a century ago, the land belonged to a number of gentlemen ranchers, including movie actor Donald Crisp, who starred in "How Green Was My Valley."

Members of the Exchange Club purchased the nucleus of the park in 1949 for $25,000 and gave it to the Boy Scouts. The emblem for the Exchange Club was a circled X—hence the name of the ranch.

About two decades ago, the Scouts, in an attempt to honor Circle X benefactor Herbert Allen, petitioned the U.S. Department of the Interior to rename Sandstone Peak. The request for "Mount Allen" was denied because of a long-standing policy that prohibited naming geographical features after living persons. Nevertheless, the Scouts held an "unofficial" dedication ceremony in 1969 to honor their leader.

Sandstone Peak—or Mount Allen, if you prefer—offers outstanding views from its 3,111-foot summit. If the five- mile up-and-back hike to the peak isn't sufficiently taxing, park rangers can suggest some terrific extensions.

Directions to trailhead: Drive up-coast on Pacific Coast Highway past the outer reaches of Malibu, a mile past the Los Angeles County line. Turn inland on Yerba Buena Road and proceed

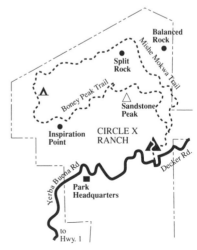

Sandstone Peak, top of the Santa Monicas

five miles to Circle X Ranch. You'll pass the park's tiny headquarters building and continue one more mile to the signed trailhead on your left. There's plenty of parking. What was once a small parking lot is now large enough to land a 747.

The Hike: From the signed trailhead, walk up the fire road. A short quarter-mile of travel brings you to a signed junction with Mishe Mokwa Trail. Leave the fire road here and join the trail, which climbs and contours over the brushy slopes of Boney Mountain. Late spring blooms include black sage, golden yarrow and wooly blue curls.

Breaks in the brush offer good views to the right of historic Triunfo Pass, which was used by the Chumash to travel from inland to coastal areas. The "drive-in movie screen" you see atop Triunfo Peak is really an old microwave relay station.

Mishe Mokwa Trail levels for a time and tunnels beneath the boughs of handsome red shanks. Growing beneath the drought-resistant chaparral plants found along the trail are some ferns. The opportunistic ferns take advantage of the shade offered by the chaparral and tap what is for the Santa Monica Mountains a relatively munificent water table located just below the surface. It's unlikely that the hiker will often find yuccas and ferns growing in close proximity on the same slope.

The trail descends into Carlisle Canyon. Across the canyon are some striking red volcanic formations, among them well-named Balanced Rock. The path, shaded by oak, and laurel, drops into the canyon at another aptly named rock formation—Split Rock. Hikers have long had a tradition of walking through the split in the rock.

Split Rock is the locale of a trail camp, shaded by oak and sycamore. An all-year creek and a spring add to the camp's charm. It's a fine place for a picnic.

From Split Rock bear right past an old outhouse—"the historic four-holer" as it is known—and begin your ascent out of Carlisle Canyon on an old ranch road. From the road's high point, you'll look straight ahead up at a pyramid-like volcanic rock formation the Boy Scouts call Egyptian Rock. To the northwest is Point Mugu State Park. You are walking on the Backbone Trail, which when completed will stretch 55 miles from Will Rogers State Historic Park to Point Mugu State Park.

The fire road turns south and you'll pass a trail camp located amid some cottonwoods. Past the camp, the fire road angles east. Look sharply to the right for a short, unsigned trail that leads to Inspiration Point. Mount Baldy and Catalina Island are among the inspiring sights pointed out by a geographical locater monument.

Continue east on the fire road and you'll soon pass the signed intersection with Boney Peak Trail. This trail descends precipitously to park headquarters. If for some reason you're in a hurry to get down, this bone-jarring route is for you.

Continue ascending on the fire road. After a few switchbacks look for a steep trail on the right. Follow this trail to the top of Sandstone Peak. "Sandstone" is certainly a misnomer; the peak is one of the largest masses of volcanic rock in the Santa Monica Mountains. Sign the summit register and enjoy the commanding, clear-day views: the Topatopa Mountains where condors once roosted, the Oxnard Plain, the Channel Islands, and the wide blue Pacific.

After you've enjoyed the view, you'll descend a bit more than a mile on the fire road back to the trailhead.

15
Nicholas Flat Trail

Leo Carrillo State Beach to Nicholas Flat
7 miles round trip; 1,600-foot elevation gain

Nicholas Flat Trail departs from Pacific Coast Highway and climbs inland up steep, scrub-covered slopes to a wide meadow and a small pond. From its high points, the trail offers good views of the Malibu coast.

Nicholas Flat Trail can also be savored for one more reason: In Southern California, very few trails connect the mountains with the sea. About eighty-five percent of all Californians live within 30 miles of the coast; in the Southland, most of the extensive coastal trail system that existed a hundred years ago has been covered with pavement or suburbs. Nowadays, to find a lot of trails that lead from Coast Highway into the mountains, you'd have to travel to the Big Sur region or the parklands north of San Francisco.

Get an early start on the Nicholas Flat Trail. Until you arrive at oak-dotted Nicholas Flat itself, there's not much shade en route. The trail crosses slopes that were scorched by a 1985 fire. In good wildflower-watching years, you might spot such fast-fading spring blooms as monkeyflowers, coyote brush, golden yarrow, bush sunflowers, hummingbird sage, and a lot of lupine along the trail.

Directions to trailhead: From the west end of the Santa Monica Freeway in Santa Monica, head up-coast on Pacific Coast Highway about 25 miles to Leo Carrillo State Beach. There's free parking along Coast Highway, and fee parking in the park's day use area. The signed Nicholas Flat trailhead is located a short distance past the park entry kiosk, opposite the day use parking area.

Pond at Nicholas Flat

74

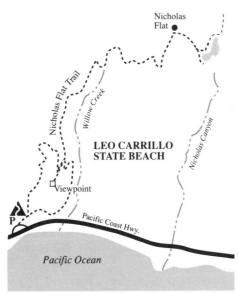

The Hike: If the state park hasn't mowed its "lawn" lately, the first fifty yards of Nicholas Flat Trail will be a bit indistinct. Immediately after its tentative beginning, the trail junctions. The right branch circles the hill, climbs above Willow Creek, and after a mile, rejoins the main Nicholas Flat Trail. Enjoy this interesting option on your return from Nicholas Flat.

Take the left branch, which immediately begins a moderate to steep ascent of the grassy slopes above the park campground. The trail switchbacks through a coastal scrub community up to a saddle on the ridgeline. Here you'll meet the alternate branch of Nicholas Flat Trail. From the saddle, a short side trail leads south to a hilltop, where there's a fine coastal view. From the viewpoint, you can see Point Dume and the the Malibu coastline. During the winter, it's a good place to bring your binoculars and scout the Pacific horizon for migrating whales.

Following the ridgeline, Nicholas Flat Trail climbs inland over chaparral-covered slope. Keep glancing over your right shoulder at the increasingly grand coastal views, and over your left at the open slopes browsed by the park's nimble deer. In the spring, the fast-fading wildflower population is dominated by that scrambling vine with the white trumpet-shaped flowers—morning glory.

After a good deal of climbing, the trail levels atop the ridgeline and you get your first glimpse of grassy, inviting Nicholas Flat. The trail descends past a line of fire- blackened, but unbowed, old oaks and joins an old ranch road that skirts the Nicholas Flat meadows. Picnickers may unpack lunch beneath the shady oaks or out in the sunny meadow. The trail angles southeast across the meadow to a small pond. The man-made pond, used by cattle during the region's ranching days, is backed by some handsome boulders.

Return the way you came until you reach the junction located 3/4 mile from the trailhead. Bear left at the fork and enjoy this alternate trail as it descends into the canyon cut by Willow Creek, contours around an ocean-facing slope, and returns you to the trailhead.

75

16

Ocean Vista Trail

3-mile loop through
Charmlee Natural Area County Park

Charmlee, a county park perched in the Santa Monica Mountains above Malibu, often has outstanding spring wildflower displays. Most of the park is a large open meadow; the flower display, given timely rainfall, can be quite good. Lupine, paintbrush, larkspur, mariposa lily, penstemon and California peony bust out all over.

Stop at Charmlee's small nature center and inquire about what's blooming where. Also pick up a copy of a brochure that interprets the park's Fire Ecology Trail. This nature trail interprets the important role of fire in Southern California's chaparral communities.

Good views are another reason to visit Charmlee. The Santa Monica Mountains spread east to west, with the Simi Hills and Santa Susana Mountains rising to the north. Down-coast you can see Zuma Beach and Point Dume and up-coast Sequit Point in Leo Carrillo State Park. Offshore, Catalina Island and two of the Channel Islands—Anacapa and Santa Cruz—can sometimes be seen.

Beginning in the early 1800s this Malibu meadowland was part of Rancho Topanga-Malibu-Sequit and was used to pasture cattle. For a century and a half, various ranchers held the property. The last of these

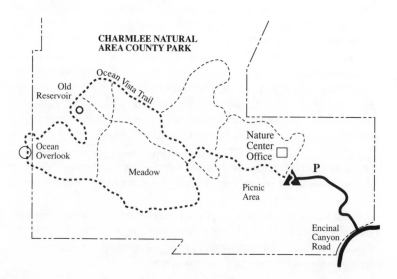

Golden Stars, spring bloomers

private landholders—Charmain and Leonard Swartz—combined their first names to give Charmlee its euphonious name. Los Angeles County acquired the Charmlee property in the late 1960s and eventually opened the 460-acre park in 1981.

For the hiker, Charmlee is one of the few parks, perhaps even the only park, that actually seems to have a surplus of trails. Quite a few paths and old ranch roads wind through the park, which is shaped like a big grassy bowl.

Because the park is mostly one big meadow fringed with oak trees, it's easy to see where you're going and improvise your own circle tour of Charmlee. Bring a kite and a picnic to this undiscovered park and relax.

Directions to trailhead: From Pacific Coast Highway, about 12 miles up-coast from the community of Malibu, head into the mountains on Encinal Canyon Road 4 1/2 miles to Charmlee Natural Area County Park.

The Hike: Walk through the park's picnic area on a dirt road, which travels under the shade of coast live oaks. The trail crests a low rise, offers a couple of side trails to the left to explore, and soon arrives at a more distinct junction with a fire road leading downhill along the eastern edge of the meadow. This is a good route to take because it leads to many fine ocean views.

Follow the road as it skirts the eastern edge of the meadow and heads south. Several ocean overlooks are encountered but the official Ocean Overlook is a rocky outcropping positioned on the far southern edge of the park. Contemplate the coast, then head west to the old ranch reservoir. A few hundred yards away is an oak grove, one of the park's many picturesque picnic spots.

You may follow any of several trails back to the trailhead or join Fire Ecology Trail for a close-up look at how Southern California's Mediterranean flora rises phoenix-like from the ashes.

17

Solstice Canyon Trail

**6-mile loop through Solstice Canyon Park
600-foot elevation gain**

Solstice Canyon Park in the Santa Monica Mountains is enjoyable year-round, but winter is a particularly fine time to ramble through the quiet canyon. From the park's upper slopes, you might even sight gray whales migrating past Point Dume.

We Southern Californians don't spend much time pondering the winter solstice, that time in the northern hemisphere when we have our shortest day, our longest night. After all, the days aren't that short, at least in comparison to those poor, sun-starved residents of Helsinki, for example, who spend all but a few hours of December days in the dark.

Solstice, to we modern city dwellers, may seem to be nothing more than a scientific abstraction—the time when the sun is farthest south of the equator. To some of the earliest occupants of Southern California, the Chumash, however, the winter solstice was a very important occasion. It was a time when the cosmic balance was very delicate. The discovery of summer and winter solstice observation caves and rock art sites, have convinced anthropologists that the Chumash possessed a system of astronomy that had both mystical meaning and practical application. To those of us who buy all our food in the supermarket, winter solstice is just a date on the calendar, but to the Chumash, who needed to know about when berries would ripen, when the steelhead would run up Malibu Creek, when game would migrate, the day was an important one.

Solstice Canyon Park opened on summer solstice, 1988. The Santa Monica Mountains Conservancy purchased the land from the Roberts family. The park is administered by the Mountains Conservancy Foundation, the operations arm of the Conservancy.

The Foundation has been working hard to transform the 550-acre Roberts Ranch into a park. Ranch roads are being converted to foot trails. Milk thistle, castor bean and other assorted nonnative plants are being eliminated. Debris, left behind by a 1982 fire, has been hauled away.

Destroyed in the fire was the Roberts family home, an extraordinary ranch-style residence that was highly praised by many home and architectural publications. The house incorporated Solstice Canyon's creek, waterfalls and trees into its unique design.

Another Solstice Canyon house—the Mathew Keller House—was built in 1865 and is the oldest house in Malibu, perhaps in the Santa Monica

Mountains. When restoration is complete, the house will become a museum and visitor center.

Solstice Canyon's third structure of note is really a strange one. It resembles a kind of futuristic farm house with a silo attached and defies architectural categorization. Bauhaus, maybe. Or perhaps Grain Elevator Modern. From 1961 to 1973 Space Tech Labs, a subsidiary of TRW, used the building to conduct tests to determine the magnetic sensitivity of satellite instrumentation. The TRW buildings are now headquarters for the Santa Monica Mountains Conservancy.

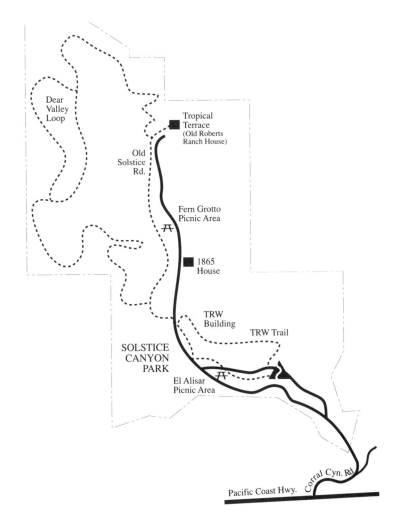

Several trails explore Solstice Canyon. TRW Loop Trail leads to the canyon bottom, where the hiker can pick up Old Solstice Road (closed to vehicular traffic) and saunter through the canyon. Sostomo Trail climbs the park's east and south-facing ridges and offers fine coastal views.

Florence Roberts, with awful meter but heartfelt sentiment, expressed her feelings about Solstice Canyon in a poem. She etched her rocking-horse rhyme on a rock stair near her house:

> *Leave behind your worries and cares,*
> *And climb with us these thirteen stairs.*
> *Our bubbling brook, our waterfall,*
> *Here we relax and enjoy it all.*

Directions to trailhead: From Pacific Coast Highway, about 17 miles up-coast from Santa Monica and 3 1/2 miles upcoast from Malibu Canyon Road, turn inland on Corral Canyon Road. At the first bend in the road, you'll leave the road and proceed straight to the very small Solstice Canyon parking lot. Beyond the parking lot, the park access road is usually closed; however, on weekends, visitors are permitted to drive in and park in a second, larger lot, located just up the road.

The Hike: Walk up the park road to a small house, which is headquarters for the Mountains Conservancy Foundation.

Near the house, join the signed TRW Trail, which switchbacks toward the strange new home of the Santa Monica Mountains Conservancy. Employees report that they much prefer this spacious, hillside office to their former, far more stressful locale downtown at 1st and Broadway.

TRW Trail crosses a paved road, ascends west, then drops south into Solstice Canyon. You'll turn right on Old Solstice Road. In a few minutes you'll pass the 1865 Mathew Keller House and in a few more minutes—Fern Grotto. The road travels under the shade of oak and sycamore to its end at the remains of the old Roberts Ranch House. Palms, agave, bamboo and bird of paradise and many more tropical plants thrive in the Roberts' garden gone wild. A waterfall, fountain and an old dam are some of the other special features found in this paradisiacal setting known as Tropical Terrace.

Just below Tropical Terrace is signed, Sostomo Trail, which ascends a chaparral-cloaked slope that still bears evidence of the 1982 fire. The trail dips in and out of a streambed, begins climbing, and offers a great view of Solstice Canyon all the way to the ocean. At a junction, the trail splits, with the right fork leading to Sostomo Overlook, while you head left toward Deer Valley. The trail crosses an open slope then tops a ridge for a great view of Point Dume. The trail briefly joins a dirt road, then resumes as a path and descends a coastal scrub-covered slope to the bottom of Solstice Canyon. A right turn on Old Solstice Road leads past El Alisar Picnic Area and returns you to the trailhead.

18

Reagan Ranch Trail

4-mile loop through Malibu Creek State Park

Before Ronald Reagan purchased what was to become the most well-known ranch in the world—Rancho del Cielo in the Santa Ynez Mountains above Santa Barbara—he owned another spread in the Santa Monica Mountains. Reagan's Ranch, now part of Malibu Creek State Park, is a delight for hikers, who can enjoy the ranch's rolling meadowland and grand old oaks, and even probe the origins of the former president's conservative political philosophy.

During the 1950s when Reagan hosted TV's "Death Valley Days," he desired a more rural retreat than his home in Pacific Palisades. He bought the 305-acre ranch in the hills of Malibu as a place to raise thoroughbred horses. Land rose greatly in value, and taxes likewise; the tax increases really piqued Reagan and influenced his political philosophy. From this point on, he would be hostile toward government programs that required more and more tax dollars to fund.

Reagan's Ranch boosted his political career in another way: it was the locale of many a barbecue and gathering attended by the well-heeled politicos who would support his gubernatorial campaign. When Reagan was elected governor in 1966, he moved to Sacramento, and sold his ranch to a movie company. Today the ranch makes up the northwest corner of Malibu Creek State Park. When the property was acquired, the Reagan ranch house was in such grim condition that it had to be destroyed. The Reagan barn still stands and is now used for offices and storage by state park employees.

Trails loop through the Reagan Ranch and connect with the main part of the state park. One path, which I've dubbed Reagan Ranch Trail, uses a combination of trails—Yearling, Deer Leg, Lookout, Crag's Road and Cage Canyon—to explore Reagan country and the heart of the park.

Winter, after rains put a little green in the grassy meadows, and spring, when lupine, larkspur and poppies pop out all over, are the best seasons for a visit.

Directions to trailhead: From Santa Monica, take Pacific Coast Highway up-coast to Malibu Canyon Road, turn inland and proceed to Mulholland Highway. Turn left and drive 3 miles to the ranch entrance at the corner of Mulholland and Cornell Road. Or from the Ventura Freeway (101) in Agoura, exit on Kanan Road and head south. Make a left on Cornell Road and follow it to its intersection with Mulholland Highway.

The trailhead is on the southeast corner. Park carefully alongside Cornell Road.

The Hike: Walk into the park on Yearling Road. The dirt road leads a quarter-mile past a row of stately eucalyptus and soon arrives at the old Reagan barn. Continue on the road which passes a corral and heads across a meadow. Soon you'll pass the first of a couple of side trails leading rightward into a grove of oaks and linking up with Deer Leg Trail. Continue straight ahead on the meadow trail.

During spring, wildflowers color the field, a 3/4-mile-long grassy strip. At the east end of the meadow, the trail dips in and out of a canyon, tunnels through some high chaparral and ascends an oak crowned ridge. Atop the ridge is a great view of Malibu Creek and the main features of the state park. Also on the ridgetop is an unsigned trail junction. You'll take the left-leading trail and begin descending southeast on well-named Lookout Trail. The trail drops to Crags Road, the state park's major trail, near Century Lake.

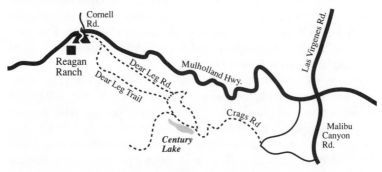

Crags Road leads east-west with Malibu Creek and connects to trails leading to the site of the old M*A*S*H set, the Backbone Trail and the park visitors center. More immediately, when you make a right on the road, you pass close to Century Lake. Near the lake are hills of porous lava and topsy-turvy sedimentary rock layers that tell of the violent geologic upheaval that formed Malibu Canyon. The man-made lake was scooped out by members of Crags Country Club, a group of wealthy, turn-of-the-century business-men who had a nearby lodge.

Walk up Crags Road about 200 hundred yards and join unsigned Cage Canyon Trail on your right. After you begin walking up the trail you'll see a sign: This trail constructed and maintained by Sierra Club. The trail makes a short and rapid ascent of the oak- and sycamore-filled canyon and soon brings you to an unsigned intersection with Deer Leg Trail. Here you bear left and begin traveling under a canopy of oaks. You'll get occasional glimpses of the rolling grassland of the Reagan Ranch below.

One attractive oak grove shades a barbecue area where the Reagans once entertained. This grove is a good place for a picnic or rest stop.

Soon you'll bear leftward at a trail junction and begin ascending the cool north slope of a hillside above the ranch. Leaving the oaks behind, the trail climbs a brushy hillside to an overlook. Enjoy the view of exclusive Malibu Lake and Paramount Ranch. The trail intersects a fire road, which you take to the right on a steep descent to the meadow near park headquarters. The road vanishes here, so walk fifty yards across the meadow to Yearling Road, which leads back to the trailhead.

A trail for the whole family along Malibu Creek

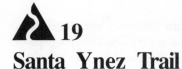 **19**

Santa Ynez Trail

Trippet Ranch to Santa Ynez Canyon
6 miles round trip; 1,000-foot elevation gain

Ferns, falls, wildflowers and dramatic sandstone cliffs are some of the delights of a ramble through Santa Ynez Canyon in the Santa Monica Mountains.

The canyon—and its waterfalls—can be reached from two trailheads; one is located at the edge of the tony Palisades Highlands development, the other is found in the heart of Topanga State Park.

The name Topanga is from the Shoshonean Indian dialect. These Indians and their ancestors occupied Topanga and adjacent canyons on and off for several thousand years, until the Spanish evicted them and forced them to settle at the San Fernando Mission.

Until the 1880s, there was little permanent habitation in the Topanga area. Early settlers tended vineyards, orchards and cattle ranches. In the 1920s, the canyon became a popular weekend destination for Los Angeles residents. Summer cabins were built along Topanga Creek and in subdivisions in the surrounding hills. For $1 round trip fare, tourists could board a Packard Auto Stage in Santa Monica and be driven up Pacific Coast Highway and Topanga Canyon Road to the Topanga Post Office and other, more scenic spots.

This hike departs from quiet and imperturbable Topanga Canyon, surrounded by urban sprawl but retaining its rural character. Santa Ynez Trail descends a ridge into Santa Ynez Canyon, then heads upstream to a 15-foot waterfall. Remember that the uphill part of this hike comes last; pace yourself accordingly.

Directions to trailhead: From Topanga Canyon Boulevard, turn east on Entrada Road; that's to the right if you're coming from Pacific Coast Highway and to the left if you're coming from the Ventura Freeway (101). Follow Entrada Road by turning left at every opportunity until you arrive at Topanga State Park. There is a state park day use fee.

If you're not feeling energetic, you can easily reach Santa Ynez Canyon via the Palisades Highland trailhead. From Sunset Boulevard in Pacific Palisades, a short distance inland from Pacific Coast Highway, turn north on Palisades Drive. As you enter the Palisades Highlands community, turn left on Verenda De La Montura. Park near the signed trailhead.

The Hike (From Topanga State Park): From the parking lot, you may proceed up the wide main trail or join the park's nature trail (a prettier way to go) and ascend past some oaks. Blue-eyed grass, owl's clover and lupine splash some springtime color on the grassy slopes. Both the nature trail and the main trail out of the parking lot lead a short quarter-mile to Fire Road 30A. Turn left on the dirt fire road and travel a short distance to signed Santa Ynez Trail. Start your descent into Santa Ynez Canyon.

High on the canyon wall, you'll get good views of the canyon and of the ocean beyond. A half-mile descent brings you to an outcropping of reddish sandstone. The main route of Santa Ynez Trail stays atop a ridgeline, but you'll notice a few steep side trails that lead to the right down to the canyon floor.

.Deer browse brushy hillsides of Topanga State Park

Soap plant, a spring bloomer with small, white, star-like flowers is abundant along the trail. This member of the lily family was a most useful plant to early residents of the Santa Monica Mountains. Indians cooked the bulbs to concoct a glue for their arrows. They also made a lather of the crushed bulbs and threw it into creeks to stun fish. White settlers stuffed mattresses with the plant's fiber.

Enjoy the views of tilted sandstone and the great bowl of Santa Ynez Canyon. As the trail nears the canyon floor it descends more precipitously. Once on the canyon bottom, turn left (down-canyon) and enter a lush environment shaded by oak and sycamore. The trail meanders with a seasonal creek to a signed junction. You'll turn left and head up-canyon on a path that crosses the creek several times. The fern-lined pools and the handsome sandstone ledges make an idyllic scene, marred only by the graffiti certain cretins have spray-painted on the boulders.

About 3/4 mile of travel brings you to the base of the waterfall. Beyond the falls are some more cascades, but continuing farther is recommended only for experienced rock- climbers; most hikers make a U-turn here and head for home.

The Hike (From Palisades Highlands): This walk departs from what I call the Designer Trailhead. Here Santa Ynez Creek, line by orange/beige artificial walls, spill over a cement creekbed. Creekside trees have been enclosed in planters, and stream-crossings are accomplished by means of cylindrical-shaped cement "stepping-stones." Once beyond this trail travesty, the path takes you into a canyon that's really quite lovely. Coast live oaks, sycamore and bay laurel line the trickling seasonal creek. Half a mile along the trail passes a pipe gate and forks. A sign points the way to Santa Ynez Falls, 3/4 mile farther up the canyon.

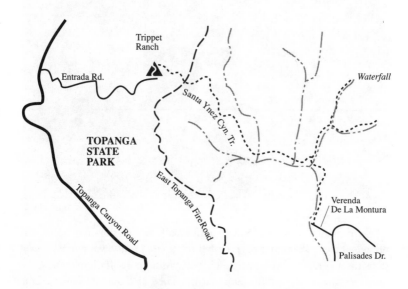

Santa Ynez Falls

20

Sullivan Canyon Trail

8-mile loop; 1,100-foot elevation gain

Sullivan Canyon above Brentwood is one of the gems of the eastern portion of the Santa Monica Mountains. Stately oaks and sycamores shade a seasonal creek and a fine trail travels the length of the canyon.

The canyon is also attractive to its owner—the Los Angeles County Sanitation District, albeit for other than aesthetic reasons. Sullivan and its neighbor, Rustic Canyon, have long been proposed as landfill sites. Protests by environmentalists have thus far derailed the dump so at least for now, Sullivan Canyon is a beautiful place to roam.

Sullivan's high and narrow canyon walls display handsome sandstone outcroppings, as well as a blue-gray bedrock known as Santa Monica slate. During winter and spring, the steep canyon walls are colored with clusters of blue, white and violet ceanothus.

Casual walkers will enjoy a nearly-flat stroll a mile or three along the canyon floor. More energetic hikers will make a loop trip by by climbing out of the canyon and traveling Sullivan's west ridge. Mountain and ocean views from the ridge are quite good.

Directions to trailhead: From the San Diego Freeway (405) in west Los Angeles, exit on Sunset Boulevard. and head west 2 1/2 miles to Mandeville Canyon Road. Turn right and after 1/4 mile turn left on Westridge Road, which

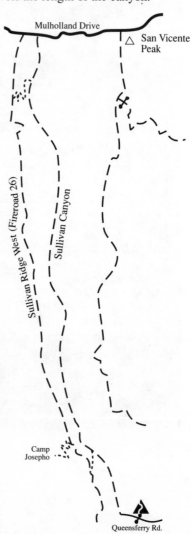

you'll follow a bit more than a mile to Bayliss Road. Turn left, travel 1/4 mile, make another left on Queensferry Road and follow this road another 1/4 mile to its end. Park near the end of the road.

The Hike: The trail begins at the end of Bayliss Road, where a frequently-traveled equestrian trail, ascending from the wilds of Brentwood, joins the road. Walk down an asphalt road (closed to vehicles) a hundred yards to cement flood control apron, then turn right and enter sylvan Sullivan Canyon.

A few minutes of walking will tell you that you've entered a very peaceful place. The wide trail meanders near a willowy streambed, beneath the boughs of antiquarian oaks and across carpets of lemon grass. Occasionally a Brentwood beauty on a prancing horse will canter by.

Three miles of tranquil trail brings you to a couple of eucalyptus trees on your left. This is a good turnaround point for those short of time or energy.

Those hikers wanting to complete this loop trip, will continue up canyon on an old dirt road. After a half-mile ascent, the road forks. The right fork leads to Mulholland Drive, which you can see about a half-mile away. You'll take the left fork and ascend a little farther to an unsigned junction with dirt Fire Road 26. A right turn offers another route to Mulholland Drive, but you'll turn left and begin descending the west ridge of Sullivan Canyon. Occasionally you'll get a glimpse to the east of Sullivan, but the better views are to the west of Rustic Canyon and the bold slopes of Topanga State Park. If it's not foggy, the coastal views are pretty good too.

The only shade on the ridge route occurs about halfway down, where you'll find a small clump of oaks and a little bench. Farther down the ridge, you'll reach a yellow gate and a paved road leading down to the Boy Scouts' Camp Josepho.

A few hundred yards past this turnoff, you'll walk under some telephone lines—your clue to begin looking sharply to your left for the unsigned connector trail that will return you to the bottom of Sullivan Canyon. As the road bears right, you'll head left for a telephone pole, pass directly under the poles two guide wires and join the footpath. The trail, quite steep but in good condition, drops several hundred feet in a quarter-mile and deposits you back on the canyon floor. Turn right, down-canyon, and travel a half-mile back to the trailhead.

*Clouds of Ceanothus
color canyon walls*

Looking north across San Fernando Valley

Chapter 5

SAN FERNANDO VALLEY

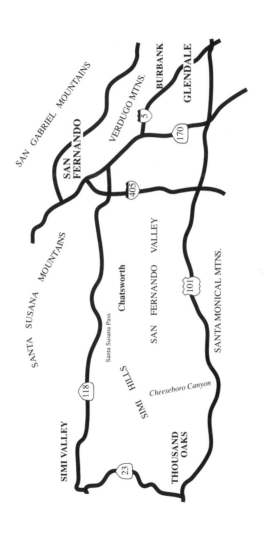

San Fernando Valley
and neighboring Simi and Conejo Valleys

It is the unique lay of the land—its geography—that in part explains why the San Fernando Valley has pursued a little bit different destiny than the the rest of Southern California.

Far back in geologic time the Valley—and most of the land around it—was flat and underwater. Over millions of years mountains rose up and enclosed it. After numerous uplifts and down-warpings, the Valley became an inland sea. Geologists speculate that two of the Valley's current openings—San Fernando Pass and Santa Susana Pass—served as inlets to this sea. Eventually the waters receded, pouring out of the Verdugo Pass at the Valley's southeast core. The path taken by these waters is today the riverbed of the Los Angeles River. One could, in fact, define the Valley as the watershed for the Los Angeles River, though this once-impressive river is now reduced to a concrete-lined flood control channel and such a definition would most certainly lack geographical grandeur.

The alluvial-filled depression we now call the San Fernando Valley is rectangular in shape, roughly twice as long as it is wide. It extends 24 miles east to west and about 12 miles north to south. (For the sake of discussion and good day hiking, we'll expand the Valley's western boundary a smidgen to take part of neighboring Conejo Valley.)

In 1769, Father Juan Crespi of the Portola expedition named the Valley De Valle Santa Catalina de Bononia de los Encinos. Mercifully, this mouthful was by the end of the century reduced to Valle de los Encinos, the Valley of the Oaks. The padres named the mission they built in 1797 after the canonized Spanish King Ferdinand III. A town and the Valley were two more places that were named after Saint Fernando.

Before the Europeans arrived, oak-dotted grassland covered much of the Valley floor. A relatively high population of Southern Shoshone and Chumash lived in the Valley and in the surrounding mountains. Game was abundant, as were acorns and seed-bearing plants. Only the lack of a dependable water supply limited the population in this land of plenty.

During the first third of the 19th Century, the Spanish and their Indian neophytes planted wheat, corn and beans, and tended horses and sheep. After the secularization of the missions, during the second third of the century, came that romantic era of the great ranchos and their huge cattle operations. In 1869, much of the southern part of the San Fernando Valley was acquired by two Isaacs—Lankershim and Van Nuys. During the last third of the century, the Valley became a giant wheat field.

When the Los Angeles Aqueduct was completed in 1913, bringing High Sierra water to the Southland, the Valley was soon transformed into an agricultural region of citrus orchards and poultry farms. By the 1930s, the irrigated fields began to give way to residential housing, a process that accelerated rapidly after World War II. Some farm communities—Winnetka, Zelzah and Owensmouth—were swallowed up, while whole new cities of stucco seemed to instantly appear.

Today's Valley cities have almost no natural boundaries. Reseda, Encino, Sun Valley and a dozen more communities are divided from each other only by signs and streets—a division that is immediately obvious to anyone who scans the Valley floor from an airplane or a nearby mountain top. The view is of an almost endless suburbia, of green lawns, glistening swimming pools, imported trees and shrubs, parking lots and shopping malls, a strange combination of tidiness and unseemliness.

The Valley surface itself takes in about 275 square miles, though it is nearly double that size if the surrounding mountains that wall off the Valley from the rest of Southern California are taken into account. And these mountains must be taken into account, for it is the mountains surrounding the Valley, not the Valley itself, where traces of the natural and human history of the region can still be found.

Walling off the San Fernando Valley on the north and northeast and protecting it from the heat of the Mojave Desert are the San Gabriel Mountains. The Santa Monica Mountains, which extend from Calabasas in the northwest to Glendale in the southeast mark the Valley's southern boundary. The Agoura Hills, Simi Hills and Santa Susana Mountains bound the Valley on the west. On the eastern edge of the Valley are the Verdugo Hills, which almost connect with the Santa Monica Mountains to the south at Verdugo Pass.

Because the Valley floor has been almost completely urbanized/suburbanized, the walker must venture into the mountains to get to know the Valley. For example, the native needle grass that once covered the floor of the San Fernando Valley is now extinct in that area, and the intrepid botanist must venture to the far corners of the Verdugo Mountains to spot clumps of this once-dominant bunchgrass.

A surprising number of trails and fire roads await the walker. One pathway actively boosted by local conservationists is the Rim of the Valley Trail, which when completed, will encircle the various mountain ranges of the San Fernando Valley.

To walk the Verdugo Mountains, Simi Hills or Santa Susana Mountains is to ascend into the unhurried past and to look down at the hectic present. Anyone who loves wild places must hope that these vestiges of Valley life lingering in the hills—sweeping grasslands, sycamore-lined creeks, soaring granite peaks—will remain for future generations to enjoy.

21

Wildwood Park Trail

To Wildwood Canyon, Lizard Rock
5 miles round trip; 400-foot elevation gain
Return via Mountclef
7 miles round trip; 600-foot gain

Wildwood Park is a tranquil retreat on the outskirts of fast-becoming-suburbanized Conejo Valley. Hikers can explore two intriguing sections of the park—gentle Wildwood Creek and Canyon and the more rugged Mountclef Ridge.

This intriguing new park with a dull name preserves 1,300 acres of canyonland and rocky cliffs. A special feature of the park is a waterfall called Paradise Falls.

Wildwood is a park-in-the-making. Plans are afoot to develop a nature center, complete with displays, exhibits and demonstrations by naturalists, and to revive a self-guided nature trail. Most of the park, however, will be left undeveloped. Quite a few school groups visit the park, which has a teepee lookout and some caves with interpretive displays inside.

Conjeo, the Spanish word for rabbit, was affixed to many geographical features in these parts. Missionary/explorer Father Font first applied it in the 18th Century. In 1803, Spanish authorities granted Rancho El Conejo to Jose Polanco and Ignacio Rodriguez. Today, a valley, a low range of mountains, a grade and a creek are among the Conejo names on the land. Wildwood Park is bounded by Conejo Creek and its two seasonal branches—Arroyo Santa Rosa and Arroyo Conejo.

Before the park came into being, it belonged to a development company that leased it out to MGM studios which owned adjacent land. The epic film "Spartacus" was filmed here, and the set for "Dodge City" and "The Rifleman" were located on what is now Wildwood Park.

The park's trail system, while unsigned, is fairly extensive. Oak Grove, Eagle Point and Santee are a few of the many trails that crisscross the park. While circling the park, you'll make use of a half-dozen paths that I've collectively dubbed Wildwood Park Trail.

Directions to trailhead: From the Ventura Freeway (101) in Thousand Oaks, exit on Lynn Road. Drive 2 1/2 miles north to Avenida Los Arboles. Turn left and proceed a mile to the park entrance, then turn left and drive a half-mile down a dirt road to the parking area.

The Hike: From the parking area, descend down the dirt fire road into Wildwood Canyon. You'll soon reach a junction. A left will take you to Meadows Cave and a picnic area. Turn right and follow the trail along Wildwood Creek.

After a short while, you'll reach a side trail on your right that leads up to Tepee Overlook. After taking a look at the teepee, which looks more like a picnic ramada than anything Native American, you can return to the creek trail the way you came or via a longer route by continuing on the dirt road past the teepee.

The creekside trail bends north with Wildwood Creek then climbs the sage- and lemonade berry-covered north canyon wall. Below is tiny Paradise Falls. Beyond the falls, both the creekside trail and Oak Grove Nature Trail meander through the oaks to a picnic area.

Beyond the picnic area, the trail heads west and crosses the creek a couple times. Approaching the park's western boundary you'll get a whiff of the Hill Canyon Sewage Treatment Plant then turn sharply north on signed Lizard Rock Trail. This path rises steeply over a wildflower-splashed grassy slope, then turns east and brings you to the base of a handsome cluster of rocks. The rock's resemblance to a lizard is dubious, but the lizard's-eye-view from atop the rock is pretty good.

Clear-day views are good from Lizard Rock and even better from the central and eastern portion of the Mountclef Range. Far to the north you can see the Los Padres National Forest backcountry and the Condor Sanctuary above Fillmore and Santa Paula. More immediately to the north are the Las Posas Hill and Little Simi Valley. To the south is Conejo Valley. To the northeast are the Santa Susana Mountains, to the east are the Simi Hills. To the west are the Camarillo Hills and Oxnard Plain.

The trail heads east down the rocky ridgeline, passes an extensive prickly pear cactus patch and continues descending toward the main part of the park. Just before you return to familiar ground—the parking area and trails leading to it—you'll arrive at the signed junction with Santa Rosa Trail. For a nice option and some great views, follow this side trail as it ascends into rocky Mountclef Range. Up-top are some lumpy, pudding-like conglomerate rocks and a panorama of both wild and suburban Ventura County.

22

Cheeseboro Canyon Trail

NPS Parking Lot to Sulfur Springs
  6 miles round trip; 100-foot elevation gain
NPS Parking Lot to Sheep Corral
  9 1/2 miles round trip; 200-foot elevation gain

It's the old California of the ranchos: Oak-studded potreros, rolling foothills that glow amber in the dry months, emerald green in springtime. It's not hard to imagine vaqueros rounding up tough Mexican range cattle.

But today this last vestige of old California, a canyon called Cheeseboro, faces an uncertain future. Though partially protected by the Santa Monica Mountains National Recreation Area, part of the canyon and much of the surrounding countryside may go the way of the ranchos; that is to say—sold, subdivided and paved over.

County Government is considering the construction of a four-lane boulevard in the lower reaches of Cheeseboro Canyon and a developer wants to build a suburb and a golf course on land bordering the park. If pro-development forces have their way, the last wildlife corridor connecting the Santa Monica Mountains to the open lands of the north will become part of Thousand Oaks Boulevard. If subdividers are successful, this little bit of parkland perched on the western rim of the San Fernando Valley will soon be an island facing the tidal wave of development sweeping the Simi Hills.

When walking beneath a canopy of oak and sycamore in the bottom of Cheeseboro Canyon, it's possible to leave people and politics far behind and enjoy this Southern California of old. But ascending the canyon's north wall on the Modello Trail brings you to a confrontation with modernity—the sight of bulldozers making molehills out of mountains.

In times past, the Chumash occupied this land. The Indians came to gather acorns, a staple of their diet. A family required about 500 pounds of acorns a year, anthropologists estimate. It was quite an operation to gather, dry, and grind the acorns into meal, then leach the meal to remove the bitter tannic acid.

From the days of the ranchos to 1985, Cheeseboro Canyon was heavily grazed by cattle. Grazing altered canyon ecology by displacing native flora and allowing opportunistic plants such as mustard and thistle to invade. As you walk through the canyon, you'll see signs indicating research areas. The National Park Service is attempting to re-colonize native flora and eradicate nonnatives.

Cheeseboro Canyon—for now—is a pleasant walk, gentle enough for the whole family. Weekdays it's an especially tranquil locale.

Directions to trailhead: From the Ventura Freeway (101) in Agoura, exit on Cheesebro Road. Loop inland very briefly on Palo Comado Canyon Road, then turn right on Cheesebro Road, which leads to the National Park Service's gravel entrance road and parking lot.

The Hike: Note your return route, Modello Trail, snaking north up the wall of the canyon, but follow the fire road east into Cheeseboro Canyon. The fire road soon swings north and dips into the canyon. You'll pass a signed intersection with Canyon Overlook Trail, a less-than-thrilling side trail that leads to a knoll overlooking the Lost Hills landfill.

After this junction, the main canyon trail, now known as Sulfur Springs Trail, winds through valley oak *(Quercus lobata)*-dotted grassland and coast live oak *(Quercus agrifolia)*-lined canyon. Watch for mule deer browsing in the meadows and a multitude of squirrels scurrying amongst the oaks.

The old road crisscrosses an (usually) all-but-dry streambed. About 3 miles from the trailhead, your nose will tell you that you've arrived at Sulfur Springs. You can turn around here or continue another 1 3/4 miles up a narrowing trail and narrowing canyon to an old sheep corral.

Return the way you came on Sulfur Springs Trail to a junction 3/4 mile from the trailhead. Join signed Modello Trail which ascends the west wall of the canyon. From the ridgetop you can get a good view of Cheeseboro Canyon and can ponder the future of what is one of the finest remaining oak woodlands in Southern California.

At a signed junction, stay with Modello Trail, which loops around the head of a ravine, then descends to the trailhead.

Coast live oak (Quercus agrifolia)

97

23

Stagecoach Trail

Chatsworth Park South to Devil's Slide
2 1/2 miles round trip; 500-foot elevation gain

One of the major obstacles to stagecoach travel between Los Angeles and San Francisco was a route out of the west end of the San Fernando Valley over the Simi Hills. About 1860, a steep road was carved out of the rock face of the hills. The steepest stretch, a peril to man and beast, was known as Devil's Slide.

The slide, the old stage road and a portion of the Simi Hills are preserved in a park in-the-making located just west of Chatsworth. In 1989, the state purchased 400 acres in the Santa Susana Pass area and added it to another 400 acres of state-owned parkland. Eventually Santa Susana State Park will be staffed with rangers, and have recreation facilities. The park represents two decades of organizing and lobbying efforts by San Fernando Valley and Simi Valley environmentalists, spearheaded by the Santa Susana Mountain Park Association.

Santa Susana as a park name is a bit confusing because it is the Simi Hills not the nearby Santa Susana Mountains that are protected by the park. Visually, the Simi Hills with their skyscraping sedimentary rock formations are quite different from the rounder, taller Santa Susana Mountains to the north of Chatsworth.

A network of trails loop through the park, but the trails are unsigned and more than a little confusing. During your first visit to the park, expect to improvise a bit. Once you get the lay of the land, subsequent visits will be easier.

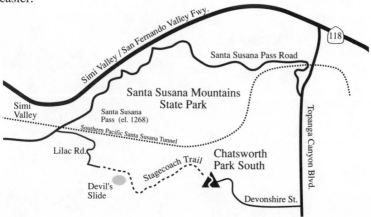

Directions to trailhead: From the Ventura Freeway (101) in Woodland Hills, exit on Topanga Canyon Boulevard and drive 6 1/4 miles north to Devonshire Street. Turn left and proceed 3/4 mile to Chatsworth Park South, a city-owned park with wide lawns and picnic areas, located next to the new state park. If you're coming from the Simi Valley-San Fernando Valley Freeway (118), take the Topanga Canyon Boulevard exit in Chatsworth, drive 1 1/2 miles to Devonshire and turn right to the park.

As you drive up Devonshire you'll notice signed Stagecoach Trail, an equestrian trail. Leave your car and pick up this trail if you wish, but it's more convenient continuing to the ample parking area in the main part of Chatsworth Park South.

The Hike: From the parking lot, walk across the wide lawn (or take one of the dirt paths that border the lawn). With the park recreation center directly behind you, navigate toward a couple of oaks and join a gravel path that begins just below a water tower on your right.

Begin a moderate ascent. When presented with confusing choices and unsigned junctions, try to keep ascending straight up the hill. Don't drift too far to the south where there's a line of electrical transmission towers, or too far to the north where the Southern Pacific railroad tracks penetrate the mountains.

A half-mile from the trailhead you'll intersect a paved road, which winds up to a small hydroelectric pumping plant. You, however, will almost immediately abandon this road at a break in a chain link fence by two telephone poles. Here you'll find the old stage road and begin to climb more earnestly toward Devil's Slide.

A century ago, the road was in much better shape. Erosion has carved wagon-wheel-sized potholes into the soft rock. The Devil's Slide is more like the Devil's Stairs these days.

Near the top of the slide is a historical marker placed by the Native Daughters of the American West commemorating "Old Santa Susana Stagecoach Road, 1859-90." This is a great place to pull up a rock, sit a spell and survey the San Fernando Valley, which spreads south and east. Just below is Chatsworth, a mixture of old ranchland and new townhouses. If you're lucky, you'll sight a freight or passenger train snaking through the Simi Hills and disappearing into the Santa Susana tunnel.

After enjoying the view, you can continue another 1/4 mile up the Stagecoach Trail and inspect the rest of Devil's Slide. Or you can retrace your steps and take one the side trails leading southeast over to the park's intriguing rock formations.

24

O'Melveney Park Trail

Bee Canyon to Mission Point
4 1/2 miles round trip; 1,400-foot gain

Billowing grass and seasonal wildflowers paint a pastoral landscape on the slopes of L.A.'s second-largest park. O'Melveney Park, located at the north end of the San Fernando Valley, is the principal recreation area in the Santa Susana Mountains. The park's peaks offer the hiker commanding clear-day views of the Los Angeles Basin.

O'Melveney Park takes its name from the well-known family of Los Angeles lawyers who once owned a "gentleman's ranch" here. Attorney John O'Melveney bought the land in 1941 and called it CJ Ranch. Cattle roamed the hills, a citrus orchard was planted, and family members enjoyed spending weekends roaming the Santa Susana Mountains. The family ranch house, barn and orchard still stand near the park entrance.

Although areas near the ranch were oil-rich, exploration on the ranch was unsuccessful. The O'Melveneys deeded half their ranch to Los Angeles, and the city purchased the rest. The 720-acre park, which opened to the public in 1981, includes a large developed picnic area and rugged wildland laced with 10 miles of trail.

In spring, a host of wildflowers—poppies, morning glory, Indian paintbrush and Mariposa lily—splash the hillsides. Fall wildflowers include the white trumpet-shaped jimson weed, scarlet California fuschia, and yellow goldenbrush. Wildlife in O'Melveney Park includes deer, golden eagle, bobcat, rabbit, raccoon, and coyote. All this flora and fauna next to super-suburban San Fernando Valley!

This hike follows a fire road to Mission Point and explores the wild parts of O'Melveney Park. Bring a city map. As you climb high into the Santa Susana Mountains, you can pick out numerous natural and man-made points of interest. Views of the Southland from 2,771-foot Mission Point are often quite good.

Directions to trailhead: Exit the San Diego Freeway (405) on Rinaldi and turn west. Turn right on Balboa Boulevard and in 3/4 miles, turn left on Jolette. Follow Jolette a mile to Sesnon Boulevard. (A right turn on Sesnon will take you to the developed part of O'Melveney Park.) Turn left on Sesnon, then right on Neon Way. Park at the end of Neon Way. The fire road leading to Mission Point starts here.

The Hike: The fire road leads you past a seasonal brook and begins to climb high above the nearby residential area. It is moderate to strenuous climbing in the first mile. Evidence of the 1971 earthquake that damaged the nearby Golden State Freeway and Van Norman Dam is present in the form of fissures and slides. Seismically, the Santa Susana Mountain range is one of California's most active areas.

As you make your ascent, you'll notice quite a difference in vegetation between north and south slopes. The canyon's dry north slopes are blanketed with sage and other coastal scrub. To the south, the hills are covered with grasses punctuated with occasional live oak or California walnut.

As you near the top, you'll pass a small stand of Aleppo pine, which is a tree native to Mediterranean countries. This pine is successful in Southern California's Mediterranean climate, too.

Close to the top, a couple washed-out dirt roads and bulldozer lines converge. (All roads lead toward Mission Point, but the "main road" is easier walking.) Navigate toward four sturdy oaks, which offer a nice picnic or rest stop.

Just past the oaks, a dirt road branches left and leads to wind-blown Mission Point. A 1932 U.S. Geological Survey Marker is atop the point. Two seasonal cow ponds are located on the southwest slope. Below Mission Point to the northwest are oil fields and natural gas underground storage areas.

Enjoy the view of the Santa Susana Mountains—including nearby Oat Mountain, highest peak in the range. The San Gabriel Mountains, Santa Monica Mountains, Santa Clarita Valley, and downtown Los Angeles are also part of the 360-degree panorama. Return the way you came.

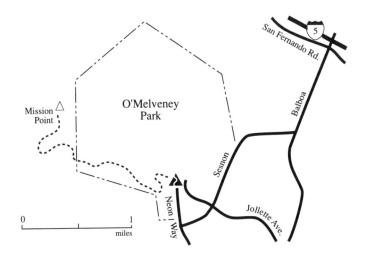

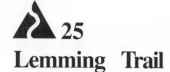

25

Lemming Trail

San Fernando Valley to the Sea
   12 miles one way; 2,000-foot elevation gain

You won't find any lemmings along the Southern California coast; the furry, short-tailed, mice-like creatures inhabit Arctic, not Mediterranean climes. The Lemming Trail takes its name not from the rodent's presence in the Santa Monica Mountains, but from its proclivity to rush headlong into the sea.

A crisp, cool winter or spring day is a great time to make like a lemming and hike from the San Fernando Valley to the sea. The Lemming Trail offers a grand tour of the Santa Monica Mountains, the only relatively undeveloped mountain range in the United States that bisects a major metropolitan area. You'll travel from Tarzana to Topanga to Temscal to the Pacific on a network of trails and fire roads and be treated to some superb valley and coastal vistas.

Though the Lemming Trail was named for a small rodent, be assured that this is no Mickey Mouse hike. Be prepared for a very long and strenuous day.

Directions to trailhead: This is a one-way walk so either a car shuttle or a helpful non-hiking friend to assist with the transportation logistics is necessary. Leave one car at Will Rogers State Beach (fee) or along Pacific Coast Highway (free) near the intersection of the Coast Highway and Temescal Canyon Road. Next proceed up-coast on PCH to Topanga Canyon Road (27) and drive inland through the canyon to Ventura Boulevard. Turn right (east) and head into Tarzana. Turn right on Reseda Boulevard and follow this road to its end. (A quick route to the Lemming trailhead is to exit the Ventura Freeway (101) on Reseda Boulevard and drive east to its end.)

The Hike: Descend to the dirt road (Fire Road 28) that meanders up the bottom of Caballero Canyon. The sycamore-dotted canyon bottom hosts an intermittent stream. After a mile, the fire road veers left and climbs to a locked gate on Mulholland Drive.

Turn right onto Mulholland and after walking a half-mile, look leftward for the Bent Arrow Trail, which will take you into Topanga State Park. Follow this trail, which at first parallels Mulholland, for 1/2 mile as it contours around a steep slope and reaches Temescal Fire Road (Fire Road 30). Turn left and begin a moderate descent. After a mile and a half, you'll pass junctions with fire roads on your right leading to Eagle Rock and

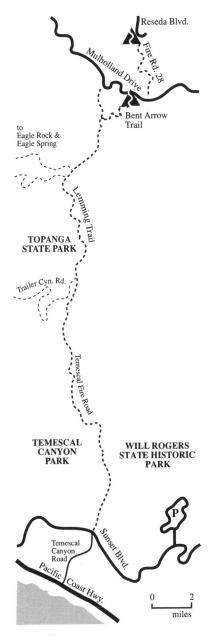

to
Eagle Rock &
Eagle Spring

Reseda Blvd.

Mulholland Drive

Fire Rd. 28

Bent Arrow
Trail

Lemming Trail

TOPANGA
STATE PARK

Trailer Cyn. Rd.

Temescal Fire Road

TEMESCAL
CANYON
PARK

WILL ROGERS
STATE HISTORIC
PARK

P

Temescal
Canyon
Road

Sunset Blvd.

Pacific Coast Hwy.

0   2
└────┴────┘
miles

Eagle Spring. Continue straight ahead past these junctions on the sharp ridgeline separating Santa Ynez and Temescal Canyons. You'll pass the junction with Rogers Road which leads to Will Rogers State Historic Park. Near the intersection of Rogers Road and Temescal Fire Road is Temescal Peak (2,126 Feet), highest peak in Topanga State Park. If you wish, scramble up a short and steep firebreak to the top for a fine view.

After one and a half miles of mostly level walking beyond the Rogers Road intersection, you'll pass Trailer Canyon Road and a mile farther south, Split Rock Road. A microwave tower, atop what locals have dubbed "Radio Peak," stands halfway between the points.

As you descend along the ridge, you'll see some rock outcroppings. A short side trip off the fire road will bring you to Skull Rock, where you can climb inside the wind-formed (aeolian) caves to cool off or picnic. From the ridgetop, the view to the southwest down at the housing developments isn't too inspiring, but the view of the rough unaltered northern part of Temescal Canyon is superb.

As you sweat it out crossing the exposed ridge, you might be amused to learn that "temescal" is what the Chumash Indians called their village sweathouse. The Chumash took as many as two ceremonial sweat baths a day, in what anthropologists speculate might have been a religious ritual. Mission fathers complained that the Chumash took too many baths and were a little too clean. More work at the mission and less relaxation in the sweathouse would be more productive, the padres thought.

Temescal Fire Road narrows and switchbacks down into Temescal Canyon. You might want to stop and cool off at the small waterfall here at the Temescal Creek crossing at the bottom of the canyon. Your route crosses over to the east side of the canyon and descends the canyon bottom on a trail shaded by oaks, willows, and sycamores.

You'll join a paved road and walk through the Presbyterian Conference Center, then join paved Temescal Canyon Road—or improvise a parallel route down canyon through a small park managed by the Santa Monica Mountains Conservancy.

After crossing Sunset Boulevard, you'll walk an easy mile through Temescal Canyon City Park to Pacific Coast Highway. Across Coast Highway is Will Rogers State Beach. Local mountaineering tradition dictates that you emulate the lemming and rush into the sea.

Make like a lemming and head for the sea

26

La Tuna Canyon Trail

La Tuna Canyon Road to Horny Toad Ridge
6 miles round trip; 1,000-foot elevation gain
La Tuna Canyon Road to Fire Wardens Grove
9 miles round trip; 1,700-foot elevation gain
Return via Hostetter Fire Road
10 1/2 miles round trip

Rising above the southeast end of the San Fernando Valley, the Verdugo Mountains are a surprisingly rugged, usually overlooked place to hike. One reason the mountains are an overlooked destination is the scarcity of hiking trails.

La Tuna Canyon Trail, constructed in the spring of 1989, is the first foot trail built in modern times to explore the Verdugo Mountains. The trail was built by the Los Angeles Conservation Corps, under the leadership of Ron Webster. The Santa Monica Mountains Conservancy, a state conservation agency, provided funds for the project.

Hikers who have hiked a lot of trails will be delighted with the look and feel of La Tuna Canyon Trail. The hand-built trail follows the lay of the land and is not at all obtrusive.

The mountains took their name from Jose Maria Verdugo, who in 1784 received one of the earliest Spanish Land grants in California. Rancho de Los Verdugo was a cattle ranch that took in land betweeen Mission San Gabriel and Mission San Fernando.

Conservationists, primarily members of SWAP (Small Wilderness Area Preservation), rallied to halt a proposed scenic parkway at the crest of the Verdugos, prevented the subdivision of the mountaintops, and preserved a portion of the mountains as parklands.

La Tuna Canyon Trail visits some quiet oak- and sycamore-lined canyons and ascends to the range's principal feature—and its main attraction for hikers—its ridgetop, which extends the length of the range. The ridgetop offers grand clear-day views of the San Fernando Valley, San Gabriel Mountains and downtown Los Angeles.

Directions to trailhead: From the Foothill Freeway (210) in Tujunga (between the communities of La Crescenta and Sunland), exit on La Tuna Canyon Road. As you head west, look sharply left, and you'll spot what looks like a frontage road paralleling the freeway. This road, closed to vehicular traffic, is the road you'll be descending from the ridgetop if you elect the longer loop option of this hike.

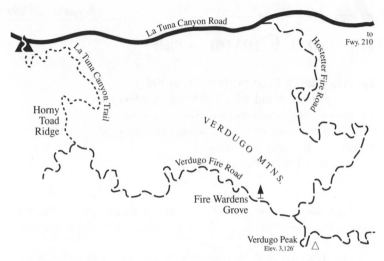

One mile from the freeway exit, you'll spot a turnout on the south side of the road with a Santa Monica Mountains Conservancy sign. (A short trail leads to a grotto and a seasonal waterfall.) Continue another 3/10 of a mile to a second turnout on your left and park.

The Hike: The unsigned trail descends into the mouth of a narrow canyon, then promptly ascends the canyon wall to a little wooden overlook. The path switchbacks out of the canyon, tops Horny Toad Ridge, then descends holly-leaved cherry-covered slopes into a second, unnamed canyon. (Not only are the charms of the Verdugos undiscovered, they're also unnamed.) Reaching the bottom of the canyon, the trail visits an oak- and sycamore-shaded glen. Beneath the trees are ferns, tangled vines and plenty of of poison oak.

At the canyon bottom, the trail joins a very steep, crumbling dirt road. Below the road are a couple of old pickup trucks; one guesses their owners drove them down the steep grade, but couldn't get them back out of the canyon. The road climbs at a 25% grade for a half-mile, then joins Horny Toad Ridge, so-named by the trail builders for the abundance of spiky-looking, brown, tan, and cream-colored horned toad lizards found here. Another half-mile's ascent along the ridge brings you to a junction with Verdugo Fire Road. Looking sharply to the east, you can see the hike's next destination—the radio towers and pine plantation near Verdugo Peak.

Turn left (east) on Verdugo Fire Road, sometimes called "Backbone Road," and begin a moderate ascent. Enjoy the great ridgetop views of the San Fernando Valley. Near the top of the range, you'll reach Fire Wardens Grove, planted by the Los Angeles County Department of Forestry more than a half-century ago. The department's Fire Wardens patrolled the Verdugos until 1953 when the agency was combined with the Los Angeles

County Fire Department. The mixed stand of conifers planted by the Fire Wardens offer some welcome shade.

From the ridge just above Fire Wardens Grove, enjoy the the views, particularly to the south, of Griffith Park, the Santa Monica Mountains and downtown L.A. On a clear day, even the Palos Verdes Peninsula, Los Angeles Harbor and Catalina Island are visible from this vantage point.

From Fire Warden's Grove, continue east on the ridge road, and you'll soon pass the second-highest peak in the Verdugos, a 3,120-foot-antennae-topped (again we have a shortage of names here) peak. Continue toward Verdugo Peak, and you'll soon reach a junction; Verdugo Fire Road continues along the top of the range, then descends to Glendale, but you turn left and begin descending on unsigned Hostetter Fire Road toward La Tuna Canyon. As you descend the north slopes of the Verdugos, and look north, particularly prominent is Mount Lukens—bristling with antennae—the highest peak within the city limits of Los Angeles. You'll also get a good look at the Glendale Freeway and narrow Verdugo Valley, which separates the mountains from its smaller sister range, the San Rafael.

A bit more than a mile's descent from the top brings you to a water tank, and two miles along to an apiary. The Foothill Freeway comes into view, the road turns to asphalt, and you'll travel the frontage road one-half mile to La Tuna Canyon Road. Here you'll head west (use caution when walking on the road shoulder) 1.3 miles back to the trailhead.

Master trail builder Ron Webster walks the trail he designed

 27

Brand Trail

Brand Park to Verdugo Overlook
6 1/2 miles round trip; 1,300-foot elevation gain

"Have you been to Glendale?"

This was the question posed in full-page advertisements that ran every Sunday in Los Angeles newspapers during the early years of this century. The man placing these ads was civic booster/real estate tycoon Leslie C. Brand, often referred to as "The Father of Glendale."

Born in St. Louis, Brand moved to the Southland in 1898 and did quite well in the insurance business, becoming president of Guarantee Title and Trust Company of Los Angeles. By 1902, he owned one thousand acres in the Verdugo Mountains.

At the base of the mountains Brand built El Miradero, a 5,000-square-foot mansion. Brand had visited the East Indian Pavillion built for the 1893 Columbia World Exposition in Chicago and was so impressed by the architecture that he decided to have something similar designed for himself. El Miradero, with its elegant white exterior, horseshoe arches and bulbous domes is a unique example of Saracenic architecture—a mixture of Spanish, Moorish and Indian styles.

Brand died in 1925, his widow in 1945, after which, by the terms of his will, Brand's property was deeded to the city of Glendale for use as a park. El Mirador is now Brand Library.

Brand Park, shaped a little bit like Italy, preserves a portion of the surprisingly rugged Verdugo Mountains, which rise above the southeast end of the San Fernando Valley. Although the 13-mile-long range is surrounded by millions of people, the cities of Burbank. Glendale, La Canada-Flintridge, Los Angeles, Pasadena and four freeways, few hikers have discovered it.

The Verdugo range, which extends northwest to southeast, is one of the mountain barriers separating the San Fernando Valley from the Los Angeles Basin. Glendale, located at the base of the mountains, usually doesn't consider itself part of the San Fernando Valley, but its geographical position in the southeast end of the valley is easily apparent when looking down upon it from the crest of the Verdugos.

Brand Trail is a fire road that offers a moderately steep ascent from El Miradero, through Brand Park to the ridgeline of the Verdugos. Fine valley views are yours from an overlook, where a strategically placed bench offers a rest for tired hikers. From Verdugo Overlook, intrepid walkers can easily extend their hike by joining one of several fire roads that travel the rooftop of the Verdugos.

Directions to trailhead: From the Golden State Freeway (I-5) in Glendale, exit on Western Avenue and head northeast on the palm-lined avenue 1 1/2 miles to Brand Library.

The Hike: Near the parking area is an ivy-covered slope where abandoned Brand Nature Trail awaits rejuvenation. You'll take the asphalt road to the left of the library that leads past the "Doctors' House," an 1880s Victorian home in the Queen Anne style that was occupied by a series of four doctors. Citizens saved this historical treasure from the wrecking ball and moved it to its present site.

A bit past a pipe gate that closes the road to vehicle traffic you'll encounter Canary Island pines, palm trees and other tropical vegetation gone wild. These trees and various tropical shrubs are what's left of Brand's estate grounds, once a fairyland of waterfalls, fountains and exotic flora.

A half-dozen roads crisscross this area. Stay on the main, widest one. A mile from the trailhead you'll pass a less attractive scene—a small sanitary landfill. Watch for rumbling trucks on the road on the weekdays.

Beyond the landfill, the road, now dirt, returns to a more natural setting. You pass a sycamore-lined canyon and reach a signed junction. Keep left on "Brand" and don't stray onto "Brand Lat."

Those parts of the hills where tilted rock outcroppings don't predominate are covered with the chaparral and coastal sage communities. Lemonade berry, toyon, ceanothus, sage, buckwheat, manzanita and tree tobacco are among the more common flora.

Two miles of ascent brings you to an oak tree, which offers the only shade en route. Keep climbing another long mile to the overlook.

A clear-day view takes in much of the San Fernando Valley and part of the Los Angeles Basin, including downtown. You can see the southeast end of the Santa Monica Montains, the Hollywood

109

Hills and Griffith Park.

From the overlook, you can can travel left (northwest) 2 miles along the ridgetop to 3,126-foot Mount Verdugo, highest peak in the range. Looking north and northwest you can see the San Gabriel Mountains and the mountains of Los Padres National Forest rising above Ojai.

"Have you been to Glendale?" asked founding father Leslie Brand

28

Dearing Mountain Trail

Wilacre Park to Coldwater Canyon Park
2 1/2 miles round trip; 500-foot elevation gain
Wilacre Park to Fryman Overlook
6 miles round trip; 700-foot elevation gain.

Wilacre Park and Fryman Overlook, Coldwater Canyon Park and Franklin Canyon Ranch—these four recreation areas comprise Cross Mountain Park. Individually and collectively, they contribute some much-needed breathing room to the San Fernando Valley side of the Santa Monica Mountains.

Betty P. Dearing Trail—or Dearing Mountain Trail as it's usually called—connects Fryman Overlook with both Coldwater Canyon Park and Wilacre Park. The trail honors a determined conservationist for her efforts to create a trail across the Santa Monica Mountains from Los Angeles to the sea.

The trail begins in the wilds of Studio City in Wilacre Park, the former estate of silent movie cowboy Will Acres. The land was saved from the bulldozer by environmentalists and the Santa Monica Mountains Conservancy in 1982. From the park's high points, great clear-day vistas of the San Fernando Valley await the urban mountaineer.

The trail continues to Fryman Overlook on Mulholland Drive, where the aforementioned valley vistas are even more terrific. From the overlook, you can follow a footpath and a suburban street back to Wilacre Park.

Between the panoramic viewpoints is Coldwater Canyon Park, headquarters of the TreePeople. The group's well-publicized tree-planting campaign has contributed a great deal to the greening of Los Angeles. You can learn about the TreePeople's work by visiting their exhibits, landscaping display, nursery and headquarters. And you can learn about the trees themselves by taking Magic Forest Nature Trail, which winds through the preserve. Benches and drinking water welcome the weary hiker.

Along Dearing Mountain Trail, you'll observe two man-made alterations of the landscape. One alteration is botanical; many exotic trees and shrubs grow on the steep slopes of Coldwater and Fryman canyons. TreePeople Headquarters was once Fire Station 108, built by the Los Angeles Fire Department in 1923. During the years the firemen were in residence, eucalyptus, pine and many other kinds of nonnative trees were planted in the area.

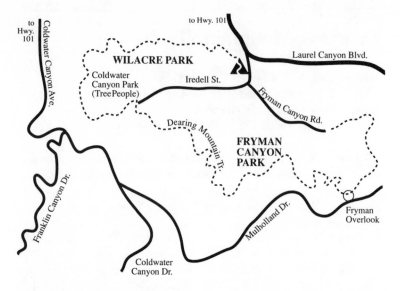

Another alteration is the terracing of hillsides to create pads for the construction of homes. Building on steep slopes is, of course, prevalent in canyons all around Southern California, but in the Coldwater-Laurel Canyon area it has reached ridiculous heights. The hiker looks up at some truly astonishing residences—homes on stilts, homes built stairstep-like down preciptious canyon walls, homes that seem certain to slide down to Ventura Boulevard after the first good rain.

Directions to trailhead: From the Ventura Freeway (101) in Studio City, exit on Laurel Canyon Boulevard and drive south 1 1/2 miles to Fryman Canyon Road. Turn right and park immediately. The unsigned trail begins at a yellow vehicle gate.

The Hike: Ascend the asphalt road past bay laurel and towering toyon, walnut trees and assorted planted pines. The road retires to dirt and soon proffers terrific clear-day vistas of the San Fernando Valley.

At a wide spot in the road, a bit more than a mile from the trailhead, you'll intersect Coldwater Canyon Park's Magic Forest Trail. You may continue on Dearing Mountain Trail, still a dirt road at this point. If you want a little break, detour right on the park's nature trail. Ascend one of the handsome stone staircases, built by the WPA in the 1930s, to the domain of the TreePeople. After learning about the group's tree-planting efforts, rejoin Dearing Mountain Trail.

A half-mile descent on the trail brings you past the backside of some homes, a yellow vehicle gate, and down to Iredell Street. Walk 50 yards on the street and rejoin Dearing Mountain Trail at another yellow gate. After a hundred yards the trail junctions. Stay left and begin a short, but very steep ascent up a terraced slope. The trail then descends to the head of a ravine that's watered by a seasonal creek and shaded by towering eucalyptus. Frogs provide musical accompaniment to the path, which traverses the canyon wall, then dips again to the bottom of another ravine. Unfortunately, this ravine and its tiny creek is located below one of Mulholland Drive's "Deadman's Curves," and has become the final resting place for a dozen wrecked autos. Minus the junkyard, this fern-lined little dell would be a pretty spot.

The trail ascends moderately up the chaparral-covered south wall of Fryman Canyon to Mulholland Drive and Fryman Overlook. From the overlook, much of the San Fernando Valley is at your feet. Beyond the valley, smog-free views also take in the Verdugo, Santa Susana and San Gabriel mountain ranges.

Fryman Overlook displays two commemorative plaques. One praises Mulholland Drive, brainchild of William Mulholland, chief engineer of the Los Angeles Department of Water and Power, who in 1913 proposed a 55-mile scenic road through the Santa Monica Mountains. Betty P. Dearing (1917-1977) is honored for her efforts to "create a nature walk from Los Angeles to the sea."

Road-builders have been more successful than trail-builders in the Santa Monicas. While Mulholland Drive was constructed in the early 1920s "to take Angelenos from the city to the ocean," the Backbone Trail across the spine of mountains has yet to be completed, despite more than twenty years of work.

Physical fitness freaks not content with the workout afforded by this hike will proceed to Fryman Overlook's exercise course for a round of hip flexor stretches, side bends and gluteus stretches. The less-energetic will head for home.

Return a short distance on Dearing Mountain Trail to a junction; instead of descending the way you came, keep straight and follow the sage- and toyon-lined path as it heads east below Mulholland Drive. The trail turns north then east again and soon junctions. Take the left fork and descend steeply down a mustard-cloaked hillside to a dirt fire road. Turn left on the fire road, which after a hundred yards continues as a cement path and descends to a yellow gate at the corner of Dona Maria Drive and Fryman Road. Follow Fryman Road 3/4 of a mile to the trailhead at Wilacre Park.

Atop Mt. Hollywood

Chapter 5

THE WILD SIDE OF L.A.

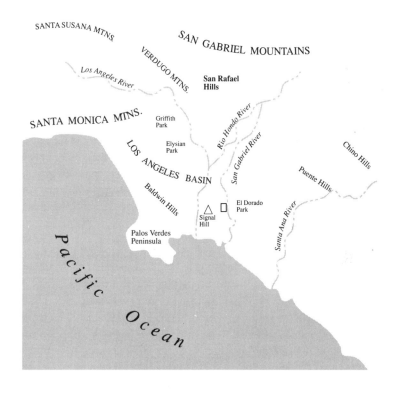

The Wild Side of L.A.

It was a paradise once, Lotus Land: Los Angeles, California. The worst insult cynic H.L. Mencken could muster was that "the whole place stank of orange blossoms." Then came the immigrants, by the thousands. They came for retirement, for health, for oil, for aerospace, for movies, for a new life and a new start. Most found enough of what they were looking for to settle in L.A. or one of its hundred suburbs.

The immigrants brought their autos and furniture and dreams and they brought a whole new landscape to the Los Angeles Basin. Few people realize that virtually every animal, vegetable and mineral in the region is imported: flowers, plants, shrubs, trees, water and energy. The trees most visitors believe are indigenous, such as eucalyptus and acacia, pepper and most palms, are imported from the wilds of Australia and South America. Even the Basin's grasses, rats, sparrows and weeds are not native.

It seems a hundred novels have opened with: "The smog hung heavy over the L.A. Basin." Los Angeles residents curse the bowl-shaped topography encircling them and hold the Basin personally responsible for their stinging eyes and scratchy throats. This, of course, is misplaced criticism, like holding the shape of the bottle responsible for the quality of the wine. It's worth taking a closer look (on a clear day) at this bowl many Southern Californians call home because this natural province shapes who we are and how we act. The Basin isn't always an eye irritant, and in fact, its geography can be quite pleasing to the eye.

Geographically, the L.A. Basin extends south from the base of the San Gabriel Mountains to the sea, and southwest from the Santa Monica Mountains to the Santa Ana Mountains. Faults border on two sides: the Palos Verdes Fault on the southwest and the Foothill Fault on the north. The Basin is divided by the Puente Hills, near Whittier. South of these hills is a coastal plain spreading toward the ocean. North is the San Gabriel Valley, surrounded by more hills and mountains—a basin within a Basin.

A short time ago, 20 million years or so, the landscape was pockmarked by furious volcanoes exploding fire, ash, and lava into the skies. One can only speculate how "smoggy" it was then! (These volcanic rocks can be seen near two trails in this guide: #39 along the Palos Verdes Hills and #22 in Griffith Park.) After Mother Nature laid a fiery foundation of bedrock over the area, this land went through a time of uplift and subsidence. During Miocene, Pliocene and Pleistocene times (2 to 20 million years ago), the ocean deposited thick sedimentary beds, which covered the igneous and metamorphic rocks.

A sea of tract houses now covers the ocean's former floor. It appears at first glance to be a relentless, monotonously flat landscape. But the lack of varied topography is an illusion. It's fun to speculate what the Basin would look like if all the sedimentary fill left behind by ancient seas were scoured out, scooped up and dumped elsewhere. If all the sediment were removed, bedrock mountains over 30,000 feet high would be unveiled.The San Gabriels would be higher than the Himalayas! At 37,000 feet, Mount Wilson would dwarf Mount Everest! So the next time life in the Big Basin gets you down and the San Gabriel and Santa Monica Mountains are lost in a smoky haze, comfort yourself by remembering that beneath your feet is a majestic mountain range.

If you take a walk on the wild side of the L.A. Basin, you'll realize how much Los Angeles needs open space. New York City has some eighteen percent of its land area in parks; San Francisco has fourteen percent (not counting the Golden Gate Recreation Area), but Los Angeles has only four percent. Still there's some surprisingly rugged open space within the L.A. city limits, and it's all the more precious because of its scarcity. It's space you never imagined when stuck in rush hour traffic on the Santa Ana Freeway. On a clear day, when the sprawled skyline of L.A. is not lost in the ozone, a hiker can see much of the Basin from these selected trails.

Metropolitan views from Baldwin Hills

29

Eaton Canyon Trail

Nature Center to Eaton Falls
3 miles round trip; 200-foot elevation gain

"It is a charming little thing, with a low, sweet voice, singing like a bird, as it pours from a notch in a short ledge, some thirty-five or forty feet into a round mirror-pool."

Eaton Falls, as admired by John Muir in 1877
—The Mountains of California

Late one August afternoon in 1877, John Muir set out from Pasadena to begin his exploration of the San Gabriel Mountains. He spent the night camped with a blindly optimistic, half-Irish, half-Spanish water prospector, who was convinced that his digging would soon result in a wealth of water. Muir was dubious of this cash flow, and the next morning bade his acquaintance farewell and began tramping up the canyon. After enjoying Eaton Falls, Muir followed bear trails, sometimes on all fours, up the chaparral-smothered ridges of the San Gabriel Mountains.

It was not the water-seeker Muir met, but Judge Benjamin Eaton, who channeled and piped the canyon's waters to nearby ranches. The judge's neighbors laughed when he planted grapevines, but the vines were quite successful and commanded a high price. San Gabriel Valley farmers knew a good thing when they saw it, and soon grapes joined oranges as the crop of choice.

Much of the canyon named for Judge Eaton is now part of Eaton Canyon County Park. The park's nature center has exhibits which emphasize Southern California flora and fauna. Kids will love the park's Naturalist's Room, which features live animals. Park nature trails explore a variety of native plant communities—chaparral, coastal sage, and oak-sycamore woodland.

Eaton Canyon County Park is a busy place on weekends. Family nature walks are conducted by docent naturalists; the park also has bird walks, natural history classes and "nature-cize" hikes

The walk up Eaton Canyon to the falls is an easy one. Eaton Canyon Trail leads through a wide wash along the east side of the canyon to a junction with Mount Wilson Toll Road. Eaton Canyon Trail was once a toll road; fees were collected from 1890 to 1911.

The hiker seeking strenuous exercise can swing right on Mount Wilson Road for a steep, 8-mile ascent of Mount Wilson.

Directions to trailhead:
From the Foothill Freeway (210) in Pasadena, exit on Altadena Drive. Proceed north 1 3/4 miles to the signed entrance of Eaton Canyon County Park. Turn right into the park and leave your car in the large lot near the Nature Center.

The Hike: From the parking lot, head north on the wide dirt road. You meander beneath the boughs of large oak trees and pass a junction with a connector trail that leads to the Mount Wilson Toll Road.

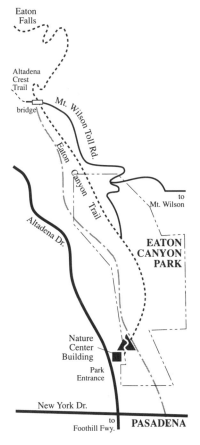

To the east, you'll spy the plateau overlooking Eaton Canyon. A hundred years ago this land belonged to wealthy capitalist and pioneer forester, public libary founder and builder of Venice, Abbott Kinney and his Kinneloa Ranch. Kinney loved this area and was a bit miffed when a nearby peak was named Mount Harvard for the university that built an observatory atop the mountain, rather than for him.

The trail leads along the wide arroyo. Eaton Canyon was widened considerably by a 1969 flood that washed away canyon walls. This flood, and the many floods before and since, have spread alluvium, or water-transported sand and rock, across the canyon floor. It takes a hearty group of drought-resistant plants to survive in this soil and Southern California's sometimes not-so-benign Mediterranean climate.

Notice the steepness of the canyon's walls. Early Spanish settlers called the canyon "El Precipio."

A mile's travel from the Nature Center brings you to the Mount Wilson Toll Road bridge. A right turn on the toll road will take you on a long, steep ascent to the top of Mount Wilson. A left turn on Mount Wilson Toll Road will bring you a very short distance to the unsigned junction with Altadena Crest Trail. This rather dull trail travels two miles above the reservoirs and backyards of residential Altadena. Walking a half-mile on Altadena Crest

Trail to a vista point will reward you with great clear-day views of the Los Angeles Basin.

To reach Eaton Falls, continue straight up Eaton Canyon wash. You'll rock-hop across the creek several times as you walk to trail's end at the falls.

When John Muir visited the canyon a century ago, the great naturalist reported: "Hither come the San Gabriel lads and lassies, to gather ferns and dabble away their hot holidays in the cool waters, glad to escape their common-place palm gardens and orange groves."

Alas, the local youth of today isn't quite as well-mannered. Cretins have desecrated some of the canyon's boulders with graffiti. After you've enjoyed the falls Muir called "the finest yet discovered in the San Gabriel Mountains," return the same way.

Eaton Falls

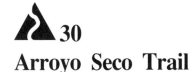 **30**

Arroyo Seco Trail

Arroyo Seco Park to Rose Bowl
3 miles round trip

Arroyo Seco is undoubtedly the best-known canyon in Southern California. It's the site of the Rose Bowl and has the dubious distinction of hosting California's first freeway, the Pasadena. The arroyo includes both ten miles of urban canyon dominated by the freeway and ten miles of wild and rugged watershed spilling from the shoulder of Mount Wilson.

In Pasadena, between the end of the freeway and the beginning of the Angeles National Forest, the arroyo takes on a third dimension, what land use planners, in the peculiar jargon of their trade refer to as "the urban/rural interface." Here the arroyo has been domesticated, but not destroyed. And here the walker will find a little leg-stretcher of a hike that recalls the Pasadena of a century ago. Rose Bowl-goers will find a fun way to reach the stadium.

Since before the turn of the century, the arroyo has been a pleasuring ground for nature-loving Pasadenans. Old photos show a verdant canyon, with trails meandering along wooded banks.

During the last decade of the last century and the first decade of this one, the banks of the Arroyo Seco hosted a way of life historians now call Arroyo Culture. Artists, writers, wealthy eccentrics and assorted nonconformists settled in this suburb, so uniquely positioned between the wilderness and fast-growing Los Angeles. Many decades before today's "Southwest Look" became so trendy, Arroyo residents gloried in Indian and Mexican cultures. They filled their homes with Indian blankets and pottery, stained glass and colored tile.

As historian Kevin Starr, in his *Inventing the Dream: California through the Progressive Era,* sums up Arroyo Culture: "To build homes on the Arroyo, as did these bohemians, was to embrace the symbol of the desert wilderness and to glory in Southern California's resistant, elemental culture. On Orange Grove Avenue the Pasadenan looked out on a lawn and a trimmed hedge. On the Arroyo Seco, he looked out on jackrabbits and chaparral."

One tireless promoter of Arroyo Culture was Charles Fletcher Lummis, city editor of the *Los Angeles Times*, editor of "Out West" magazine and founder of the Southwest Museum. (You can see the Lummis Home at 300 East Avenue 43.)

Another booster was George Wharton James, author of *Wonders of the*

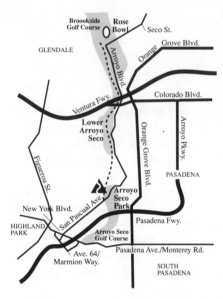

Colorado Desert and innumerable articles about the natural and cultural history of the southwest. Two of the many writers whose careers were influenced by their contact with Arroyo Culture included Mary Austin and a young Occidental College student/blossoming poet, Robinson Jeffers.

Pasadena purchased the arroyo from the Pasadena Land & Water Company in 1912. Over the years, the arroyo hasn't always been so "seco"; during some winters, quite a torrent rushed down the arroyo. Devil's Gate Dam and Reservoir were built to capture the arroyo's runoff and a cement channel built to direct its flow. As a result of these flood control measures, the trail along Arroyo Seco is no wilderness adventure, but it does afford a pleasant walk into Pasadena's past.

Directions to trailhead: From the Pasadena Freeway in South Pasadena, exit on Marmion Way/Avenue 64. Bear left and follow the signs to York Avenue. Turn right on York and then almost immediately turn left on San Rafael Avenue. Drive three-quarters of a mile to Arroyo Seco Park, where there's plenty of parking. Best bet for hikers is the small lot near the softball field. Arroyo Seco Trail departs from San Pasqual Stables, just up the avenue on the left side of the road. Don't park in the stables' lot.

The Hike: The trail, signed "Horseback Riding Trail," begins at the north end of the stable grounds. A 50-yard walk brings you to a small bridge over the arroyo flood control channel. Here you may choose which side of the arroyo you'd like to walk upon; equestrian trails parallel both sides of the channel for about a mile.

Arroyo Seco Trail passes native oak, alder and sycamore, as well as arboreal imports from faraway lands—eucalyptus, palm and pepper trees. Pasadenans have been cultivating gardens at the arroyo's edge for about a century, and some mighty strange flora has escaped from these gardens and sprouted on the canyon walls and bottom. Bougainvillea, bird of paradise, and dozens of other exotic plants now decorate the arroyo.

High above you, atop the arroyo walls, are some fine old homes—

Bavarian, Victorian, Tudor and Anyone's Guess in style—and all but hidden by the profligate vegetation.

As you approach an archery range, note the huge castle-like structure high on the arroyo's east bank. This is the Vista del Arroyo Hotel, finished in 1936 and now a federal government office building.

The trail takes you beneath a trio of bridges arching over the Arroyo Seco. Unlike the arroyo flood control channel, the bridges are an aesthetic triumph. Particularly pleasing to the eye is the Colorado Boulevard Bridge, known in the 1930s as "Suicide Bridge." Many wealthy Pasadenans were hard hit by the 1929 stock market crash and decided to leave this world by leaping off the bridge. Seventy-nine people were reported to have taken a dive. Arroyo homeowners, upset by the effect this leaping was having on their property values and the unseemliness of it all, pressed the city to correct the situation. The city responded in 1937 by building a high fence and stationing a guard on the bridge.

Somewhat ironically, the most natural part of the arroyo that you'll encounter along this trail is found beneath the Colorado Boulevard and Ventura Freeway bridges.

Eastside and westside arroyo trails join together near a spillway and finally depart from the straight line course of the cement flood control channel. The path follows a little creek, which hints at what the arroyo might have looked like before its ecology was forever altered by engineers.

Arroyo Seco Trail emerges from the greenery near the corner of Arroyo Boulevard and Seco Street. The Rose Bowl is dead ahead. Walk along Arroyo Boulevard a short distance to Brookside Park, where you can picnic in the shadow of the Rose Bowl.

A signed "Horseback Riding Trail" continues north another mile, first passing through the Rose Bowl parking lot, then continuing alongside West Drive past Brookside Golf Course. Skip this boring path, eat your lunch at Brookside Park and return the same way.

Bridges of the Arroyo Seco, pleasing to the eye

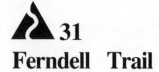 **31**

Ferndell Trail

Ferndell Canyon to Griffith Observatory
   2 1/2 miles round trip; 500-foot elevation gain
Ferndell Canyon to Mount Hollywood
   5 miles round trip; 1,000-foot elevation gain

Griffith Park, one of the largest municipal parks in the world, holds plenty of surprises for the hiker. Among these surprises is well-named Ferndell, where a brook bubbles through a woodsy, fern-lined glen.

Another surprise is the grove of coast redwood (*Sequoia sempervirens*) that thrives in the bottom of the dell. The redwoods complement the native sycamore and alder, which shade this oasis in the heart of the Hollywood Hills.

Hopefully, your sense of surprise won't be lessened when you discover that human engineering, not Mother Nature, is responsible for the life-giving brook that waters Ferndell. Recycled water from Griffith Observatory's cooling system is released from the top of the hill and sent merrily on its way down to the dell.

Still, the urban mountaineer can be grateful for the brook, which attracts numerous birds including brown towhees, robins and jays. Around sunrise and sunset, Griffith Park's deer often descend from the hills for a drink.

Moco-Cahuenga Canyon is believed to be the Indian name for Ferndell. The name's origins are a bit fuzzy, but Moco was supposedly the meeting ground of the Cahuenga Indians.

This day hike visits two of the park's most interesting sights. First, the trail climbs to Griffith Observatory, where you can tour a little museum and catch the planetarium show. More ambitious hikers can continue to the top of Mount Hollywood, highest peak in the park, for great views of the metropolis.

   Directions to trailhead: This day hike begins at the south end of Griffith Park off Loz Feliz Boulevard. One way to go: Exit the Hollywood Freeway (101) on Sunset Boulevard and head east to Western Avenue. Turn left and follow Western north until it jogs right onto Los Feliz Boulevard.

Turn left on Ferndell Drive and park alongside the drive. If parking is scarce, continue up the road a little farther to Ferndell Picnic Area.

   The Hike: Join the path to the east of Ferndell Drive. Large sycamores shade the trail which ascends alongside the moss-covered banks of a brook, past tiny waterfalls, to Ferndell Picnic Area. The picnic ground has plenty of tables and is a great place for a post-hike lunch stop.

As you walk toward the redwoods and past the picnic area, stay to the right, east, side of the brook.

(Two other trails that ascend from Ferndell should be noted. One trail follows the left, west, bank of Ferndell Brook. A second trail, which departs from the end of the picnic area where Western Canyon Road makes a wide left turn, climbs to an intersection with the trail that connects Mount Hollywood with the Observatory; this path is a good, optional return route.)

Your trail, officially known as Lower West Observatory Trail, lingers for a time alongside the east bank of Ferndell Brook, then begins to climb out of the dell. Gaps in the eucalyptus and chaparral allow good views of the Hollywood sign above and the city below. Three-fourths of a mile from Ferndell is an unsigned three-way junction. You'll bear right, continue a quarter-mile to another junction and bear left, then ascend another quarter-mile to the Observatory.

From the Observatory, enjoy clear-day views of Hollywood and its hills, Century City, the Wilshire corridor and downtown, as well as the beach cities to the south and west.

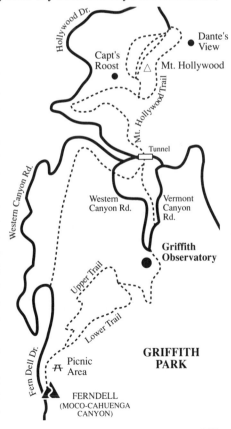

Those hikers bound for Mount Hollywood should walk to the north end of the Observatory parking lot, where a handsome trail sign points the way to Mount Hollywood. The path soon begins ascending a tree-shaded ridge. After a quarter-mile's travel, you'll cross a ridge that's above the Mount Hollywood Drive tunnel. Here you'll pass a junction with a trail leading left down Western Canyon to Ferndell. (This is the optional return route mentioned above.)

Continuing your ascent, you'll climb west, then east.

By now you've figured out that Mount Hollywood is not the mountain crowned by the historic Hollywood sign, where disappointed screen actresses leap to their deaths. You can, however, see the sign quite well as you near the summit of Mount Hollywood.

After ascending a long westward switchback, you'll reach a junction and fork left, heading north then west around the shoulder of Mount Hollywood. You'll pass Captain's Roost, a eucalyptus-shaded rest stop, then take the first right turn up the fire road to the top of Mount Hollywood. Wonderful sunsets can be observed from the 1,625-foot peak, and on clear days the entire Basin is spread out before you from the San Gabriel Mountains to the Pacific Ocean.

To return via a different route: Leave the peak and join the first fire road leading right. Soon you'll pass Dante's View, a two-acre retreat of pine, palm and pepper trees high on the south-facing slope of Mount Hollywood. From Dante's, you descend to the trail that brought you up from the Observatory.

32

Baldwin Hills Trail

3-mile loop through Kenneth Hahn
State Recreation Area; 300-foot elevation gain

From a distance, the Baldwin Hills appear to have little attraction for the walker. Oil wells work the hills, whose slopes have been scarred by roads and bulldozers. But the oil is petering out, the hillsides are being ecologically rehabilitated, and a park is in the making.

Located in the west/central part of Los Angeles, Kenneth Hahn State Recreation Area—named for the long-time Los Angeles County Supervisor—is a park developed and operated by Los Angeles County. It takes in hills and canyons between La Brea and La Cienega Boulevards. Few Southern Californians seem to know about Baldwin Hills, but the clean, well-kept, developed part of the park is no secret to nearby residents, who enjoy weekend picnics and barbecues on the expansive lawns. Anglers cast for catfish in the park's pond, which is stocked every couple weeks.

A highlight for hikers of all ages and abilities is a path that leads through the park's Olympic Forest. The forest includes at least one tree for each of the 140 nations that participated in the 1984 Olympic Games. Los Angeles also hosted the Olympics in 1932, at which time the Baldwin Hills park site served as the Olympic Village hosting the athletes. An interpretive display near the forest describes the trees and gives some history of the Olympic Games.

Walkers will enjoy viewing sea hibiscus from Seychelles, oleander from Algeria,

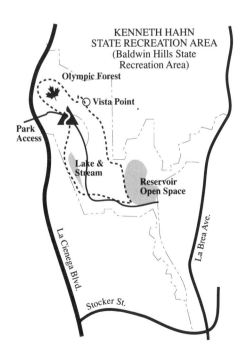

KENNETH HAHN
STATE RECREATION AREA
(Baldwin Hills State
Recreation Area)

Olympic Forest

Vista Point

Park
Access

Lake &
Stream

Reservoir
Open Space

La Cienega Blvd.

La Brea Ave.

Stocker St.

sweet bay from Greece and the Cajeput from Papua New Guinea. You'll probably be able to figure out which countries are represented by the Italian stone pine and Cedar of Lebanon.

The Baldwin Hills offer one more attraction for the walker: great clear day views of the Santa Monica Mountains, the whole sweep of Santa Monica·Bay, the San Gabriel Mountains and much of the L.A. metropolis. While the Baldwin Hills are only 500 feet high, they offer dramatic, unobstructed views of the basin. If you want to get the lay of the land, take a city or county map along on this hike.

Directions to trailhead: From the Santa Monica Freeway (10) in Los Angeles, exit on La Cienega Boulevard and drive south a few miles to Kenneth Hahn State Recreation Area. Park in the lot signed "Olympic Forest."

The Hike: From the interpretive displays posted at the edge of the parking lot, take the path into the Olympic Forest. The forest is divided into a half-dozen habitats, including desert, tropical and temperate environments. Contemplate the paper mulberry from Tonga, the carob from Cyprus, the date palm from Egypt. The forest is yet another proof of the oft-repeated adage that "anything can and does grow in Southern California."

After your around-the-world tree tour, ascend on a path leading toward some rather forlorn palms. Here at a man-made oasis, you'll find a waterfall cascading into a little grotto. From the palm oasis, you'll continue your ascent on trail and dirt road to a picnic ramada perched on the hilltop. Near the ramada is a pine grove planted by "Top Teens of America, Inc."

The view from the summit includes the Wilshire corridor, Century City, Westwood and the Hollywood sign. You'll spot sailboats tacking this way and that as they head out to sea from Marina del Rey. And you'll get an air traffic controller's view of the amazing number of jets zooming in and out of LAX.

A dirt road crosses the hilltop plateau and passes two more picnic ramadas. Enjoy the striking views of Palos Verdes Peninsula and Catalina Island. The road, then a footpath, follows a fence beside some high-tension power lines.

Rabbits and quail are frequently sighted in the hills, which are covered with California sagebrush, black mustard, coyote bush and prickly-pear cactus. The native plant community—coastal sage scrub—has been greatly altered by the hand of man, so much so that botanists describe Baldwin Hills flora as being in a condition called "disclimax." Introduced "weeds" such as castor bean, milk thistle and tree tobacco have invaded the canyon bottoms. The hills host a number of domestic plants gone wild, including agave, hottentot-fig, nasturium and lantana.

The trail passes near the old Baldwin Hills Dam, which failed a quarter-century ago. Overlooking the empty reservoir back of the dam is an observation tower, which resembles a castle from the Middle Ages. Fennel, chamise and dandelions have pushed through the cracked cement bottom of the reservoir. The county is converting the reservoir into parking and picnic areas.

Near the dam, you'll meet a road coming up from the developed part of the park. Join a paved path, which parallels this road, and descend a handsomely landscaped hillside to the main park picnic area. Improvise a route past the pond, bubbling brook and picnic grounds back to Olympic Forest and the trailhead.

Trekking above Olympic Forest into Baldwin Hills

33

Signal Hill Trail

4-mile loop of Signal Hill; 300-foot elevation gain

Signal Hill has long been synonymous with oil. Atop this Long Beach prominence a great oil field was discovered in 1921. Alamitos #1, as the discovery well was known, produced 600 barrels a day. Soon Signal Hill was covered with derricks, which produced 250,000 barrels a day.

The hill is a quieter place now, though a number of active wells are still pumping black gold. Because Signal is the only hill for miles around, it has long been a popular conditioning walk for hikers trying to stay in shape.

Sierra Club outings leaders report that often more than a hundred hikers turn out for evening strides around the hill. Signal Hill is anything but a natural environment, but the great views of harbor and city and the camaraderie of the trail usually add up to a fun trip.

During the 1940s, the hill was the property of rancher John Temple, who called his spread Los Cerritos—"Little Hills." The hill was renamed in 1889 when the Coast Survey of 1889 used it as a signal point.

Signal Hill and its geologic cousins to the north—Baldwin Hills—were uplifted as a result of activity from the Newport-Inglewood Fault Zone. One result of this fault activity was that oil accumulated beneath various anticlines, or domes of rock.

Signal Hill—the mountain—has been cleaned up some since its heyday, and its slopes now host more houses than oil wells. Still, day hikers should use caution, avoid drilling equipment and respect "No Trespassing" signs. There isn't a single path around the hill; rather, you improvise a route on Signal's dirt and paved roads.

To fully enjoy the great clear-day views, bring binoculars and a city map.

Directions to trailhead: From the San Diego Freeway (405) in Long Beach, take the Cherry Ave/Signal Hill exit. Head south on Cherry one-half mile to Willow. Turn right and after a mile, make a right on Redondo, then right on aptly-named Hill Street. Proceed to the base of Signal Hill. Depending on your time and/or inclination, you can park at the base of the hill or closer to the top.

The Hike: Follow Panorama Drive or the dirt road below it in a counterclockwise direction. You'll pass oil wells, get a view to the north of the San Diego Freeway, the planes arriving and departing from Long Beach Airport, and many square miles of suburbia. Eucalyptus and palm trees line the up-and-down dirt roads. Lemon grass and California poppies add a little color to the ugly hillsides.

Your route crosses Burnett Street and you join a dirt road on the west side of the hill. Growing on this slope is a zany mixture of flora—banana palms and California fan palms, Canary Island pines, lemonade berry, brittle bush and gazanias.

Only the hawks(!) circling overhead have a better view than you. The view west takes in the Palos Verdes Peninsula. Catalina Island, thirty miles away, is visible on a clear day.

Looking south and west you can identify the Queen Mary and its three stacks and count a number of man-made oil islands. Dominating the coast is the massive Los Angeles/Long Beach harbor complex and the tall cranes used for loading containerized cargo. Several bridges spanning the harbor are also in view, including the Vincent Thomas Bridge which connects San Pedro and the Harbor Freeway with Terminal Island.

After circling the hill and seeing the sights, you'll end up at the corner of Hill and Temple Streets. Here you'll find the plaque commemorating the success of Southland's oil pioneers and Alamitos #1: "...a success which has, by aiding in the growth and expansion of the petroleum industry, contributed so much to the welfare of mankind."

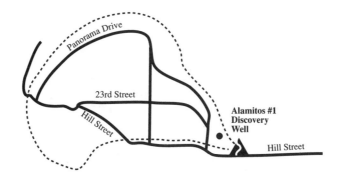

34

El Dorado Nature Trail

2-mile loop through El Dorado Nature Center

Southern Californians have long lamented the destruction of the natural world caused by freeway construction. But in one community, freeway building resulted in the formation of a unique nature center.

Back in the mid-1960s, during construction of the San Gabriel River/ San Diego Freeway interchange, earth movers were moving millions of cubic yards of earth. Thanks to concerned citizens and conservationists, some of that earth was moved to form 800-acre El Dorado Regional Park and 80-acre El Dorado Nature Center. The park is everything a big park should be, with wide lawns, ball fields and picnic areas. The Nature Center is a surprise—an oasis in the midst of the metropolis.

Surely this land has undergone a strange evolution: from San Gabriel River floodplain to beanfields to freeway interchange to nature preserve. Only in Southern California!

Next to its beach, El Dorado Nature Center is Long Beach's biggest natural attraction. Established in 1969, this man-made wildlife sanctuary includes two lakes and a stream, tree-lined meadows and low rolling hills. It's a serene habitat for flora and fauna as well as a tranquil retreat for humans.

Nature trail loops around park's two ponds

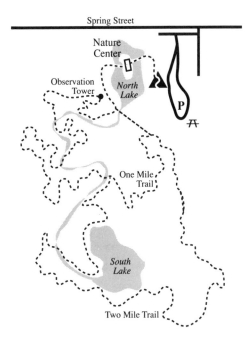

Several ecological zones are represented in the nature preserve, which for the most part, emphasizes native California flora. Walkers can tour oak woodland, grassy meadow, and chaparral communities, which are representative of Southern California plant communities, and can meander among redwoods and a white alder grove—vegetation typical of the northern part of the state.

El Dorado Nature Center, a small museum perched on an island, is a good place to learn about Southern California's plant life and wildlife. This satellite museum of the Natural History Museum of L.A. County features a "hands on" ecology exhibit and a gallery that displays the work of nature artists and photographers.

Kids will particularly enjoy a visit to the nature center. The museum's exhibits, interpretive walks and even the pint-sized drinking fountains were designed with the smaller nature lover in mind.

Two miles of easy trail circle El Dorado. A one-mile nature trail is keyed to an interpretive pamphlet available from the museum. Another mile of trail loops around the preserve's two ponds.

Bird-watchers flock to the preserve because more than 150 resident and migratory bird species have been sighted. A bird checklist is available at the museum.

Directions to trailhead: From the San Diego Freeway (405), exit on Studebaker Road and travel north about 2 1/2 miles to Spring Street. Take a right on Spring and proceed 3/4 of a mile to the entrance of El Dorado Park Nature Center. You can park in the lot by the nature center museum for a fee, or for free along Spring Street.

The Hike: Pick up a nature trail interpretive pamphlet from the museum, then head out across the bridge into the reserve. Enjoy the native plant communities, including a cattail-lined creek and a chaparral-cloaked hillside. And keep an eye out for two nonnatives that have been part of the Southland scene for more than a century and seem like natives—the large, plume-like pampas grass from South America and the ubiquitous eucalyptus. Be sure to get the "big picture" from the Observation Tower, the preserve's highest point.

When you reach a trail junction, you can proceed straight ahead on the "One Mile" nature trail or bear right for a two-mile hike. The second mile of trail meanders past the park's ponds before returning to the Nature Center building.

Ducks patrol El Dorado's waterways

134

35

Bonelli Park Trail

6-mile loop of Frank G. Bonelli Park

A half-century ago, the Los Angeles Angeles Flood Control District built Puddingstone Dam in the San Jose Hills near San Dimas. Completed in 1928 for the purpose of capturing and storing rainwater and storm runoff, the dam created a 250-acre lake. The new lake soon attracted swimmers and fishermen, and has remained a popular destination for more than 60 years.

As the population of the San Gabriel Valley mushroomed during the 1950s and 1960s, the State Department of Parks and Recreation began purchasing land around the reservoir. Puddingstone Reservoir State Park as it was known, remained a little-developed, low-key place until 1970, when the property was transferred to Los Angeles County.

Today, the park features the aquatic amusement park Raging Waters, a golf course, giant RV campground and a hot tub rental establishment. Plans are in the works for a hotel, cocktail lounge and a second golf course.

The 2,000-acre park, the county's second-largest, has long been the center of controversy between those who want to further develop the park and those who would prefer that the park's hills and canyons remain wild. These conflicting sentiments are even etched onto the lakeside plaque dedicated to former county supervisor and park namesake Frank G. Bonelli. The plaque proclaims that the park is dedicated for "use as a county regional recreation and wilderness area for the enjoyment of all."

As most outdoors enthusiasts know, the words "recreation" and "wilderness" mean different things to different people. For the last decade and a half, the County Parks Department has leaned heavily toward intensive recreation at the park, which is visited by more than two million people each year.

Considering that two of the park's borders are the Foothill and San Bernardino Freeways, and drag boat races are held on Puddingstone Reservoir, Bonelli offers more peace and solitude than one might expect. Fourteen miles of trail cross the park's chaparral-covered hills and lead through quiet canyons shaded by oak and walnut groves. Plantations of pepper, eucalyptus, cedar and pine have been planted in the park. Wildlife includes squirrels, cottontail rabbits, blacktail rabbits, raccoons and deer. About 130 bird species have been sighted in the park.

Bonelli's trail system is poorly marked and oriented toward equestrians, not pedestrians. It's the hiker with a sense of direction—and a sense of humor—who will most enjoy a walk in this park. Trails and trail junctions are rarely signed, but the paths don't stray too far from park roads and landmarks, so you won't get lost. Your best bet for hiking Bonelli is to pick up a park map (out-of-date but it locates major features) from headquarters and improvise your own route.

Directions to trailhead: Frank G. Bonelli Regional Park has two main entrances. (1) Exit the San Bernardino Freeway (10) on Ganesha Boulevard, then turn left (west) on Via Verde Park Road. Continue a couple of miles to park headquarters, where you can pick up an equestrian trails map. You can park in Picnic Valley off Via Verde Park Road or continue following this road out of Bonelli to the Caltrans parking lot located just west of the Foothill Freeway. (2) Exit the Foothill Freeway (210) on Via Verde Road. Park in the Caltrans lot just west of the freeway. There is a vehicle parking fee; no charge to walk in.

The Hike: From the Caltrans parking lot, cross (with caution) to the south side of Via Verde Road and follow the sidewalk over the freeway overpass into the park. Look right (south) for the path signed "Equestrian Trail." If you want to pick up a park map, you'll continue a short distance farther up Via Verde Road to the headquarters. The trail enters the bougainvillea-draped mouth of the underpass beneath Via Verde. Ever-adapative mud swallows have affixed their nests to the ceiling of the underpass.

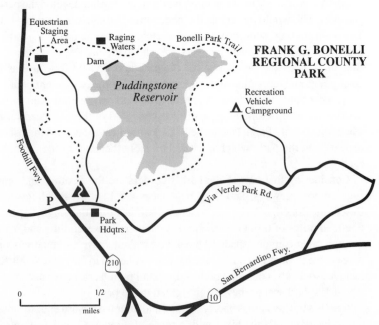

Emerging from the underpass, you'll follow the horse trail into a quieter world. The din of the freeway fades away, and you can hear the call of the birds. Crossing slopes covered with ceanothus, thistle and prickly pear cactus, the trail soon offers its first view of Puddingstone Reservoir. Depending on the day's ozone level, the San Gabriel Mountains rise majestically or murkily before you.

In spring, the hills are green and brightened with mustard and California poppies, but most of the year, they're bare and brown.

The trail descends into a shallow, walnut-shaded canyon, and crosses a (usually dry) creek. Nearing the park's equestrian center, the path emerges from the greenery and reaches a fork located by a thicket of blackberry bushes. The left fork ascends a hillock, dead-ending at an overlook high above Raging Waters. On clear days, this overlook offers a panorama from Mount Baldy to San Bernardino. You'll take the right fork, proceed along a fence line, then switchback up a jimson weed- and monkeyflower-dotted slope to Boater Picnic Area. The trail descends an oak- and pine-shaded draw, passes a fig tree, then joins a fire road that leads near the Raging Waters amusement park.

Crossing Puddingstone Road, near the entrance to Raging Waters, you'll pick up the signed Equestrian Trail, which soon deposits you at a boat-launching area on the north side of the reservoir. Now your improvisation begins in earnest.

Join the paved walkway and head east along the north shore of the reservoir. When the walkway gives out, pick up the unmarked dirt trail that continues east then south along the moist, willow-choked lakeshore. Perched on the hill above you is the park's campground. You'll join a paved bike path and pass several picnic areas.

After passing through well-named Picnic Valley, walk up Eucalyptus Park Road to its junction with Via Verde Park Road. At this point you're just about opposite park headquarters. A right turn and a short walk along Via Verde will return you to the trailhead.

36

Marshall Canyon Trail

7-mile loop through Marshall Canyon
800-foot elevation gain

Marshall Canyon, a county park in-the-making, offers some fine hiking in the foothills of the San Gabriel Mountains. Marshall Canyon and its neighbor, Live Oak Canyon, are shaded with oak, alder and sycamore. From atop the canyon walls, there are great clear-day views of the mountains to the north and San Gabriel Valley to the south.

For several years this semi-wild area above San Dimas and Claremont has been something of a secret—frequented only by a few horseback riders and a very few hikers. Los Angeles County Department of Parks and Recreation planners say their intention is to leave Marshall Canyon more or less alone—that is to say undeveloped, with minimum facilities. In the parlance of land use planners, Marshall Canyon will remain as "open space"—something to be thankful for in the fast-growing eastern edge of the metropolis.

A good network of equestrian/hiking trails explores the brushy ridges and lush canyon bottoms of the park. Much of the network is fire roads, which may sometimes be closed during the dry summer months.

Depending on your time and inclination, you can fashion a number of loop trips ranging from 2 to 8 miles. Park trails and roads are unsigned, so expect to improvise a little.

Directions to trailhead: Follow the Foothill Freeway (210) to its end, continuing east on Highway 30 and still farther east on Foothill Boulevard. Turn left, north on Wheeler Avenue, ascend to Golden Hill Road and turn right. You'll see signs for Marshall Canyon Golf Course. Just before the road turns right toward Live Oak Reservoir, turn left into a dirt parking lot. On weekends, you're likely to find a few horse trailers in the lot.

The Hike: The trail begins at the east end of the lot and soon begins descending into the Marshall Canyon. During winter, the snow-covered peaks of the San Gabriel Mountains framed by oaks are a picturesque sight.

Just before a creek crossing, the trail splits. Marshall Canyon is to the left, Live Oak Canyon to the right. (The trails intersect again, so you may choose either.)

Marshall Canyon Trail crosses the creek a couple times, then rises out of the canyon as a dirt road. You'll pass a side road leading to the park's nursery, and a couple side trails offering access to the canyon bottom.

Rather than traveling a northeast course through the canyon, it's enjoyable to wind along in a half-circle toward a prominent water tower and partake of the fine ridgetop views.

Atop the ridgeline, the trail rollercoasters along. You turn left on signed Miller Road, then descend into Live Oak Canyon. You'll reach a three-way junction and continue a hundred yards along the main fire road to a picnic area. Enjoy this oak-shaded retreat, then double back and look sharply right for an unsigned footpath descending into Live Oak Canyon.

The canyon's oaks are accompanied by sycamores, walnuts, cottonwoods, mosses and ferns. It's a most delightful half- mile descent to the canyon bottom. You'll continue your descent to an unsigned junction. The right fork follows Marshall Canyon back to the trailhead. Bear left and meander along with Live Oak Canyon 1 1/2 miles back to the trailhead.

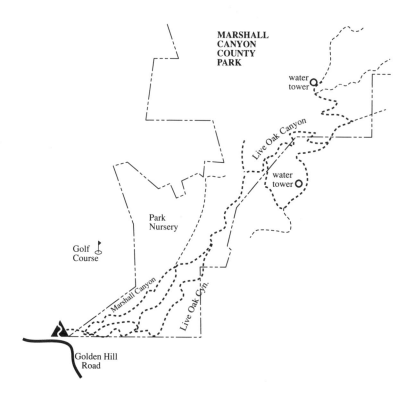

*For more than a century Southern Californians have
enjoyed the pleasures of the San Gabriels*

Chapter 6

SAN GABRIEL MOUNTAINS

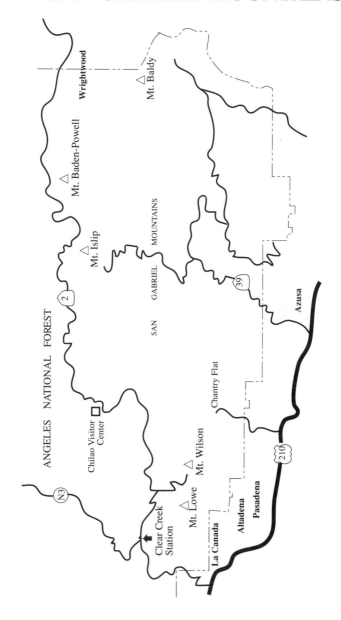

San Gabriel Mountains

The San Gabriel Mountains bless L.A. by keeping out desert winds, and curse it by keeping in the smog. Most of the range is included in the 700,000 acres of the Angeles National Forest, the most heavily used national forest in the U.S. The San Gabriels twist atop the San Andreas Fault. Geologists claim these mountains are the most fractured and shattered in California. The range consists of crystalline metamorphic and granitic blocks, sixty miles long and twenty miles wide, extending from Soledad Pass to Cajon Pass. The Los Padres mountain ranges are to the west and the San Bernardino range is to the east. The San Gabriels vary extensively in temperature. Along the northern rim at the edge of the Antelope Valley, the mountains seem an extension of the Mojave Desert. However, some alpine areas with peaks near 10,000 feet know snow from one winter to the next.

John Muir found it tough going in the San Gabriels: "The slopes are exceptionally steep and insecure to the foot and they are covered with thorny bushes from five to ten feet high." Muir was referring to the dominant plant community of the San Gabriels—the chaparral—that elfin forest of burrs and brambles which covers much of the sun-drenched lower slopes of the mountains. Higher elevations bring easier traveling and a wealth of taller trees: mountain laurel, oaks, pines, cedar. The arroyos are another special feature of the San Gabriels. These boulder-strewn washes seem dry and lifeless in the bottomland; however, as hikers follow their course upward, they'll soon find the arroyo's banks are verdant and graceful with a tangle of ferns, lilies and wildflowers.

As early as the 1880s, it became obvious to Southern Californians the mountains should be protected from the destruction of indiscriminate logging and other ventures. In 1892, the San Gabriel Timberland Reserve was proclaimed by President Harrison. It was the first forest reserve in California, and the second in the U.S. (The first was Yellowstone.)

On of the first trail construction projects in the San Gabriels began in 1864 when Benjamin Wilson revamped an old Indian path to his timbering venture on the mountain that now bears his name. Later, other Indian trails were improved. William Sturtevant, who came to California from Colorado in the early 1880s and became a premier packhorseman and trail guide, linked and improved several Indian trails and made it possible to cross the mountains from west to east. Until Sturtevant figured out a route, most people did not know that a network of Indian trails reached from the desert to the L.A. Basin.

More trails were built at the turn of the century when Southern California's "Great Hiking Era" began. With Rough Rider Teddy Roosevelt urging Americans to lead "the strenuous life," Southlanders challenged the nearby San Gabriels. Mountain farmers and ranchers, fighting against the odds of fire, flood and distance to market, began capitalizing on the prevailing interest in the great outdoors. As more and more hikers headed into the backcountry, the settlers began to offer food and accommodations. Soon every major canyon on the south side of the mountains had its resort or trail camp and many had several. Most resorts were not big business, with the exception of the Mount Wilson and Echo Mountain complexes which featured luxury hotels and observatories. The majority were run by rugged entrepeneurs who offered rustic accomodations, hearty meals, and good fellowship. Visitors thronged to the resorts on weekends and holidays. Many stayed all summer.

The Depression brought about a golden age of public campground construction. These camps, tied to an ever-increasing network of highways, eventually doomed the private resorts and trail camps. Angeles Crest Highway, built between 1929 and 1956 by a motley assortment of Depression laborers, prison road gangs and various construction crews, linked many of the best high mountain picnic and camping areas.

Today, only a few stone foundations and scattered resort ruins remind the hiker of the "Great Hiking and Resort Era." Though the modern mountaineer will not be greeted with tea, lemonade or something stronger, or a hearty welcome from a trail camp proprietor, the mountains still beckon. That bygone era left us a superb network of trails—more than 500 miles of paths linking all major peaks, camps and streams.

Rising above the smog and din of the Big Basin, the San Gabriels still delight. When we manage to pry the fingers of our more mechanized citizens off their steering wheels and send them tramping through the San Gabriels, a second great hiking era may begin.

37

Grizzly Flat Trail

Big Tujunga Creek to Grizzly Flat
5 miles round trip; 900-foot elevation gain

During the last century, a large population of grizzlies roamed the San Gabriel Mountains. The bears frightened early miners and settlers, and in later years, had many a run-in with sportsmen and forest rangers. Big Tujunga Canyon was particularly attractive habitat to the big bears; in fact, the last wild grizzly in Southern California was killed in the lower reaches of the canyon in 1916.

These days you won't find any grizzlies atop Grizzly Flat, just a few hikers enjoying a pine-shaded retreat in the Angeles National Forest. Grizzly Flat Trail explores Tujunga Canyon, then rises into the storied hills where notorious highwayman Tiburcio Vasquez eluded a posse in 1874. Vasquez, after robbing a San Gabriel Valley rancher, rode over the top of the San Gabriels, descended north along a then-unnamed creek to Big Tujunga Canyon, and made good his escape. The unnamed creek, which cuts through the eastern edge of Grizzly Flat, has since been known as Vasquez Creek.

Big Tujunga Canyon—or "Big T" as it's sometimes nicknamed—has certainly felt the hand of man. Its creek has been dammed and diverted by the Los Angeles County Flood Control District. The purpose of these flood control efforts is to control the run-off of Big Tujunga Creek and prevent it from rushing into the eastern lowlands of the San Fernando Valley.

Damming a wild, but seasonal, mountain stream such as Big Tujunga solves one problem but creates another: when rains swell the creek, millions of cubic yards of sand and gravel are carried downstream and clog up flood control structures. Obviously, to be effective, a flood control reservoir should not be filled with rock debris. So the debris must be hauled away. But where?

The urban mountaineer may ponder a not altogether facetious question: If Los Angeles and its flood control projects keep growing and we keep carting away rock debris, will we one day haul our mountains entirely away?

Grizzly Flat Trail departs from Stonyvale Picnic Area, one of the less-visited locales in the front range of the San Gabriel Mountains. The trail, while not difficult, does require four crossings of Big Tujunga Creek, and should be avoided after heavy rains and during times of high water.

Directions to trailhead: From the Foothill Freeway (210) in Sunland, exit on Sunland Boulevard and head west to Foothill, continuing west to Mount Gleason Avenue. Turn left and drive 1 1/2 miles to a stop sign. Turn right, proceed 6 miles to Vogel Flat Road, and turn right again. The road drops to a stop sign. To the right is a Forest Service fire station. Turn left and park by the Stonyvale Picnic Area.

The Hike: The trail, signed with the international hiking symbol, begins at a vehicle barrier at the east end of Stonyvale Picnic Area. Almost immediately you cross Big Tujunga Creek. Small trail markers keep you on the path, which crosses a boulder field and fords the creek three more times.

A bit more than a mile from the trailhead, Big Tujunga creek and canyon bend northeast, but the trail heads right, south. Soon you'll pass an abandoned trail register and begin ascending up oak- and chaparral-covered slopes. After a mile, you'll dip to a seasonal fern-lined creek, then ascend briefly to grassy Grizzly Flat. The Forest Service planted pines here in 1959, shortly after a fire scorched the slopes above Big Tujunga.

From Grizzly Flat you can make your way northeast a few hundred yards to spruce-shaded Vasquez Creek. Picnic here or at Grizzly Flat and return the same way.

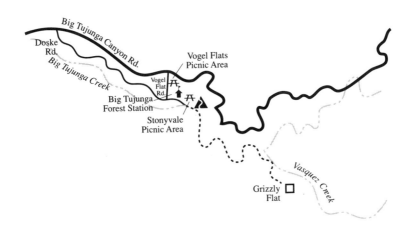

38

Stone Canyon Trail

Vogel Flats Campground to Mount Lukens
8 miles round trip; 3,200-foot elevation gain

Mount Lukens, a gray whale of a mountain beached on the eastern boundary of Los Angeles, is the highest peak within the city limits. A hike up this mile-high mountain offers a great aerobic workout and terrific clear-day views of the metropolis.

Theodore P. Lukens, for whom the mountain is named, was a Pasadena civic and business leader, and an early supporter of the first scientific reforestation effort in California. A self-taught botanist, Lukens believed that burnt-over mountainsides could be successfully replanted. During 1899 alone, Lukens and fellow mountaineers planted some 65,000 seeds in the mountains above Pasadena. He started an experimental nursery atop Heninger Flats that grew thousands of knobcone pine, spruce and other trees for replanting in burnt-over areas in the San Gabriel and San Bernardino Mountains. Today, this nursery furnishes a large percentage of the young trees planted in Southern California mountains.

After the death of Lukens in 1918, a 5,074-foot peak was named to honor the one-time Angeles National Forest Supervisor and Southern California's "Father of Forestry."

Stone Canyon Trail is by far the nicest way to ascend Mount Lukens. (Other routes are via long wearisome fire roads.) The trail climbs very steeply from Big Tujunga Canyon over the north slope of Lukens to the peak.

Carry plenty of water on this trail; none is available en route. A city map—the Auto Club's "Los Angeles and Vicinity" is one good one—is fun to unfold on the summit to help you identify natural and man-made points of interest.

One warning: In order to reach the beginning of the Stone Canyon Trail, you must cross the creek flowing through Big Tujunga Canyon. During times of high water, this creek crossing can be difficult and dangerous— even impossible. Use care and your very best judgement when approaching this creek.

Directions to trailhead: From Foothill Boulevard in Sunland, turn north on Mount Gleason Avenue and drive 1 1/2 miles to Big Tujunga Canyon Road. Turn right and proceed 6 miles to signed Vogel Flats Road. Turn right and drive into the Forest Service's Vogel Flats Campground and Picnic Area. Turn right on the Forest Service road. Leave your car in one of the many day use parking spaces, near water, restrooms and picnic tables; or proceed another quarter-mile through a private residential area to the end of the road where parking is limited to a few cars and there are no facilities.

The Hike: From the Forest Service parking area, walk a quarter-mile northwest along the paved road past some cabins. The road ends at a barrier and you continue on a trail which travels 150 yards or so along and above the Big Tujunga Canyon creekbed. Look leftward for 1) A good place to cross the creek 2) a metal trail registry on the other side of the creek that marks the beginning of the Stone Canyon Trail 3) well-named Stone Canyon itself, which resembles a waterfall of white boulders. Stone Canyon Trail runs just to the left of Stone Canyon.

After you've signed the trail registry, begin the vigorous ascent, which first parallels Stone Canyon, then switchbacks to the east above it. Pausing now and then to catch your breath, you'll enjoy the view of Big Tujunga Canyon.

The trail leads through chamise, ceanothus and high chaparral. The 1975 Big Tujunga Fire scorched the slopes of Mount Lukens. Stone Canyon Trail could use a few more shady big cone spruce and a little less brush. Theodore Lukens and his band of tree planters would today be most welcome on the mountain's north slopes!

Three-and-a-half miles from the trailhead, you'll intersect an old fire road and bear left toward the summit. Atop the peak is a forest of radio antennae.

If you have the current Angeles National Forest map, you might notice the words "Sister Elsie" next to the peak. Before the peak was renamed for Lukens, Sister Elsie Peak honored a beloved Roman Catholic nun who was in charge of an orphanage for Indian children located in the La Crescenta area.

Enjoy the sweeping panorama of the Santa Monica and Verdugo Mountains, Santa Monica Bay and the Palos Verdes Peninsula, and the huge city spreading from the San Gabriel Mountains to the sea.

39

Gabrielino Trail

West Fork Campground to DeVore Trail Camp
2 miles round trip; 200-foot elevation gain

Downriver, the San Gabriel (along with its sister streams the Santa Ana and the Los Angeles) is best-known for depositing the alluvium that now covers the surface of the Los Angeles Basin. Upriver, the San Gabriel has two major forks, each with a claim to fame. East Fork is known for its gold, West Fork for its trout.

West Fork, its course determined by one of Southern California's more significant faults, the San Gabriel, is one of the best fishing rivers in Southern California. The river can be reached from a couple different directions, but most fishermen, as well as hikers and bicyclists, join the West Fork Scenic Trail which departs from Rincon Ranger Station off Highway 39.

A less well-known section of the West Fork is its upper part, which courses behind one of the tall shoulders of Mount Wilson. The canyon cut by the West Fork is woodsy and wild, a tranquil place sure to please. Down by the riverside, a maple- and oak-shaded trail leads from West Fork Campground to DeVore Trail Camp.

Both West Fork and DeVore camps have colorful histories. Right at the turn of the century, San Gabriel Mountains pioneer Louis Newcomb built a log cabin at West Fork that became California's first, and the nation's second National Forest ranger station. (The first ranger station was built in 1899 in Montana's Bitterroot National Forest.)

Old West Fork Camp, not to be confused with modern-day West Fork Campground, was a tiny wilderness hostelry operated by Ernest and Cherie DeVore. Opened in 1913, Camp West Fork was popular with hikers and fishermen for about a decade. Ownership squabbles resulted in its closure. Nothing remains of the trail resort but its peaceful setting, where the Forest Service has constructed a primitive camp.

The hike between West Fork and DeVore camps is an easy saunter that samples the best of the West Fork of the San Gabriel River. You'll be hiking a short segment of the 28-mile-long Gabrielino Trail, named after a local Indian tribe, which leads from Red Box Ranger Station on Angeles Crest Highway to Chantry Flats Ranger Station above Sierra Madre.

Directions to trailhead: From the Foothill Freeway (210) in La Canada, exit on Angeles Crest Highway (2) and ascend into the San Gabriel Mountains. As you pass a junction with the Angeles Forest Highway (N3)

you'll spot the Angeles National Forest's Clear Creek Information Station, a good place to pick up a map or to inquire about the latest trail conditions. Fourteen miles from La Canada, you'll leave the Angeles Crest Highway at Red Box Ranger Station and turn right on the signed road leading to Mount Wilson. After you make your right, bear immediately left onto dirt West Fork Road. The dusty road is potholed and bumpy, but suitable for most passenger cars with good ground clearance. Use caution and courtesy when negotiating the road's narrow spots. Six miles of driving brings you to West Fork Campground, where you'll find a modest amount of parking and the signed Gabrielino Trail.

The Hike: After cutting through the campground, you'll cross the West Fork and begin following it downriver (east). After a severe storm, the West Fork can turn into a raging river, but most of the year it's mellow and shallow. You'll probably be able to keep your feet dry as you boulder-hop across the river a dozen different times on the way to DeVore. Halfway along, you might be surprised to find a seasonal waterfall located above one of the bends of the river.

Your pleasant stream-side saunter ends at DeVore Trail Camp. An old fisherman's trail continues quite some distance along the San Gabriel River—all the way to Coswell Reservoir, in fact—but it is in poor condition, and just below DeVore is quite overgrown with poison oak.

West Fork Ranger Station barn, 1914

149

▲40

Millard Canyon Trail

To Millard Canyon Falls
        1 mile round trip
To Dawn Mine
        5 miles round trip; 800-foot elevation gain

Hidden from the metropolis by Sunset Ridge, lush Millard Canyon is one of the more secluded spots in the front range of the San Gabriel Mountains. A cold stream tumbling over handsome boulders and a trail meandering beneath a canopy of alder, oak and sycamore, are a few of the many attractions of Millard Canyon.

The historical record is sketchy in regard to squatter Millard, who settled at the mouth of the canyon that now bears his name in about 1862. Millard eked out a living by keeping bees and hauling firewood down to Los Angles. He reportedly spent about a decade in the canyon, then left suddenly in 1872 after his wife and child died.

Millard Canyon is best-known as the site of the Dawn Mine which, unfortunately for its investors, produced more stories than gold. The mine was worked off and on from 1895, when gold was first discovered, until the 1950s. Enough gold was mined to keep ever-optimistic prospectors certain that they would soon strike a rich ore-bearing vein, but the big bonzana was never found.

You can explore Millard Canyon by two different routes, which lack an official name, but are often referred to as Millard Canyon Trail. An easy half-mile path meanders along the canyon floor to 50-foot Millard Falls. This is a pleasant walk that provides a good introduction to the delights of the San Gabriel Mountains.

Experienced hikers will enjoy the challenge of following an abandoned trail through Millard Canyon to the site of the Dawn Mine. Enough of the old trail remains to keep you on track, but it's slow going with many stream crossings en route.

Directions to trailhead: From the Foothill Freeway (210) in Pasadena, exit on Lake Avenue. Drive north four miles, at which point Lake veers left and becomes Loma Alta Drive. Continue a mile to Chaney Trail and turn right. Proceed another mile to a junction atop Sunset Ridge. If you're taking the hike to Dawn Mine, you'll bear right at this junction and park just outside the gate blocking Sunset Ridge Fire Road. If you're bound for Millard Canyon Falls, you'll stay left at the junction and descend to a parking lot at the bottom of the canyon.

The Hike: To Millard Canyon Falls. From the parking area at the bottom of Millard Canyon, you'll walk a hundred yards up a fire road to Millard Canyon Campground. Walk through the campground and pick up the signed trail leading to the falls. The trail heads east along the woodsy canyon bottom, crosses the stream a couple times, and arrives at the base of the waterfall. Don't try to climb up, over, or around the falls; people have been injured attempting this foolhardy ascent.

The Hike: To Dawn Mine. From the Sunset Ridge parking area, head up the fire road. Enjoy the clear-day ridgetop views of the metropolis. You'll soon pass a junction on your left with a trail leading down to Millard Canyon Campground.

A short quarter-mile from the trailhead, you'll spot the signed Sunset Ridge Trail, which you'll join and begin descending into Millard Canyon. A few minutes of walking down the well-graded path will reward you with an eagle's-eye-view of Millard Canyon Falls.

Near the canyon bottom, you'll meet a trail junction. Sunset Ridge Trail continues along the canyon wall, but you bear left and descend past a cabin to the canyon floor. As you begin hiking up-canyon, turn around and take a mental photograph of the trail that brought you down to the canyon; it's easy to miss on your return trip.

As you pick your way stream-side amongst the boulders and fallen trees on the canyon floor, you'll follow vestiges of the old trail. Typically, you'll follow a fifty- or hundred-yard stretch of trail, boulder-hop for a bit, cross the stream, then pick up another length of trail.

The canyon floor is strewn with lengths of rusting pipe and assorted mining machinery. Several pools, cascades, and flat rocks suggest a stream-side picnic.

After hiking a bit more than a mile up-canyon, you'll find that Millard Canyon turns north. From this turn, it's a bit less than a mile to the Dawn Mine site. Don't go into the mine shaft. Darkness and deep holes filled with water make it very dangerous.

Return the same way, and remember to keep a sharp lookout for the trail that leads out of the canyon back to the trailhead.

41
Winter Creek Trail

Season: All Year

Chantry Flat to Hoegees Camp
6 miles round trip; 300-foot elevation gain

Cascades, currants and woodwardia ferns are a few of the delights of historic Winter Creek Canyon, which has been popular with Southern Californians for nearly one hundred years.

Before the turn of the century, packer/entrepreneur Wilbur Sturtevant set up a trail camp in one of the woodsy canyons on the south-facing slope of Mount Wilson. This peaceful creek-side refuge from city life was called Sturtevant's Winter Camp. In later years the name Winter was given to the creek whose headwaters arise from the shoulder of Mount Wilson and tumble southeasterly into Big Santa Anita Canyon.

In 1908, Arie Hoegee and his family built a resort here that soon became a popular destination for Mount Wilson-bound hikers; it remained so until it was battered by the great flood of 1938. A trail camp named for the Hoegees now stands on the site of the old resort and offers the modern-day hiker a tranquil picnic site or rest stop.

A hike along Winter Creek is a fine way to greet the arrival of winter. One of a half-dozen trails accessible from the popular Chantry Flat trailhead located just above Altadena in the Angeles National Forest, Winter Creek Trail offers a pleasant family hike in the front range of the San Gabriel Mountains.

Directions to trailhead: From the Foothill Freeway (210) in Arcadia, exit on Santa Anita Avenue and drive six miles north to its end at Chantry Flat. The trail begins across the road from the parking area. A tiny store at the edge of the parking lot sells maps and refreshments.

The Hike: (See Trail 42 map.) Descend 3/4 mile on the paved fire road, part of the signed Gabrielino Trail, into Big Santa Anita Canyon. At the bottom of the canyon, you'll cross a footbridge near the confluence of Big Santa Anita and Winter Creeks.

After crossing the bridge, look leftward for the signed Lower Winter Creek Trail. Following the bubbling creek, the trail tunnels beneath the boughs of oak and alder, willow and bay. The only blemish on the pristine scene is a series of check dams constructed of giant cement "Lincoln logs" by the Los Angeles County Flood Control District and Forest Service in the early 1960s. Fortunately, during the last quarter-century, moss, ferns and other creek-side flora have softened the appearance of the dams and they now fit much better into the lovely surroundings.

You'll pass some cabins, built just after the turn of the century and reached only by trail. For more than seven decades, the needs of the cabin owners have been supplied by pack train. Today, one of the more colorful sights in the San Gabriel Mountains is that of packers Dennis and Jody Lonergan urging their obstinate donkeys up the Winter Creek Trail.

When you see man and beast moving through the forest, it's easy to imagine that you've stepped three-quarters of a century back in time, back into Southern California's great Hiking and Trail Resort Era. The Lonergans operate one of the last working pack strings in Southern California, continuing a tradition that would surely make early packers Sturtevant and Chantry proud.

After crossing Winter Creek, you'll arrive at Hoegees Camp. A dozen or so tables beneath the big cone spruce offer fine picnicking. Almost all signs of the original Hoegees Camp are gone, with the exception of flourishing patches of ivy. (In later years, Hoegees was renamed Camp Ivy.)

Walk through the campground until you spot a tiny tombstone-shaped trail sign. Cross Winter Creek here and bear left on the trail. In a short while you'll pass a junction with Mount Zion Trail, a steep trail that climbs over the mountain to Sturtevant Camp and Big Santa Anita Canyon.

After recrossing the creek, you'll pass a junction with a trail leading to Mount Wilson and join the Upper Winter Creek Trail. This trail contours around a ridge onto open chaparral-covered slopes. This stretch of trail offers fine clear-day views of Sierra Madre and Arcadia. The trail joins a fire road just above Chantry Flat and you follow this road through the picnic area back to the parking lot where you left your car.

*Ivy along trail recalls
days when Hoegees was
named "Camp Ivy"*

42

Mount Zion Trail

From Chantry Flat, a loop around Mount Zion via Gabrielino, Winter Creek and Mount Zion Trails
9 miles round trip; 1,500-foot elevation gain

Zion, the name of one of the hills of Jerusalem on which the City of David was built, and which became the center of Jewish life and worship, is also the name of a peak in the San Gabriel Mountains above Arcadia.

Mount Zion Trail was one of many paths constructed by turn-of-the-century pioneer packer/entrepreneur Wilbur Sturtevant. Sturtevant had constructed Sturtevant's Winter Camp, a creekside refuge from city life on the banks of Winter Creek, and Camp Sturtevant in upper Santa Anita Canyon. Obviously he needed to connect his camps, so in 1896 he began constructing a three-mile link in the Sturtevant Trail that would later be known as Mount Zion Trail. The first mile and a half of trail up Mount Zion from Winter Creek was a killer construct—a thousand-foot climb over the steep and rocky shoulder of Mount Zion.

Long after Sturtevant finished his trail, the pioneer was asked why he elected to climb over Mount Zion rather than around it. Replied Sturtevant: "Well, I'm a pretty stubborn sort of man; a fellow told me it would be better to go around, so I went over."

At least stubborn Sturtevant had an easier time of it building the second half of his trail, which led down Mount Zion into Santa Anita Canyon. Here the slope was gentle, the trail shaded by tall trees.

For two decades, until a trail was built up Santa Anita Canyon in 1916, Mount Zion Trail was the primary route to Camp Sturtevant and the backcountry beyond. A 1953 fire scorched Mount Zion, and subsequent rains, landslides and erosion destroyed part of the trail. By the 1960s, chaparral had covered the trail and made it impassable. Fortunately, this historic path was rescued from oblivion by Sierra Club volunteers and an informal group of San Gabriel Mountains afficionados who call themselves the "Big Santa Anita Gang." Mount Zion Trail was reconstructed and reopened to public use in the spring of 1987.

Mount Zion Trail allows the modern mountaineer to make a grand loop by connecting the Winter Creek and Gabrielino Trails. Those hikers not quite up for a 9-mile trip can enjoy a shorter 5 mile-loop along the Winter Creek Trail, or a walk along the Gabrielino Trail to Sturtevant Falls. With a half-dozen interconnecting trails accessible from Chantry Flat Picnic Area, you can plan your own perfect hike.

Directions to trailhead: From the Foothill Freeway (210) in Arcadia, exit on Santa Anita Avenue and drive six miles north to its end at Chantry Flat. The trail begins across the road from the parking area. A tiny store at the edge of the parking lot sells maps and refreshments.

The Hike: Descend three-quarters of a mile on the paved fire road, part of the signed Gabrielino Trail, into Big Santa Anita Canyon. At the bottom of the canyon, you will cross a footbridge near the confluence of Big Santa Anita and Winter creeks.

After crossing the bridge, look left for the signed Lower Winter Creek Trail. Following the bubbling creek, the trail tunnels beneath the boughs of oak and alder, willow and bay.

After crossing Winter Creek, you'll arrive at Hoegee Camp, 2 1/2 miles from the trailhead. In 1908, Arie Hoegee and his family built a resort here that soon became a popular destination for Mount Wilson-bound hikers. The resort was a casualty of the great flood of 1938, but a trail camp named for the Hoegees stands on the site of the old resort and offers the modern-day hiker a tranquil picnic site or rest stop.

Walk through the campground until you spot a tiny tombstone-shaped trail sign. Cross Winter Creek here and bear left on the trail. After a short while, you'll arrive at a signed junction with Mount Zion Trail. Those in

155

the mood for a shorter walk can decide here to loop back to Chantry Flat via the signed Upper Winter Creek Trail. The more energetic will now begin the ascent to Zion.

Mount Zion Trail wastes little time in its steep ascent of the chaparral-cloaked mountain. You'll get good over-the-shoulder views of the canyon cut by Winter Creek. About 1 1/2 miles of climbing brings you to a signed junction. Here you'll find a small interpretive display that explains the history of the Mount Zion segment of the Sturtevant Trail and the short side trail that leads to the peak. Follow the summit trail a hundred yards through the manzanita to the 3,575-foot peak, where you can sign a summit register and enjoy fine clear-day views.

Return to Mount Zion Trail and enjoy a pleasant, shady descent of a bit more than a mile into Big Santa Anita Canyon. In the canyon bottom you'll reach a junction. Here the Sturtevant Trail heads up canyon to Sturtevant Camp, now Methodist Camp, and on to Mount Wilson. You'll head down canyon to Spruce Grove Camp, a shady spot with plenty of picnic tables. Another mile of travel brings you to Cascade Picnic Area.

Below the picnic area, your trail, the Gabrielino Trail, forks. The leftward, lower trail, which heads through the heart of Santa Anita Canyon, is prettier, while the upper trail, which zigzags along the canyon wall is easier walking and offers good views. The trails rejoin in a mile and proceed down-canyon as one.

Once you reach the canyon bottom, you can detour on a short side trail to one more tribute to Wilbur Sturtevant— Sturtevant Falls, a silver stream that cascades 50 feet to a natural rock bowl.

After recrossing the Winter Creek footbridge, trudge up the paved fire road back to the trailhead.

43

Silver Moccasin Trail

Chilao to Horse Flats Campground
    2 miles round trip; 200-foot elevation gain
Chilao to Mount Hillyer
    6 miles round trip; 1,000-foot elevation gain

Even on the Angeles National Forest map, the trail looks intriguing: a red dashed line zigs and zags through the heart of the San Gabriel Mountains and connects Chantry Flat and Shortcut Station, Chilao, Cloudburst and Cooper Canyon. Designed by the Los Angeles Area Council of the Boy Scouts of America, the 53-mile-long Silver Moccasin Trail, extends from Charlton Flat to the mountain named for the founder of the Boy Scouts, Lord Baden-Powell. Scouts who complete the week-long trek earn the prized Silver Moccasin award.

One pretty stretch of the Silver Moccasin Trail tours the Chilao country, a region of giant boulders and gentle, Jeffrey pine-covered slopes. Another path—Mount Hillyer Trail—leads to the top of 6,162-foot Mount Hillyer. From the top, you'll get great views to the north of the desert side of the San Gabriels.

During the early 1870s, stagecoach-robber/horse-and-cattle thief Tiburcio Vasquez and his gang hid out in the Chilao country. The stolen horses were pastured in secluded grassland we now call Horse Flats. Vasquez, last of a generation of bandits to operate out of the Southern California backcountry, was captured in 1874. Many reporters visited Vasquez in his Los Angeles jail cell, and the highwayman soon found himself quite a celebrity. He was not an ordinary ciminal, he told the press but a patriotic Californio whose goal was to rid Southern California of the gringo influence. Southern Californians loved Vasquez's stories and knew that in a small way, he represented the end of the Wild West; never the less, he was sent to the gallows in 1875.

Tiburcio Vasquez

One exhibit at the Chilao Visitor Center answers a trivia question that perplexes all day hikers who depart from Chilao area trailheads: What exactly does Chilao mean? As the story goes, one of Vasquez's men, Jose Gonzales, lived in a log cabin in the area where the visitor center now stands. Gonzales guarded the hideout and horses. His battle with a huge bear, which he killed using only a knife, earned him the name Chillia—roughly translated as "hot stuff." The name over the last century of use evolved into Chilao.

Chilao Country, great place to hide out for awhile

Located just off Angeles Crest Highway near the trailhead, the Angeles National Forest Chilao Visitor Center is well-worth a visit for the latest in trail, road and weather information. Exhibits interpret flora, fauna and forest history; behind the station is a short nature trail.

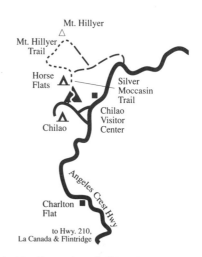

Directions to trailhead: From the Foothill Freeway (210) in La Canada, exit on Angeles Crest Highway (2) and wind 27 miles up the mountain road to the signed turnoff for the Chilao Visitor Center. Turn left and follow the paved road past the visitor center a half-mile to signed Silver Moccasin Trail on your right. Parking at the trailhead is limited to a few cars, but there's a wide turnout located just up the road.

The Hike: The trail ascends a manzanita- and yucca-covered slope to the top of a minor ridge. A mile from the trailhead, the trail widens and you reach a signed junction. Here Silver Moccasin Trail swings southeast toward Angeles Crest Highway and Cooper Canyon, but you go right with a retiring dirt road one hundred yards to Horse Flat Campground. The camp, with plenty of pine-shaded picnic tables, is a good rest stop.

Just as you reach the gravel campground road, you head left with the signed Mount Hillyer Trail. The path switchbacks up slopes covered with pine, incense cedar and scrub oaks. Some big boulders suggest a perfect hideout, whether you're fleeing the sheriff or the stresses of modern life.

Up top, Mount Hillyer may remind you of what Gertrude Stein said of Oakland: "There's no there there." The summit is not a commanding pinnacle, but a forested flat. With all those trees in the way, you'll have to walk a few hundred yards along the ridgeline to get your view of the green bandito country to the south and the brown, wrinkled desert side of the San Gabriels to the north.

44

Mount Islip Trail

Angeles Crest Highway to Little Jimmy Trail Camp
3 miles round trip; 500-foot elevation gain
Angeles Crest Highway to Mount Islip
5 miles round trip; 1,100-foot elevation gain

Mount Islip, (pronounced eye-slip) is not named, as you might guess, for a clumsy mountaineer, but for Canadian George Islip, who homesteaded in San Gabriel Canyon a century ago. The mountain is by no means one of the tallest San Gabriel Mountains peaks, but its relatively isolated position on the spine of the range makes its stand out. The summit offers the hiker fine views of the middle portion of the Angeles National Forest high country and of the metropolis.

On the trail to Mount Islip

Mount Islip has long been a popular destination for hikers. The mountain was particularly popular with Occidental College students who, in 1909, built a huge cairn (heap of boulders) dubbed the "Occidental Monument" atop the summit. The monument, which had the name Occidental on top, stood about two decades, until the Forest Service cleared the summit of Mount Islip to make room for a fire lookout tower. Today, the monument and the fire lookout are long-gone, but the stone foundation of the fire lookout's living quarters still remains.

One early visitor to the slopes of Mount Islip was popular newspaper cartoonist Jimmy Swinnerton (1875-1974), well-known in the early years of this century for his comic strip "Little Jimmy." By the time he was 30-something, hard-working, hard-drinking Swinnerton was suffering from the effects of exhaustion, booze, and tuberculosis. His employer and benefactor William Randolph Hearst sent Swinnerton to the desert to dry out. Swinnerton, however, found the summer heat oppressive so, loading his paintbrushes onto a burro, he headed into the San Gabriel Mountains.

"I wouldn't exactly call Jimmy an outdoorsman," opines Swinnerton's biographer, Santa Barbara author and art dealer Harold Davidson. "But no question about it, he loved the mountains and the clean air really improved his lungs."

Swinnerton spent the summers of 1908 and 1909 at Camp Coldbrook on the banks of the north fork of the San Gabriel River. Often he would set up camp high on the shoulder of Mount Islip near a place called Gooseberry Spring, which soon became known as Little Jimmy Spring. His campsite, for many years known as Swinnerton Camp, now bears the name of Little Jimmy Trail Camp.

During the two summers Swinnerton was encamped in the San Gabriels, he entertained passing hikers with sketches of his popular Little Jimmy character.

You can reach Mount Islip from the south side of the mountains, the way Jimmy Swinnerton did, or start from the north side from Angeles Crest Highway. This day hike follows the latter route, which is a bit easier than coming up from the Crystal Lake/Camp Coldbrook area.

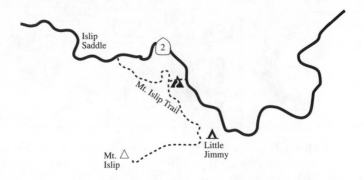

Directions to trailhead: From the Foothill Freeway (210) in La Canada, exit on Angeles Crest Highway (2) and follow the winding road into the mountains. Proceed to signed Islip Saddle. (At the saddle, on the north side of the highway, is a large parking area. If you want, you can start your hike to Mount Islip at the trailhead across the road from the parking area. An old trail heads west, paralleling the highway for a mile, then veers upward to meet the trail leading to Little Jimmy Trail Camp.)

From Islip Saddle, a mile and a half drive east on Angeles Crest Highway brings you to the signed trailhead for Little Jimmy Trail Camp on the right (south) side of the road. There's parking on both sides of the highway.

The Hike: Your trail, at first, is a dirt road (closed to all but Forest Service vehicles). Jeffrey and sugar pine shade the route. A half-mile ascent brings you to a three-way junction. To your right is the old crest trail coming up from Islip Sadddle. The forest road you've been following continues to Little Jimmy Trail Camp.

Bear left on the signed trail to Little Jimmy. The trail stays just below and parallel to the road as it ascends a mile over forested slopes to Little Jimmy Trail Camp. The camp, popular with scout troops, has tables, stoves and restrooms. A side trail leads 1/4-mile southeast to all-year Little Jimmy Spring.

At the west end of camp, pick up the signed trail to Mount Islip. A half-mile of switchbacks through piney woods brings you up to a sharp ridgeline. From atop the ridge, you'll enjoy great views of Crystal Lake, the San Gabriel Wilderness, and the canyons cut by Bear Creek and the San Gabriel River.   The trail turns east and follows the ridge for another half-mile to the 8,250-foot peak. Summit views include the ski areas of Krakta Ridge and Mount Waterman to the west and Mount Baden-Powell to the east.

▲45
Sunset Peak Trail

Glendora Ridge Road to Sunset Peak
5 miles round trip; 1,200-foot elevation gain

Mount Baldy, highest peak in the San Gabriel Mountains, is visible from much of the Southland. Its summit gleams white in winter and early spring; in fact, Baldy is so big and bare that is seems to be snow-covered even when it's not.

As spry octagenarian, long-time peak-bagger Sam Fink admired the panoramic view from the summit, he declared, "Sunset Peak gives you the best view of Old Baldy."

Fink knows his views. When I encountered him atop Sunset Peak, he was making his 82nd trip up this trail. Fink began leading Sierra Club trips into the San Gabriels back in the 1930s and has been day hiking for well over a half-century. Sunset Peak and its view of Baldy has long been a favorite with Fink, though it takes second-place to Mount Baldy itself, which he says he has climbed 103 times.

"I'm not as fast as I used to be," Fink grouses, "but I still get to the top."

When snow covers the San Gabriel high country, consider the short hike to Sunset Peak. For most of the winter and early spring, the 5,796-foot peak seems to be strategically positioned just below the snow line and just above the smog line. You'll get great clear-day views of Claremont and the San Gabriel Valley below and of Baldy and its neighboring peaks above.

Sunset views, as the name of the peak suggests, are often glorious. If you plan an evening hike, bring warm clothing and flashlights.

Directions to trailhead: From the San Bernardino Freeway (10) in Claremont, exit on Indian Hill Boulevard and head north. Drive 2 miles to Foothill Boulevard (old Route 66 for the nostalgic). Turn right and proceed 3/4 mile Mills Avenue, then turn left and follow Mills 2 miles to a stop sign, where the avenue becomes Mount Baldy Road; continue another 8 miles to Glendora Ridge Road, which you'll spot on your left just short of the hamlet of Mount Baldy. Turn left and follow Glendora Ridge Road a mile to a gravel parking lot on the right. The trailhead is on the opposite (left) side of the road.

The Hike: Sunset Peak Trail, a Forest Service fire road closed to vehicles, begins at a bullet-riddled stop sign and a candy-cane striped barrier. The trail ascends moderately, but steadily up the pine- and big cone spruce-shaded north side of Sunset Peak.

About halfway to the peak, you'll ascend out of the shade into chaparral country. A 1975 fire scorched these upper slopes, and it will be a while before tall trees grow here again.

A very steep fire break offers a route to the summit, but it would be wise to ignore it and continue on the main trail. A half-mile from the top, at a wide bend in the road, the trail swings sharp left.

Just below the peak the fire road gives way to a steep footpath and you'll ascend a final hundred yards to the summit. Up top are a couple of cement pillars and other debris, remains of a Forest Service fire lookout tower that was abandoned because of several reasons: Smog hindered visibility and the Forest Service has for some years been replacing human lookouts with more automated surveillance. Also, a fire burned the peak.

The view of the metropolis below is notoriously undependable; however, the panorama of peaks above is always an inspiring sight.

 **46**

Ski Hut Trail

Manker Flat to San Antonio Falls
1 mile round trip; 200-foot elevation gain
Manker Flat to San Antonio Canyon Overlook
6 1/2 miles round trip; 2,600-foot elevation gain
Manker Flat to Mount Baldy summit
8 1/2 miles round trip; 3,800-foot elevation gain

Three saintly mountains—San Gorgonio, San Jacinto and San Antonio—tower over the City of the Angels. Lowest of the three, but by far the best-known, is Mount San Antonio, more commonly called Mount Baldy. The 10,064-foot peak, highest in the San Gabriel Mountains, is visible from much of the Southland. Its summit gleams white in winter, and early spring, gray in summer and fall. Old Baldy is so big and bare that it appears to be snow-covered even when it's not.

Legend has it that the padres of Mission San Gabriel, circa 1790, named the massive stone bulwark after Saint Anthony of Padua, Italy. The 13th-Century Franciscan friar evidently was a favorite of California missionaries: A number of geographical features in Monterey County and around Southern California were christened San Antonio. In the 1870s, San Antonio Canyon and the nearby high country swarmed with gold seekers, who gave the massive peak a more earthy name—Old Baldy.

Several trails lead to the summit. The most difficult is the Bear Flat (or Old Baldy) Trail, which gains 5,500 feet as it climbs the south ridge of Baldy to the top. The most popular route gets a head start with the Mount Baldy ski lift, then follows Devil's Backbone Trail to the summit.

This day hike utilizes a pretty but not-so-well-known trail that leads up San Antonio Canyon to the top of Baldy. Locals call it the Ski Hut Trail because the Sierra Club maintains a hut halfway up the path. The trail doesn't have an official name and it's not on the Angeles National Forest map.

Hikers of all ages and abilities will enjoy the half-mile walk to San Antonio Falls. After a little rain, the three-tiered, 60-foot waterfall is an impressive sight.

Beyond the falls the hiking is strenuous, definitely not for the inexperienced or out-of-shape. Hikers who want more than the "leg-stretcher" walk to the falls but aren't quite up for an assault on the peak can choose two intermediate destinations: the Sierra Club ski hut, where there's a cool spring, or a high ridge overlooking San Antonio Canyon.

Old Baldy

Hikers in top form, with good trail sense (the last mile of trail to the peak is rough and tentative), will relish the challenge of the summit climb. A clear-day view from the top offers a panorama of desert and ocean, the sprawling Southland and the southern High Sierra.

Directions to trailhead: Take the San Bernardino Freeway to Claremont, exit on Mountain Avenue and head north, joining Mount Baldy Road in San Antonio Canyon, and winding about 11 miles to Manker Campground. One-third mile past the campground entrance, look to the left for an unsigned paved road with a vehicle barrier across it. Park in the dirt lot just below the beginning of the road.

The Hike: Walk up the fire road, which is closed to all motor vehicles except those belonging to ski-lift maintenance workers. After a modest ascent, you will hear the sound of falling water and soon behold San Antonio Falls. If you decide to hike down to the base of the falls, watch for loose rock and use caution on the rough trail.

Resume walking along the road (unpaved beyond the falls). After about 10 minutes of walking at a moderate pace, look sharply left for an unsigned trail. Ducks (piles of rock) on both sides of the road mark the trail. (If you find yourself heading north up Manker Canyon and getting good views of the ski lift, you missed the turnoff.)

The no-nonsense trail ascends very steeply along the side of San Antonio Canyon. You'll get great over-the-shoulder views of the canyon bottom and of Mount Baldy Village. Trail connoisseurs will appreciate this path, which, despite its steepness, has a hand-hewn, unobtrusive look and follows the natural contours of the land. Jeffrey pine, ponderosa pine and fir shade the well-constructed path, which is seasonally decorated with red Indian paintbrush and creamy yucca blossoms.

From the ski lift road, it's 1 3/4 miles by trail to the Sierra Club ski hut. Near the hut, which was built in 1935, is a cool and refreshing spring.

Just past the ski hut the trail crosses a tiny creek, then snakes through a boulder field. Beyond the boulders, the trail ascends via a half-mile series of steep switchbacks to a ridgetop overlooking the headwaters of San Antonio Canyon. There's a great view from the tree-shaded ridgetop, and if you aren't quite up for an assault on the peak, this is a good picnic spot or turnaround point.

Peak-baggers will continue up the extremely rugged trail for another mile to the summit. The trail is rough and tentative in some places, but rocks piled in cairns help you stay on course. You'll get good view of Devil's Backbone, the sharp ridge connecting Mount Harwood to Mount Baldy.

Boulders are scattered atop Baldy's crown. A couple of rock windbreaks offer some shelter. Enjoy the view of San Gabriel and San Bernardino Mountain peaks, the Mojave and the metropolis.

Depending on your energy and inclination, you can either return the same way or take the Devil's Backbone Trail to Mount Baldy Notch. From the Notch, you can follow the fire road down Manker Canyon back to the trailhead or ride down the ski lift.

Chapter 7

SOUTHERN CALIFORNIA COAST

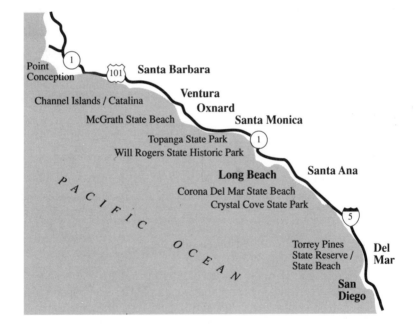

Southern California Coast

The moon rules a province of living things on the margin of the restless Pacific. The moon is twenty-seven million times smaller than the sun, yet it exerts twice the sun's power over the tides. A multitude of tidal creatures, from crabs to grunion, observe a lunar day. These shoreline animals swim, feed, and mate in harmony with Southern California's twice-daily ebb and flow of the tide.

This lunar rhythm is illustrated by the behavior of a creature familiar to Southern California beachgoers, the sandhopper or beach flea. At the peak of each high tide, when waves sweep the hopper's habitat, it emerges from the sand to swim and feed in the surf. A few hours later, as the tide recedes, the hopper burrows in the sand and awaits the tide's return. You may jump to the conclusion that the hopper is merely responding to getting wet or staying dry, but that isn't the case. Temperature and pressure changes delivered by waves are what motivate the sandhopper. Scientists at Scripps Institute of Oceanography found that sandhoppers kept in a jar of sea water remained sedentary at the bottom of the jar during the low tides. Other experiments have left scientists with the conviction that some creatures have internal biological clocks that trigger their movements.

Another coastal creature observing a lunar day is the grunion. Grunion spawn only in Southern California between Point Conception and Baja. Actual spawning occurs only for a few hours between March and August. Through evolutionary successes in feeding and mating, crabs, gulls, grunion, sandhoppers and a million more shoreline dwellers have adapted to a lunar cycle. Biologists are trying to find out what makes these creatures tick, trying to discover these biological clocks and how they work. So far, the clocks remain ghosts, perhaps the result of enzyme action or cell chemistry.

If the lunar time were only a matter of academic interest of affected only the lives of a few sandhoppers or grunion, it would be easy to ignore. But the moon's power governs the qualiity of out lives and the quality of our beaches far more than we imagine. Understanding the moon's gravitational pull on the water and the rhythm or the tides is important to all of us who love our southern coast. More than eighty percent of Southern Californians live within thirty miles of the coast. We love our beaches; in fact, we may be loving them to death. Tidal processes are something we've chosen to ignore in our rush to develop the coast, and as a result, we're losing our beaches, despite our best efforts.

Consider how beaches are made. The moon pulls Pacific tides against cliffs and grinds rock into sand. Without cliff erosion, there would be no beaches. However, when building occurs on the beach, this erosion can't take place. Beaches are dynamic ecosystems, forever expanding and contracting, yet they are treated by developers as steady-state systems. Dunes, marshes and sandstone cliffs are surveyed and beach lot boundaries laid out in straight lines. The shoreline is then blacktopped and condominium-ized. Motels, marina, and parking lots spring up at water's edge. Once beachfront investments are made, property rights predominate over natural tidal rhythms. Attempts to stablize the beach are initiated—dunes are leveled, inlets and channels are dredged, groins, sea walls and jetties— often more expensive than the property they are designed to protect—are erected. The beach, which once maintained itself, can do so no longer. Beaches disappear in some places and, with them, beachfront property. Concerned citizens then try to "save the beach," answering Nature's warning with more groins and more jetties, becoming more involved in a costly and ultimately futile cycle. Someday we'll learn an important lesson—the best way to save the beach is to leave it alone!

For the day hiker, our southern coast offers not only those white sand beaches depicted on postcards, but a wide variety of shoreline features— the palms of La Jolla and Santa Monica, the cliffs of Torrey Pines and Palos Verdes. Above Santa Barbara, the Santa Ynez Mountains march toward the Pacific, and at Point Mugu, the Santa Monica Mountains do likewise.

The trailless beach is ever-changing. Tidepool exploring, viewing the unique organisms that have adapted to the twice-daily change in tides, is one of the highlights of a beach walk. Another is beachcombing—picking through the flotsam and jetsam for treasures cast ashore. After a storm, the keen-eyed beachcomber may find a unique piece of driftwood, a pretty shell, a Japanese fishing ball, or treasure from an ancient wrecked ship.

What would our feeding, sleeping and mating habits be today if we lived in harmony with the tide's ebb and flow? Would it change our wristwatches, calendars, and television-watching habits? Would we have a little more respect for the sanctity of our beaches if our bodies, like those of sandhoppers, were found to contain biological clocks keeping time with the moon? The restless ocean holds answers to questions we have not yet learned to ask.

 **47**

Point Sal Trail

Point Sal State Beach to Point Sal
5 miles round trip

When your eye travels down a map of Central California coast, you pause on old and familiar friends—the state beaches at San Simeon, Morro Bay, and Pismo Beach. Usually overlooked is another state beach—remote Point Sal, a nub of land north of Vandenberg Air Force Base and south of the Guadalupe Dunes. Windy Point Sal is a wall of bluffs rising 50 to 100 feet above the rocky shore. The water is crystal-clear, and the blufftops provide a fine spot to watch the boisterous seals and sea lions.

Point Sal was named by explorer Vancouver in 1792 for Hermenegildo Sal, at that time commandante of San Francisco, The state purchased the land in the 1940s. There are no facilities whatsoever at the beach, so remember, if you pack it in, pack it out.

This hike travels Point Sal State Beach, then takes to the bluffs above rocky reefs. At low tide, you can pass around or over the reefs; at high tide the only passage is along the bluff trail. Both marine life and land life can be observed from the bluff trail. You'll pass a seal haul-out, tidepools, sight gulls, cormorant and pelicans, and perhaps see deer, bobcat and coyote on the ocean-facing slopes of the Casmalia Hills.

The trail system in the Point Sal area is in rough condition. The narrow bluff trails should not be undertaken by novice hikers, the weak-kneed or those afraid of heights. Families with small children and less experienced trekkers will enjoy beachcombing and tidepool-watching opportunities at Point Sal and the pleasure of discovering this out-of-the-way beach.

Directions to trailhead: From Highway 101 in Santa Maria, exit on Betteravia Road. Proceed west past a commercial strip and then out into the sugar beet fields. Betteravia Road twists north. About eight miles from Highway 101, turn left on Brown Road. Five miles of driving on Brown Road (watch for cows wandering along the road) brings you to a signed junction; leftward is a ranch road, but you bear right on Point Sal Road, partly paved, partly dirt washboard (impassable in wet weather). Follow this road about 5 miles to its end at the parking area above Point Sal State Beach.

Be advised that Point Sal Road is sometimes closed during the rainy season. The Air Force sometimes closes the road for short periods during its missile launches.

The Hike: From the parking area, follow one of the short steep trails down to the beautiful crescent-shaped beach. Hike up-coast along the windswept beach. In 1/3 mile, you'll reach the end of the beach at a rocky reef, difficult to negotiate at high tide. A second reef, encountered shortly after the first, is equally difficult. Atop this reef, there's a rope secured to an iron stake to aid your descent to the beach below. The rope is also helpful in ascending the reef on your return.

Unless it's very low tide, you'll want to begin following the narrow bluff trail above the reefs. The trail arcs westward with the coast, occasionally dipping down to rocky and romantic pocket beaches sequestered between reefs.

About 1 1/2 miles from the trailhead, you'll descend close to shore and begin boulder-hopping. After a few hundred yards of boulder-hopping, you'll begin to hear the bark of sea lions and get an aviator's view of Lion Rock, where the gregarious animals bask in the sun. Also be on the lookout for harbor seals, often called leopard seals because of their silver, white, or even yellow spots.

Your trek continues on a pretty decent bluff trail, which dips down near a sea lion haul-out. (Please don't approach or disturb these creatures.) You'll then ascend rocky Point Sal. From the point, you'll view the Guadalupe Dunes complex to the north and the sandy beaches of Vandenberg Air Force Base to the south. Before returning the same way, look for red-tailed hawks riding the updrafts and admire the ocean boiling up over the reefs.

Energetic hikers can follow a trail which passes behind Point Sal, joins a sandy road, and descends to a splendid beach north of the point. Here you'll find a two-mile-long sandy beach to explore. This unnamed beach is almost always deserted except for a few fishermen and lots of pelicans.

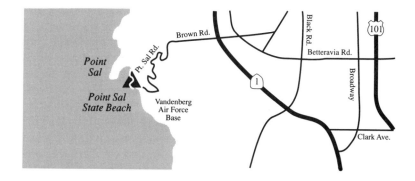

48

McGrath Beach Trail

McGrath State Beach to McGrath Lake
    4 miles round trip
McGrath State Beach to Oxnard Shores
    8 miles round trip
McGrath State Beach to Channel Islands Harbor
    12 miles round trip

McGrath State Beach and McGrath Lake were named for the McGrath family which had extensive land holdings in the area dating from 1874. Located on the western city limits of Oxnard, the 2-mile-long state beach extends south from the Santa Clara River.

A small lake in the southern portion of the park helps to attract more than two hundred species of birds, including white-tailed kites, marsh hawks, owls, and herons. Such rare birds as ospreys, white wagtails and black skimmers have been sighted here. The Santa Clara Estuary Natural Preserve on the northern boundary of the park also offers a haven for birds and habitat for weasels, skunks, jackrabbits, opossum, squirrels and mice, plus tortoises and gopher snakes.

Near the state beach entry kiosk, a small visitors center has exhibits about the areas plant and wildlife.

This walk takes you on a nature trail through the Santa Clara River Estuary, visits McGrath Lake and travels miles of sandy beach to Channel Islands Harbor.

Directions to trailhead: To reach McGrath State Beach, visitors southbound on U.S. 101 should take the Seaward Avenue offramp to Harbor Boulevard, turn south on Harbor and travel 3/4 mile to the park. Northbound visitors should exit Highway 101 on Victoria Avenue, turn left at the light, Olivas Park Drive, then right to Harbor Boulevard. Turn left on Harbor and proceed 3/4 mile to the park. The signed nature trail leaves from the day use parking lot. Signposts along the nature trail are keyed to pamphlet, available from the entry kiosk.

There is a state park day use fee.

The Hike: From the parking lot, follow the nature trail through the estuary. The river banks is mass of lush vegetation, especially willow and silverweed. In 1980 the Santa Clara River area was declared a natural preserve, primarily to protect the habitat of two endangered species of birds—the California least tern and Belding's Savannah Sparrow.

When you reach nature trail signpost 11, join a nearby trail that leads

atop an old levee, first along the river, then down-coast along the periphery of the state beach campground. This trail joins a dirt road and continues down-coast, but the far-more aesthetic route is along water's edge, so trudge over the dunes and walk along the shoreline.

Along the beach, visitors enjoy sunbathing or surf fishing for bass, corbina, or perch. In two miles you'll spot McGrath Lake, tucked away behind some dunes.

As you continue south, more sandy beach and dunes follow. You pass a huge old Edison power plant, and arrive at Oxnard Shores, a development famous for getting clobbered by heavy surf at high tide. The beach is flat and at one time was eroding at the phenomenal rate of 10 feet a year. Homes were built right on the shoreline and many have been heavily damaged. New homes are built on pilings, so the waves crash under rather than than through them.

Past Oxnard Shores, a mile of beach walking brings you to historic Hollywood Beach. "The. Sheik," starring that great silent movie idol Rudolph Valentino, was filmed on the desert- like sands here. Real estate promoters of the time attempted to capitalize on Oxnard Beach's instant fame and renamed it Hollywood Beach. They laid out subdivisions called Hollywood-by-the-Sea and Silver Strand, suggesting to their customers that the area was really a movie colony that might become a future Hollywood.

This walk ends another mile down-coast at the entrance to Channel Islands Harbor.

▲49

Portuguese Bend Trail

Del Cerro Park to Badlands Slide Area
2 1/2 miles round trip; 400-foot elevation gain

"In Palos Verdes one has the impression of entering
a paradise designed by the Spanish for the annointed of heaven."
—Louis Bromfield, "Vogue," 1930

The little-known and infrequently traveled trails of the Palos Verdes Peninsula offer the hiker a tranquil escape from metropolitan life. During March, the hills are colored an emerald green and sprinkled with wildflowers, and you might spot a migrating California gray whale on the horizon.

One short loop trip, suitable for the whole family, explores the hills above Portuguese Bend, one of the most geologically interesting (and unstable) areas in Southern California. Earth movement during 1956-57 wrecked approximately 100 homes. At one point, the rate of land movement was slightly over an inch a day!

Portuguese Bend takes its name from the Portuguese men who practiced the risky, but lucrative, business of shore whaling. Most of the hardy whalers who worked the waters off Palos Verdes Peninsula from the 1850s to the 1880s were of Portuguese descent. Many a whale was slaughtered, but the Peninsula whaling operation was abandoned not because of a lack of gray whales but because of a shortage of fuel with which to process blubber into oil.

The Peninsula is famous for its rocky cliffs, which rise from 50 to 300 feet above the ocean and form thirteen wave-cut terraces. These terraces, or platforms, resulted from a combination of uplift and sea-level fluctuations caused by the formation and melting of glaciers. Today the waves, as they have for so many thousands of years, are actively eroding the shoreline, cutting yet another terrace into the land.

You don't have to be a geology student to enjoy a walk in the Palos Verdes hills. The route I've dubbed Portuguese Bend Trail links various paths and fire roads and offers great clear-day views of the Peninsula and Catalina Island.

Directions to trailhead: From the San Diego Freeway (405) in Torrance, exit on Crenshaw Boulevard and head south. Continue on Crenshaw past Pacific Coast Highway, and into the hills of Rancho Palos Verdes. Park at boulevard's end at the side of the road or at nearby Del Cerro Park. The trail begins at a steel gate which separates the end of Cren-

176

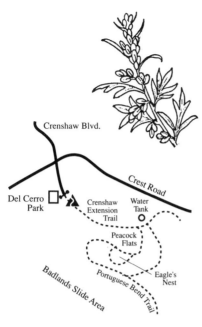

Crenshaw Blvd.

Crest Road

Del Cerro
Park

Crenshaw
Extension
Trail

Water
Tank

Peacock
Flats

Badlands Slide Area

Portuguese Bend Trail

Eagle's
Nest

shaw Boulevard from the beginning of a dirt fire road.

The Hike: Walk down the unsigned fire road, which is officially named Crenshaw Extension Trail. Leaving red-roofed million-dollar residences behind, you'll look ahead to a million-dollar view. The green hills, bedecked with lupine in spring, roll to the sea. Geology students will note several marine terraces, while botany students will observe the Peninsula's unique blend of native brush and imported flora gone wild.

A half-mile descent from the trailhead brings you to a water tank and an unsigned three-way intersection. The leftward trail climbs to a fire station. The trail dead-ahead will be your return route on this walk. Continue right with Crenshaw Extension Trail, which soon drops into a wildflower-splashed meadow known as Peacock Flats. It's doubtful you'll see a peacock here, but you might hear the shrill call of the "watchdog of the Peninsula" from other parts of the trail. The aggresssive birds are popular pets around here.

Above Peacock Flats, two short trails lead up a hill topped with a dozen pine trees. From the crest of this hill, known as Eagle's Nest, you'll have grand clear-day views of Catalina. The nest is close to the southwesternmost point of the Peninsula, meaning Catalina is but seventeen nautical miles away, and meaning you can identify many of the island's geographical features.

Return to the main trail which heads northwest then makes a long horseshoe bend to the southeast. After descending past a stand of eucalyptus and a water tank, you'll begin crossing the geologically unstable terrain known as Badlands Slide Area.

A water pipe on the left parallels the dirt road at this point. Look sharply left for an unsigned trail that climbs to the east. After a steep and tentative start, the trail widens and ascends at a more moderate pace atop a canyon wall. Sweet-smelling fennel lines the path, which turns north and climbs to the above-mentioned three-way trail junction. Retrace your steps on Crenshaw Extension Trail to the trailhead.

177

50

Avalon Canyon Loop Trail

6 1/2 miles round trip; 1,000-foot elevation gain

The islophile expecting a lush landscape is often surprised by Catalina Island's backcountry. Catalina's vegetation is sparse, spartan. Catalina resembles a Greek island—one of the Cyclades, perhaps—far more than a tropical South Seas paradise.

Catalina shares the semi-arid conditions of Southern California, but hosts a surprising amount of plant life. About 600 species, 400 or so of them native plants, grow on the island. By taking a walk above Avalon, you can study the island's botany at the Botanical Garden, then venture into the interior to view Catalina's special flora in its natural habitat.

Each year about a million people travel to Catalina, but few of these visitors are hikers. The adventurer who strides out of Avalon will leave the crowds behind and be treated to superb island and mainland panoramic views.

The route out of Avalon, which I have dubbed, "Avalon Canyon Loop Trail" leads to the Botanical Garden, a showcase for plants native to Catalina and the Channel Islands. At the head of the canyon is the imposing Wrigley Memorial, a huge monument honoring chewing gum magnate William Wrigley, who purchased most of the island in 1919.

Families with children, and those visitors looking more for a walk than a hike will enjoy the trip as far as the Botanical Garden. More adventurous hikers will undertake the second, much more strenuous part of this loop trip; it utilizes fire roads and Hermit Gulch Trail and offers a sampling of Catalina's rugged and bold terrain.

Directions to trailhead: Several boat companies offer ferry service to Catalina, with departures from San Diego, Newport Beach, Long Beach and San Pedro. Usually, least expensive round trip fare is offered by Catalina Cruises, which operates out of San Pedro and Long Beach. The 22-mile crossing to Catalina takes about 2 hours. Catalina Express, which offers the fastest boats (90 minutes to Avalon), also operates out of both Long Beach and San Pedro. For more information about ferryboat schedules, island services and accomodations, call the Catalina Island Chamber of Commerce.

If you intend to hike into the Catalina backcountry (anywhere past the Botanical Garden) you must secure a free hiking permit from the Los Angeles County Department of Parks and Recreation. The department operates an information center in the Island Plaza, located at 213 Catalina

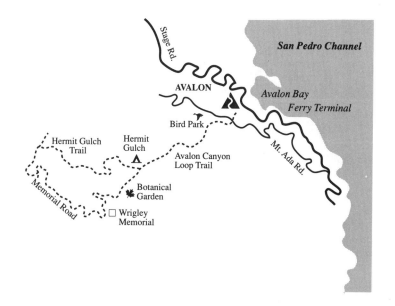

Street. You can pick up a trails map here and secure your permit at the office.

The Hike: Head uphill along Catalina Street, which soon joins Avalon Canyon Road, passes a few residences, and begins a 1 1/2 mile ascent toward the Botanical Garden. On your right, you'll soon pass one of William Wrigley's many contributions to the island, Bird Park, which once held thousands of unusual birds in the "largest bird cage in the world." Bird Park is now a campground. On the left side of the road, bleacher bums will stop and pay homage to the one-time spring training camp of Wrigley's beloved Chicago Cubs.

You'll reach Hermit Gulch Campground and soon come to the end of the road at the Botanical Garden. Enter the Garden (an admission fee is charged). The garden began in the 1920s, when Wrigley's wife, Ada, began planting native and exotic plants in Avalon Canyon. More recently, the garden has greatly expanded, emphasizing native Southern California flora. Particularly interesting are plants endemic to Catalina, including Catalina mahogany, Catalina manzanita, Catalina live-forever, and Catalina ironwood.

When you've memorized at least three native plant species, proceed up the dirt path to the Wrigley Memorial. At one time, Wrigley's body was entombed here. If you wish, climb up the many stairs to the 232-foot-wide, 130-foot-high monument, and enjoy the great view of Avalon Harbor.

At this point, intrepid hikers will not proceed back to Avalon for some liquid refreshment, but pass through an unlocked gate below and to the right of the memorial and stride up Memorial Road. Scrub oak, manzanita and

179

Avalon Harbor

lemonade berry—and many more of the same plants, sans identification plaques, that you studied at the Botanical Garden—line the fire road.

The vigorous ascent on Memorial Road offers better and better views of Avalon Harbor. It's likely your approach will flush a covey or two of quail from the brush. Practiced birders might recognize the Catalina quail, a slightly larger and slightly darker subspecies than its mainland relatives.

Memorial Road reaches a divide, where appropriately enough, you'll intersect Divide Road. Bear right. From the 1,000-foot high divide, you'll have commanding views of both sides of the island and of the mainland. The mainland sometimes has an interesting look from this vantage point. The major topographical features of the Southern California area—the Santa Monica and San Gabriel Mountains—but not a trace of civilization.

Continue along the divide, which bristles with prickly pear cactus. The slopes below are crisscrossed with trails made by the island's many wild goats. After about 3/4 of a mile of walking atop the divide, you'll bear right on unsigned Hermit Gulch Trail. This trail is difficult to spot and the early going steep. The trail descends 2.4 miles along a waterless canyon back to Avalon Canyon Road and Hermit Gulch Campground. Turn left and saunter downhill to the comforts of Avalon.

51

Crown of the Sea Trail

Corona Del Mar Beach to Arch Rock
2 miles round trip
Corona Del Mar Beach to Crystal Cove
4 miles round trip
Corona Del Mar Beach to Abalone Point
7 miles round trip

In 1904, George Hart purchased 700 acres of land on the cliffs east of the entrance to Newport Bay and laid out a subdivision he called Corona Del Mar—"Crown of the Sea." The only way to reach the townsite was by way of a long muddy road that circled around the head of Upper Newport Bay. Later, a ferry carried tourists and residents from Balboa to Corona Del Mar. Little civic improvement occurred until Highway 101 bridged the bay and the community was annexed to Newport Beach.

This hike explores the beaches and marine refuges of "Big" and Little Corona Del Mar, and continues to the beaches of Crystal Cove State Park.

Consult a tide table. Best beach-walking is at low tide.

Directions to trailhead: From Pacific Coast Highway in Corona Del Mar, turn oceanward on Marguerite Avenue and travel a few blocks to Corona Del Mar State Beach. There is a fee for parking in the lot.

Surfers enjoy the breaks off Corona Del Mar

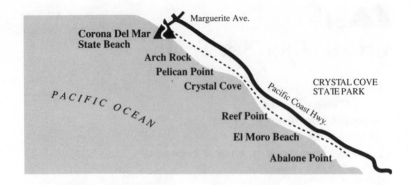

The Hike: Begin at the east jetty of Newport Beach, where you'll see sailboats tacking in and out of the harbor. Snorkelers and surfers frequent the waters near the jetty. Proceed down-coast along wide, sandy Corona Del Mar State Beach.

The beach narrows as you approach the cove that encloses Little Corona Del Mar Beach. Snorkeling is good below the cliffs of Big and Little Corona beaches. Both areas are protected from boat traffic by kelp beds and marine refuge status.

A mile from the jetty, you'll pass well-named Arch Rock, which is just offshore and can be reached at low tide. The beach from Arch Rock to Irvine Cove, 2 1/2 miles to the south was purchased by the state from the Irvine Corporation, and is now part of Crystal Cove State Park. Trails lead up the bluffs. From December to about March, the blufftops offer a good vantage point from which to observe the California gray whale migration.

Continuing your stroll down the undeveloped beach and past some tidepools brings you to the tiny resort community of Crystal Cove, site of a few dozen beach cottages. The wood frame cottages have been little altered since their construction in the 1920s and were recently collectively named to the National Register of Historic Places. "Cove" is something of a misnomer because the beach here shows almost no coastal indentation.

Rounding Reef Point, you'll continue your beach walk along El Moro Beach. The sandy beach is sometimes beautifully cusped. El Moro is a misspelling of the Spanish word morro, meaning round, and describes the round dome of Abalone Point which lies dead ahead. The point, a rocky promontory located just outside Laguna Beach city limits, is made of eroded lava and other volcanic material distributed in the San Joaquin Hills. It's capped by a grass-covered dome rising two hundred feet above the water.

Return the same way or ascend one of the coastal accessways to the blufftops of Crystal Cove State Park. You can use blufftop trails for a portion of your return route.

52
Torrey Pines Beach Trail

Scripps Pier to Torrey Pines State Beach
10 miles round trip

Before or after this walk, check out the Aquarium Museum at Scripps Institute of Oceanography. In the Aquarium, all manner of local sea creatures are on display. Underwater video cameras provide views of activity in the nearby marine reserve. Located near the entrance of the Aquarium is a dryland tidepool, where the tide rises and falls in 2-hour intervals. Kelp planted in the pools provide hiding places for bright orange Garibaldi, rockfish, and red snapper. Starfish, barnacles, and sea anenomes cling to the rocks. A wave generator simulates surf conditions.

This walk begins at Scripps Pier, passes along Torrey Pines City Beach, known locally as Black's Beach, once swimsuit- optional, now suits-only. After hiking below some spectacular cliffs and along Torrey Pines State Beach, you'll arrive at Torrey Pines State Reserve, home to the rare and revered *Pinus torreyana*.

Torrey Pines State Reserve

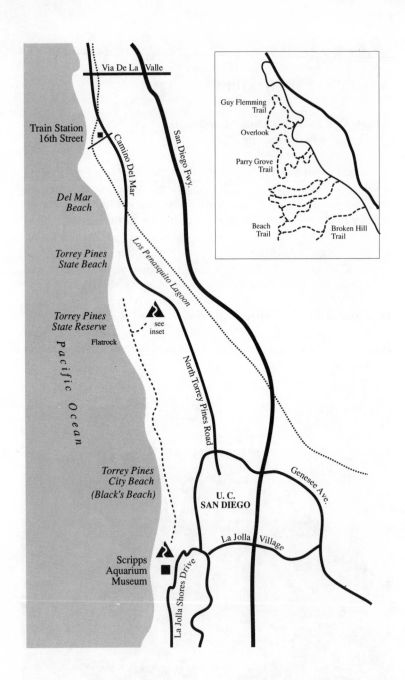

Via De La Valle

Train Station
16th Street

Camino Del Mar

San Diego Fwy.

*Del Mar
Beach*

*Torrey Pines
State Beach*

Los Penasquito Lagoon

*Torrey Pines
State Reserve*

Flatrock

see
inset

P a c i f i c   O c e a n

North Torrey Pines Road

*Torrey Pines
City Beach
(Black's Beach)*

Genesee Ave.

**U. C.
SAN DIEGO**

La Jolla Village

Scripps
Aquarium
Museum

La Jolla Shores Drive

Inset:

Guy Flemming
Trail

Overlook

Parry Grove
Trail

Beach
Trail

Broken Hill
Trail

Plan your hike for low tide, particularly during winter, when beach sand is carried away by high waves. The beach just north of Scripps Aquarium and pier are passable only at low tide.

Directions to trailhead: Exit Interstate 5 on La Jolla Village Road, traveling west past UC San Diego to North Torrey Pines Road. Turn right, then make a left on La Jolla Shores Drive, following it to the Aquarium turnoff on your right. Parking is sparse and metered near the Aquarium.

The Hike: As you look south from Scripps Pier, you'll see long and flat La Jolla Shores Beach, a wide expanse of white sand where the water deepens gradually. This is a family beach, popular during the summer with swimmers.

Hiking north, the going is rocky at first; the surf really kicks up around Scripps Pier. Soon the beach widens, growing more sandy, and the spectacular curry-colored cliffs grow higher and higher.

A glider port once stood atop the bluffs. Manned fixed-wing gliders were pulled into air, then they rode the currents created by offshore breezes rising up as they meet the cliffs. Nowadays, brave adventurers strap themselves to hang gliders and leap off the cliffs and, unless the wind shifts, come to a soft landing on the beach below.

The 300-foot cliffs tower over Black's Beach, named for William Black, the oil millionaire who owned and developed most of the land on the cliffs. During the 1970s, Black's Beach enjoyed fleeting notoriety as the first and only public beach in the country on which nudity was legal. Called "a noble experiment" by sun worshipers and "a terrible fiasco" by the more inhibited, the clothing-optional zone was defeated at the polls.

After passing below more handsome bluffs, you'll spot a distinct rock outcropping called Flat Rock. Here you may join a bluff trail that leads up to Torrey Pines State Reserve.

Torrey Pines State Reserve Trails: Atop the bluffs of Torrey Pines State Reserve lies a microcosm of old California, a garden of shrubs and succulents, an enclave of life that the Indians lived.

Most visitors come to view the 3,000 or so *Pinus torreyana*, but the reserve also offers the hiker a striking variety of native plants. If you enjoy interpretive nature trails, the reserve has some nice ones. Protect the fragile ecology of the area by staying on established trails.

Be sure to check out the interpretive displays at the park museum and the native plant garden near the head of the Parry Grove Trail. Plant and bird lists, as well as wildflower maps (Feb.-June) are available.

Chapter 9

ORANGE COUNTY

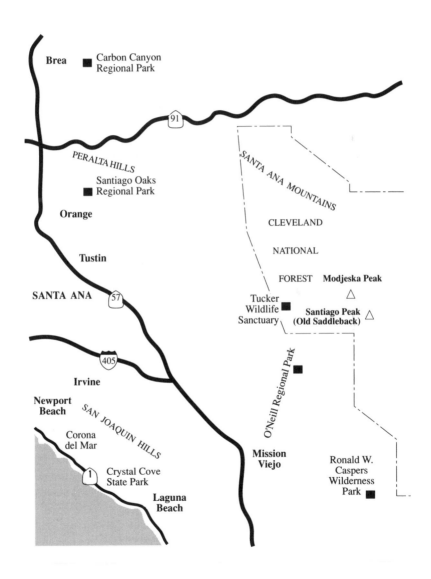

Orange County

Orange County shares its coastline and coastal plain with neighboring Los Angeles County, but has a distinct geographical identity. This geography, which in the decades since World War II has been almost unbelievably altered by the hand of man, nevertheless still holds some intrigue for the lover of wild places.

The orchards that gave Orange County its name are nearly gone, but the hills and mountains occupying half the County still afford invigorating vistas. This guide seeks out what remains of the pastoral in the County's hills and canyons.

San Mateo Point is the northernmost boundary of San Diego County, the southern boundary of Orange County. When the original counties of Los Angeles and San Diego were set up in 1850, the line that separated them began on the coast at San Mateo Point. When Orange County was formed from southern Los Angeles County in 1889, San Mateo Point was established as the southern point of the new county. The northern boundary is Seal Beach. Riverside County and the Santa Ana Mountains form the eastern boundary.

During the last decade of the 19th Century and the first few decades of the 20th, the County was known for its fruited plain watered by the Santa Ana River. (Although the Santa Ana for most of its length is now a cement-lined flood control channel, it was once a substantial river and even today is Southern California's leader in average annual run off.) Citrus and other fruits, flowers and vegetables were successfully grown on the fertile coastal plain. Valencia orange groves, protected from the wind by long rows of eucalyptus, stretched across the plain to the foothills.

Today the coastal plain has been almost completely covered by residential and commercial development. Once huge farms and ranches such as Laguna Niguel, Moulton, Mission Viejo and Irvine are now suburbs. Although 782-square mile Orange is not one of California's larger counties, it is the state's second most populous, right behind Los Angeles County.

In a county with more than two million residents and with most of its flatland developed, hikers must head for the hills to find untouched or less-touched places. In the backcountry, where level land and water is scant, there has been little settlement.

Protecting the last of Orange County's ecological heritage is Crystal Cove State Park and a half-dozen county parks. Oak woodland, chaparral slopes and grassy meadows are among the natural communities found in these parks.

From cactus to oak — a botanical diversity

Hiking and getting to know this land is a good way to shed some stereotypes about Southern California in general, and Orange County in particular. One stereotype—that Orange County is nothing more than a monotonous urban-suburban sprawl—vanishes when you witness first-hand the ecological diversity of the backcountry. Another stereotype—that Orange County's history is all Anglo—disappears when you walk into the land's Spanish, Indian, German, Polish and Japanese heritage. The names on the land—from Flores to Modjeska to Anaheim—speak of this rich tapestry of cultures.

The special places—and the trails exploring them— protected by the County's parks are priceless assets to the megalopolis.

53

Carbon Canyon Nature Trail

2 miles round trip

Carbon Canyon Regional Park offers some much-needed "breathing room" for fast-growing northeastern Orange County. The park has both a natural area with trails that connect to nearby Chino Hills State Park, and a more developed part with wide lawns, tennis courts, ball fields, picnic grounds and a lake.

The park spreads up-canyon behind Carbon Canyon dam. As Orange County grew, so did the need for flood control, and in 1959, a dam was built at the mouth of the canyon. If, as a result of winter storms, the Santa Ana River rises too high, the dam's floodgates will be closed, thus sparing communities downstream of the dam, but flooding the park.

A century ago, the arrival of the Santa Fe Railroad precipitated a minor land boom. Farmers and ranchers rushed to the area. Cattle and sheep were pastured in the canyon now called Carbon.

But it was another boom—an oil boom—that put Carbon Canyon on the map. E.L. Doheny, soon to become one of L.A.'s leading boosters, discovered oil in the area in 1896. His company and several others drilled the foothills of Orange County. The name Carbon was applied to the canyon because of the many dried-up oil seeps in evidence.

Santa Fe Railroad tracks were extended to the mouth of Carbon Canyon in order to haul out the oil. At the end of the tracks was the oil town of Olinda, boyhood home of the great baseball pitcher Walter Johnson. "Big Train," as the hurler was known, pitched for the Washington Senators, and led the American League in strikeouts from 1912 to 1919. Olinda boomed until the 1940s when the oil fields began to play out.

The undeveloped part of Carbon Canyon Regional Park is a narrow corridor along Carbon Canyon Creek. A one-mile nature trail leads creekside through an interesting mixture of native and foreign flora. At the park entrance station you can pick up an interpretive pamphlet, which is keyed to numbered posts along the trail, and details points and plants of interest.

During the summer months, early morning and late afternoon are the most comfortable times to hit the Carbon Canyon Nature Trail. Rewarding the hiker at trail's end is a small, shady redwood grove.

Directions to trailhead: From the Orange Freeway (57) in Brea, exit on Lambert Road. Drive 4 miles east on Lambert (which changes to Carbon Canyon Road east of Valencia Avenue) to the park entrance. There's a vehicle entry fee.

The Hike: From the parking area, walk back to the entrance station, you'll spot the signed trail in a stand of pine, just east of the park entrance. On closer inspection, you'll discover that the pines are Monterey pines, native to California but not to this area. This stand is a holdover from a Christmas tree farm that was operated before the park opened in 1975.

From the pines, the nature trail descends to the Carbon Canyon creekbed. After crossing the creek, the trail forks. (The path to the left leads toward Telegraph Canyon and to a network of hiking trails that crisscross Chino Hills State Park. The 8-mile length of Telegraph Canyon, home of native walnut groves, is well worth exploring.) Carbon Canyon Nature Trail heads right with the creekbed. Creek-side vegetation is dominated by mustard, castor bean and hemlock. You'll also find two exotic imports—the California pepper tree, actually a native of Peru, and some giant reeds, bamboo-like plants that harm the native plant community because they take a great deal of the scarce water supply.

At the trail's mid-point, there's a distinct, but unmarked, side trail that angles across the creekbed to the developed part of the park. If for some reason you want to call it a day, here's your exit point.

As you near trail's end you'll get brush-framed glimpses of Carbon Canyon Dam. The trail ascends out of the creekbed to the park's redwood grove. The redwoods, planted in 1975, have a lot of growing to do before they rival their majestic cousins to the north.

Turn-of-the-century oil boom put Carbon Canyon on the map

▲ 54

Anaheim Hills Trail

Santiago Oaks Regional Park to Robbers Roost
3 1/2 miles round trip; 700-foot elevation gain

"Who determines the names of natural features? Fundamentally, names are a part of language, and the eventual power rests with the people."

George Stewart, *Names on the Land*

Geologists and mapmakers have long referred to the long, low ridge extending west from the Santa Ana Mountains and rising above Santa Ana Canyon as the Peralta Hills, but almost no one uses that name anymore. Today the hills are the known as the Anaheim Hills.

The hills honor, or did honor, Juan Pablo Peralta and his family, original owners of the huge Rancho Santiago de Santa Ana. Peralta is an excellent name, historic and euphonious. It recalls the Latin expression *Per Alta*, "through the high things." Sounds like a university motto, doesn't it?

Anaheim, which German settlers in 1858 named after the river Santa Ana plus the suffix heim (home), already names a city, a boulevard, a bay, a stadium and much more. Perhaps it's time for concerned day hikers and Orange Countians to rally to save the Peralta Hills. (Alas, it is not merely the name of the hills, but the hills themselves that are fast- disappearing beneath the suburban sprawl.)

Other names from the past still remain. Santiago Oaks Regional Park, Santiago Creek and Santiago Canyon are derived from the old Rancho Santiago de Santa Ana. One intriguing name for a rocky knob overlooking the regional park is Robbers Roost. From this lookout, such infamous 19th Century outlaws as Joaquin Murietta and Three-Finger Jack kept watch over rural Orange County. The outlaws would ride down from the hills to rob the Butterfield Stagecoach or ride into the hills to escape the sheriff.

Santiago Oaks Regional Park preserves 125 acres of pastoral Orange County, including an oak woodland that attracts many species of birds.

You can sample the park's ecosystem with Windes Nature Trail. The 3/4 mile trail and its Pacifica Loop offer a glimpse of the county's coastline. A nature center, located near the trailhead, is well-worth a visit.

A network of fire roads and equestrian trail crisscross the park and extend into the Anaheim Hills. While the hills seem destined for suburban development, for now, at least, you can enjoy a ramble up to Robbers Roost and steal a last look at fast-vanishing rural Orange County.

Directions to trailhead: From the Newport Freeway (55) in Orange, exit on Katella. Turn east on Katella, which undergoes a name change in a half-mile to Villa Park Road, then a second name change to Santiago Canyon Road. A bit more than two miles from the freeway, turn left on Windes Drive and drive a mile to Santiago Oaks Regional Park. An "Iron Ranger," a self-service entrance gate, collects your vehicle entry fee.

The Hike: From the end of the parking area, you'll spot Windes Nature Trail on your right, then swing left and cross Santiago Creek on some man-made stepping-stones. You'll pass a number of trails leading left into the woods, but for now stay with the main trail along the creek. Along with the native oaks, you might spot some more uncommon flora, including eucalyptus and pepper trees, and even a small grove of Valencia oranges.

Soon you'll see an old dam. With the aid of Chinese laborers, the Serrano and Carpenter Water Company built a clay dam here in 1879. This dam was destroyed by floods, and replaced in 1892 with a more substantial structure of river rock and cement.

Bear left, uphill, and ascend steeply up a dirt road to the park's north boundary gate. Beyond the gate you'll ascend to an unsigned junction and bear left, then ascend a prickly pear cactus-dotted slope to a junction signed with an equestrian symbol and turn right. After passing under some transmission lines, the equestrian trail reaches Robbers Roost.

From the 1,152-foot peak, you can look over the Peralta Hills and trace the path of Santiago Creek. Not so long ago, the view would have taken in hundreds of cattle, orange groves, and barley fields. Nowadays the panorama is considerably less pastoral.

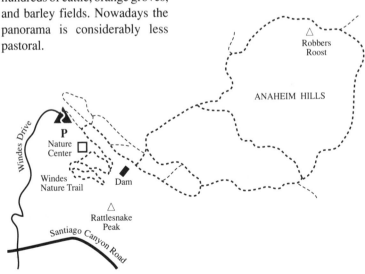

⚡55

Moro Canyon Trail

Park Headquarters to top of Moro Canyon
7 miles round trip; 700-foot elevation gain

Extending three miles along the coast between Laguna Beach and Corona del Mar, and inland over the San Joaquin Hills, 3,000-acre Crystal Cove State Park attracts bird-watchers, beachcombers and hikers.

The backcountry of Crystal Cove State Park is part of the San Joaquin Hills, first used by Mission San Juan Capistrano for grazing land. Cattle raising continued under Jose Sepulveda when the area became part of his land grant, Rancho San Joaquin, in 1837. In 1864, Sepulveda sold the land to James Irvine and his partners and it became part of his Irvine Ranch. Grazing continued until shortly after the state purchased the property as parkland in 1979.

Former Irvine Ranch roads now form a network of hiking trails that loop through the state park. An especially nice trail travels the length of Moro Canyon, the main watershed of the park. An oak woodland, a seasonal stream and sandstone caves are some of the attractions of a walk through this canyon. Bird-watchers may spot the roadrunner, quail, Cooper's hawk, California thrasher, wrentit and many more species.

After exploring inland portions of the state park, allow some time to visit the park's coastline, highlighted by grassy bluffs, sandy beaches, tidepools and coves. The Pelican Point, Crystal Cove, Reef Point and Moro Beach areas of the park allow easy beach access. An offshore area adjacent to the park has been designated an underwater park for divers.

Directions to trailhead: Crystal Cove State Park is located off Pacific Coast Highway, about two miles south of the town of Corona Del Mar or one mile north of Laguna Beach. Turn inland on the short park road, signed "El Moro Canyon." Drinking water, restrooms, interpretive displays and plenty of parking is available at the ranger station. There is an entrance fee. Pick up a trails map at the ranger station. At the station, you can consult the schedule of ranger-led interpretive walks, which explore both inland and coastal sections of the state park.

The Hike: Below the ranger station, near the park entry kiosk pick up the unsigned Moro Canyon Trail, which crosses the grassy slopes behind a school and trailer park down into Moro Canyon. At the canyon bottom, you meet a fire road and head left, up-canyon.

The hiker may observe such native plants as black sage, prickly pear cactus, monkeyflowers, golden bush, lemonade berry and deer weed. Long before Spanish missionaries and settlers arrived in Southern California, a native Indian population flourished in the coastal canyons of Orange County. The abundance of edible plants in the area, combined with the mild climate and easy access to the bounty of the sea, contributed to the success of these people, whom anthropologists believe lived off this land for more than four thousand years.

The canyon narrows, and you ignore fire roads joining Moro Canyon from the right and left. You stay in the canyon bottom and proceed through an oak woodland, which shades a trickling stream. You'll pass a shallow sandstone cave just off the trail to the right.

About 2 1/2 miles from the trailhead, you'll reach the unsigned junction with a fire road. If you wish to make a loop trip out of this day hike, bear left on this road, which climbs steeply west, then northeast toward the ridgetop that forms a kind of inland wall for Muddy, Moro, Emerald and other coastal canyons.

When you reach the ridgetop, unpack your lunch and enjoy the far reaching views of the San Joaquin Hills and Orange County coast, Catalina and San Clemente Islands. You'll also have a raven's-eye-view of Moro Canyon and the route back to the trailhead. After catching your breath, you'll bear right (east) along the ridgetop and quickly descend back into Moro Canyon. A 3/4-mile walk brings you back to the junction where you earlier ascended out of the canyon. This time you continue straight down-canyon, retracing your steps to the trailhead.

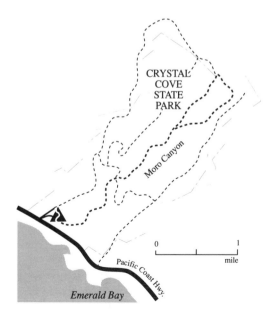

195

56
Harding Trail

Tucker Wildlife Sanctuary to Goat Shed Overlook
3 miles round trip; 600-foot elevation gain
Tucker Wildlife Sanctuary to Laurel Spring
10 miles round trip; 2,300-foot elevation gain

The story of Modjeska Peak and Modjeska Canyon in Orange County began in Warsaw, Poland in the 1870s. Count Karol Bozenta Chlapowski edited a fiercely nationalistic patriotic journal, "The Country." The Count got into hot water for his literary rebellion against the cultural and political imperialism of Czarist Russia and Germany. He and his wife, acclaimed actress Helena Modrzejewski, along with novelist Henryk Sienkiewicz (*Quo Vadis?*) and other Polish writers and artists, yearned for the freedom of America and the climate of Southern California.

The Count purchased an Orange County farm and the dreamy Polish aristocrats emigrated to the new world. While the setting and company was artistically inspiring, the immigrants had difficulties with some of the practical aspects of ranch life. No one, it seemed, knew how to milk a cow or care for citrus trees. Siekiewicz preferred writing to working in the fields, Helena enjoyed singing and acting far more than cooking, and the Count lost a lot of money in a short time. Even utopian colonies have to pay their bills.

Helena mastered English, shortened her name to Modjeska, and under the Count's management, began her tremendously popular stage career. In 1888, Madame Modjeska and the Count returned to Orange County; this time they bought a ranch in Santiago Canyon and hired professionals to run it. Madame called her ranch Arden after the enchanted forest in Shakespeare's "As You Like It." New York architect Stanford White was commissioned to design a dream home, which looked out over a little lake, across which glided swans. The happy couple spent their mornings riding over the ranch and inspecting the orange groves and vineyards, and their afternoons with friends in discussion of art, literature and the issues of the day. Evenings were given over to music recitals or Madame's performances of one of her favorite parts—Camille, Cleopatra or Lady MacBeth.

For two decades, the Chlapowski/Modjeska household was a center of artistic and literary life in Southern California.

Today, a state historical marker on Modjeska Canyon Road commemorates their home. A few years ago, the home was purchased by Orange

Madame Helena Modjeska

County, which may some day restore the residence and open it to the public.

The natural history of Modjeska Canyon is as intriguing as its human history. In 1939, Dorothy May Tucker, a canyon resident, willed her land to the Audubon Society and the Tucker Bird Sanctuary was created. California State University Fullerton took over its operation in 1969.

The sanctuary is best-known for its hummingbirds, which may be viewed from an observation porch. Because the sanctuary includes a

mixture of coastal scrub, chaparral and oak woodland environments, it attracts a diversity of bird life. Nearly two hundred species have been spotted in the sanctuary.

Two short nature trails wind through the preserve. One trail interprets chaparral flora, and the other leads along the banks of Santiago Creek. Among the trailside exhibits is one interpreting the life of water bugs, and explaining the difference between a mayfly nymph and a dragonfly nymph.

Tucker Wildlife Sanctuary is the trailhead for Harding Trail, a dirt road that ascends the western slopes of the Santa Ana Mountains. The trail, formerly known as Harding Truck Trail, is used by Cleveland National Forest fire crews and their trucks, but is closed to all other vehicles.

Old Saddleback, comprised of 5,687-foot Santiago Peak and 5,496-foot Modjeska Peak, forms the eastern boundary and highest portion of Orange County. You can reach the peaks via Harding Trail, but this would mean a 20-mile hike. A more reasonable destination, halfway up the mountain, is Laurel Spring, a tranquil rest stop tucked under the boughs of giant bay laurel. En route to the spring, you'll get great views of Madame Modjeska's peak and canyon, as well as much of rural Orange County.

Directions to trailhead: From the San Diego Freeway (5) in El Toro, exit on El Toro Road (S-18). Drive inland on the road, which after about 7 miles bends north and continues as Santiago Canyon Road. Eight-and-a-half miles from the freeway, veer right onto Modjeska Grade Road, travel a bit more than a mile, then turn right and follow Modjeska Canyon Road a mile to its end at Tucker Wildlife Sanctuary. Park in the gravel lot by a tiny observatory. The trail, signed forest road 5S08, begins at a locked gate on the north side of the road.

Flores Peak

The Hike: Harding Trail immediately begins a no-nonsense ascent above Modjeska Canyon, which, in all but its lower reaches, is officially known as Harding Canyon. To the northwest is Flores Peak, named for outlaw Juan Flores. Flores and his gang in 1857 robbed a San Juan Capistrano store, killed its owner, and then killed Sheriff John Barton. The gang fled to the Santa Ana Mountains, with General Don Andres Pico and his posse in hot pursuit. The gang was captured, but Flores escaped for a time; he was later caught.and hanged in Los Angeles.

As you ascend, notice the lumpy, pudding-like clumps of conglomerate rock revealed by the road cuts. After a mile, the trail descends a short distance (the only elevation loss on the way to Laurel Spring), rounds the head of a canyon, and ascends to the remains of a funny-looking wood structure that locals call the Goat Shed. Enjoy the view of Modjeska Canyon. If you're feeling a bit leg-weary, this is a good turnaround point.

Chaparral-lined Harding Trail continues climbing east along a sharp ridgeline. To your left, far below, is deep and precipitous Harding Canyon, and to your right—Santiago Canyon. Four-and-a-half miles from the trailhead, Harding Trail offers clear-day views of the southern end of the Los Angeles Basin, the San Joaquin Hills and the central Orange County coastal plain, the Pacific Ocean and Catalina Island. The view serves notice that you're nearing Laurel Spring. A narrow trail descends 50 yards from the right side of the road to the spring. The spring (unsafe drinking water), waters an oasis of toyon, ferns and wonderfully aromatic bay laurel.

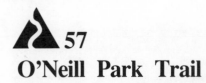 **57**

O'Neill Park Trail

Trabuco Canyon to Ocean Vista Point
3 miles round trip; 600-foot elevation gain

The soldier marching with Captain Gaspar de Portola's 1769 expedition who lost his firearm in this hilly region would no doubt be astonished at the number of Orange County place names inspired by his mistake. Trabuco, which means "blunderbuss" in Spanish, now names a canyon, a creek, a plain, a trail, a road and even a ranger district of the Cleveland National Forest.

If the unknown soldier who lost his blunderbuss trekked this way again he would be amazed at the names on the land, and even more amazed at the land itself, so drastically has it changed. Maybe though, he would recognize Trabuco Canyon, at least that part of it saved from suburbanization by O'Neill Regional Park. Here the modern trekker can explore a small slice of the pastoral Southern California of two centuries ago.

This land of grassy meadows, rolling hills and oak woodland was originally part of Rancho Trabuco, two leagues granted to Santiago Arguello in 1841 by Mexican Governor Alvarado. The rancho had various lessees and owners until it was purchased by James Flood, a wealthy businessman and his partner Richard O'Neill, a packing house owner. O'Neill built up quite a ranching empire here and elsewhere in California. O'Neill's Orange County property passed to various heirs who, in turn,

gave 278 acres of Tra-buco Canyon to Orange County for a park in 1948. Today, after vari-ous gifts and purchases, the park encompasses 1,700 acres of woodland and brushy hills, taking in Trabuco Canyon and neighboring Live Oak Canyon.

A good way to learn about the ecology of Trabuco Canyon is to walk the park's 1 1/2-mile (round trip) nature

O'Neill Park

trail. Trabuco Creek Trail, with stops keyed to a pamphlet available at the park's entry station, meanders through an oak/sycamore woodland and explores Plano Trabuco, or Trabuco Flat, a level alluvial surface deposited by runoff from the slopes of the Santa Ana Mountains.

Another way to explore a bit of rural Orange County is to hike the park's various fire roads and trails on a route I've dubbed O'Neill Park Trail. The trail ascends to Ocean Vista Point, which offers fine coast and canyon views.

Directions to trailhead: From the San Diego Freeway (5) in El Toro, exit on El Toro Road and drive 7 1/2 miles to Santiago Canyon Road (S-18). Turn right and proceed 3 miles to O'Neill Regional Park. There is a vehicle entry fee. Park in the day use lot near the entrance.

The Hike: From the entry station, walk north on a service road that parallels Live Oak Canyon Road. Soon you'll head left on a paved road that ascends toward some water tanks. After a quarter-mile's travel, leave the pavement and turn right on a dirt road. Two turns bring you to a junction with a dirt road on your right (an optional return route from the top).

Continue your ascent along a ridge. Over your shoulder are two scenes typical of rural Orange County: Red-tailed hawks circling over classic Southland ranching country in one direction, and suburbs-in-the-making in the other.

Continue on a last steep ascent toward what appears to be a Star Wars movie set, but is actually Ocean Vista Point, sometimes known as "Cellular Hill." Up top, communications hardware helps car phoners complete their calls.

From the 1,492-foot summit, enjoy clear-day coastal views from Santa Monica Bay to San Clemente, with Catalina Island floating on the horizon.

For a different return route, head back two hundred yards and make a left at the first fork. Descend to an unused kid's camp, then follow the park's service road back to the trailhead.

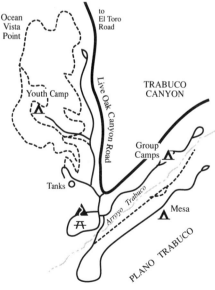

58

Bell Canyon Trail

4-mile loop through Caspers Wilderness Park
Wilderness permit required

This hike is rated X. Adults only.

Caspers Wilderness Park regulations restrict minors to picnic areas and the park visitor center, and allow only adults (18 and over), in groups of two or more, to hike park trails. Visitors must also obtain a wilderness permit. The permit states that the park is "characterized by certain inherent dangers" and that "your safety cannot be guaranteed."

The unusual rules and the permit system are a response to a 1986 mountain lion attack of a six-year-old boy. The highly-publicized incident also resulted in an outpouring of support for the beleaguered mountain lion population, and a questioning of the meaning of the word "wilderness."

It's highly unlikely that you will glimpse a mountain lion in Caspers Wilderness Park. The big cats are scarce and elusive. Suburban sprawl and human intrusion have drastically reduced the number of mountain lions in Orange County, and in every other place in the Southern California backcountry. The animal's small numbers will likely be a comfort to some nervous individuals, and a disappointment to those hikers who would welcome the opportunity to observe one of the graceful creatures.

Visitors to the 7,600-acre park in the Santa Ana Mountains near San Juan Capistrano will, however, have a good chance of sighting other wildlife: Deer, rabbits and coyote, as well as more furtive animals such as foxes and bobcats. Bird-watchers will want to consult the park's bird list and test their skill by identifying the many species found in the hills and canyons.

Crisscrossing Caspers Wilderness Park are thirty miles of trail, which explore grassy valleys, chaparral-cloaked ridges and native groves of coastal live oak and sycamore.

In winter and spring the valleys are usually a deep green, sprinkled with lupine and blue-eyed grass. In dry years, the grassland quickly assumes its summer gold color.

Centerpiece of the park is oak-lined Bell Canyon. Acorns from the oaks were an important food source for the Juaneno Indians who lived in the canyon. As the legend goes, the Indians would strike a large granite boulder with a small rock to make it ring. The sound could be heard for a mile through what is now known as Bell Canyon. "Bell Rock" is now housed in Bowers Museum in Santa Ana.

Bell Canyon, San Juan Canyon, and surrounding ridges were once part of Starr-Viejo Ranch, which was purchased by Orange County in the early 1970s. The park honors Ronald W. Caspers, Chairman of the Orange County Board of Supervisors, who was instrumental in preserving the old ranch as a park. Reminders of the park's ranching heritage include a windmill and a wooden corral where the branding and loading of cattle took place. The windmill still pumps a little water, which helps park wildlife make it through the long hot Santa Ana Mountains summers. During summer, the area around the windmill is the park's best bird-watching spot.

To learn more about the region's human and natural history, drop by the park's visitor center. Exhibits interpret Native American life, birds, mammals, geology, and much more. On weekends, park rangers lead nature walks.

The mostly level, Nature Trail-Oak Trail-Bell Canyon Trail-loop described below is only one of many possible day hikes you can fashion from the park's extensive trail network. The park's map is keyed to numbered posts located at trail junctions, so it's easy to design a hike that suits your time or energy level.

If you're an early riser and beat the heat, ascend one of the park's exposed ridges—via West Ridge Trail or East Ridge Trail. The latter trail connects to Bell Canyon Trail. From the higher ridges, a fine view is

yours. To the north are the mile-high twin peaks of Saddleback Mountain, highest in Orange County. To the west and south you can see the town of San Juan Capistrano, the wide blue Pacific, and on an exceptionally clear day, San Clemente Island.

Directions to trailhead: From Interstate 5 in San Juan Capistrano, take the Highway 74 (Ortega Highway) exit. Drive eight miles inland to the entrance to Caspers Wilderness Park. There is a vehicle entrance fee. Each adult in your party must obtain a wilderness permit at the entry kiosk. Remember, no solo hiking, and no kids on the trails.

From the entry kiosk, take the park road 1 1/2 miles to its end at the corral and windmill. There's plenty of parking near the signed trailhead for Nature Trail.

The Hike: Nature Trail loops through a handsome grove of antiquarian oak. You might see woodpeckers checking their store of acorns, which the birds have stuffed in hidey-holes in the nearby sycamores. Beneath the oaks are some huge patches of poison oak, but the trail steers clear of them.

You'll pass a junction with a left-branching trail that leads to Gunsight Pass and West Ridge Trail, and soon arrive at a second junction. (If you want a really short hike, keep right at this junction and you'll loop back to the trailhead via Nature Trail.)

Head north on signed Oak Trail, which meanders beneath the oak and sycamore that shade the west wall of Bell Canyon. The trail never strays far from (bone-dry) Bell Creek, its streambed, or sandy washes. During drought years, it's difficult to imagine that in the last century, black bears used to catch spawning steelhead trout in Bell Creek.

Fragrant sages perfume the trail, which is also lined with lemonade berry and prickly pear cactus. Colorful, but fast-fading, spring blooms include blue dick, monkeyflower, thistle, Indian pink, lupine, and the humble pineapple weed.

Oak Trail reaches a junction at Post "12." You may take a short connector trail east to Bell Canyon or head north on another short trail, Star Rise, and join Bell Canyon Trail. A wide dirt road, Bell Canyon Trail travels the canyon floor.

To return to the trailhead, you'll head south on Bell Canyon Trail, which passes through open oak-dotted meadows. Red-tailed hawks roost atop spreading sycamores. The trail returns you to the parking area, within sight of the beginning of Nature Trail, where you began your walk.

Windmill recalls Bell Canyon's ranching days

Aspens, San Bernardino Mountains

Chapter 10

SAN BERNARDINO MOUNTAINS

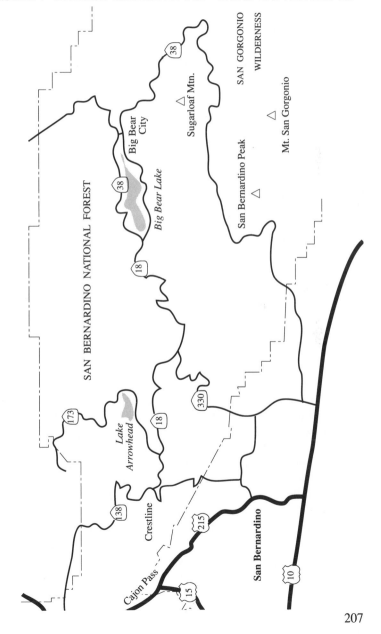

San Bernardino Mountains

When that restless breed of American—the trapper, the trader, the Army mapmaker—pushed westward, they had to reckon with arid country beyond the lower Colorado River. The Mojave Desert gave sustenance to few, and mercy to none. And if crossing the desert's uncharted sands wasn't enough of a problem, another formidable obstacle barred the way west—the San Bernardino Mountains. Sheer granite cliffs, thorny chaparral, snowbound passes. The San Bernardinos today suffer the indignities of the sewer line and the television antenna, and may seem a little too accessible. However, the high peaks still challenge the hardy.

The San Bernardino range is a vast fault block about sixty miles long and thirty miles wide, extending in a southwesterly direction across Southern California. The western portion is plateau-like with some rather broad uplands—unusual for Southern California mountains. At its western end, the mountains terminate abruptly at Cajon Pass, which separates the range from the San Gabriel Mountains. Geologists speculate that the two ranges may originally have been one. Rocks on both sides of the pass suggest the earth's convulsions wrenched the mountains fifteen to twenty-five miles apart. The earth is still shuddering in this area; the San Andreas Fault runs through the pass. It's an excellent place to observe fault features and view this Maker and Shaker of continents.

Although the two ranges look something alike at first glance, they aren't the same age. The San Gabriels are more sheer, more faulted. The San Bernardinos are younger, less fractured by earthquakes.

The southern slopes of the San Bernardinos consist of high ridges cut by many deep stream gorges. At the western end of the highest ridge is San Bernardino Peak. The ridge culminates toward the east in Mount San Gorgonio (Old Grayback, 11,499'), the highest peak in Southern California. To the south, San Gorgonio Pass separates the San Bernardinos from the San Jacinto Range. The discovery of the pass in 1853 enabled Los Angeles to be tied to the rest of the United States by railroad line.

By the mid-nineteenth century, industrious Mormons and other settlers invaded the San Bernardinos. They drove the Serrano and Cahuilla Indians into the desert. Newcomers clear-cut miles of forest, dammed and channeled the wild rivers into irrigation ditches, and dynamited the mountains in search of gold. But not all visitors blasted, mined and milled.

Some came to relax in the alpine air and enjoy the good life. Summer tents and homes clustered around high-country lakes. To many people, the San Bernardinos no longer seemed so remote, so formidable.

A large portion of the San Bernardino Mountains was protected by the establishment of the San Bernardino Forest Reserve, created by President Benjamin Harrison in 1893. Subsequently, the name "Reserve" was changed to "National Forest." In 1908, the San Bernardino National Forest and Angeles National Forest were brought together and administered under the latter's name, but in 1925, President Coolidge divided them.

The San Bernardino National Forest is a huge parcel of land, bigger than the state of Rhode Island, the second-largest national forest in California (first is Los Padres). It's also one of the most heavily used national forests in the nation. One year, more than seven million people visited the San Bernardino Mountains. It was as if everyone in the L.A. Basin visited once.

The Rim of the World Highway, leading from San Bernardino to Lake Arrowhead and Big Bear Lake, opened up the mountains to recreation on a large scale. Chiseled into rock walls, the road takes many a switchback and hairpin turn, following the crest of the range and ascending to more than 7,000 feet. Even the highway's primitive forerunners—with their forty-one percent grades—didn't stop thousands of guns and fishing rods from assaulting the wilderness. Big Bear and Arrowhead Lakes became one of Southern California's most popular resort areas. The rustic hotels, spas and lodges delighted Southern Californians in the same manner the Catskills and Berkshires served the needs of New Yorkers.

There are many quiet places in the 700,000-acre San Bernardino National Forest where the hiker can behold waterfalls, stunning fields of flowers, and golden eagles soaring above lofty crags. The San Gorgonio Wilderness contains all the delights of these mountains, and none of its "civilization." The San Gorgonio Wild Area was created by a law in 1931 as a place free of restaurants and roads, camps and resorts. In 1965, Congress declared it a Wilderness.

Seventy-one miles of hiking trails wind through the high-country wilderness. The 56,000-acre Wilderness is a lonely refuge from the glass and chrome world far below. On the high spine of the range, Mount San Gorgonio and other 10,000-plus foot peaks—Dobbs, Jepson, Charlton and San Bernardino—stand shoulder to shoulder. When you reach the summit on one of these peaks, you'll be only ninety miles from downtown L.A. and two miles high, but the city will seem more remote than the map indicates, and you'll feel much higher.

Heaps Peak Trail

3/4-mile loop through Heaps Peak Arboretum

San Bernardino National Forest is a huge parcel of land; it's larger than the entire state of Rhode Island. The National Forest, which takes in the San Bernardino and San Jacinto Mountains, is the second-largest in California (first is Los Padres), and is one of the most heavily used recreation areas in the nation.

A huge portion of the San Bernardino Mountains was protected by the establishment of the San Bernardino Forest Reserve, created by President Benjamin Harrison in 1893. Subsequently, the name "reserve" was changed to National Forest. In 1908 the San Bernardino National Forest and the Angeles National Forests were brought together under the latter's name, but in 1925, President Coolidge divided them.

San Bernardino National Forest is not only huge, it's botanically diverse; the forest hosts ecological communities ranging from sagebrush to subalpine, from Joshua tree to limber pine. One of the best places to learn about National Forest flora is at Heaps Peak Arboretum, located near the tiny San Bernardino Mountains community of Running Springs. Most of the arboreteum is filled with mixed stands of pine and fir—the typical forest community of these parts. In addition, the arboretum grows trees and shrubs that are representative of other parts of the forest.

A walk through the arboretum is a relaxing—and quite educational—experience. Numbered stops along the trail are keyed to a pamphlet which can be picked up at the trailhead. The entertaining pamphlet, published by the Rim-of-the-World Interpretive Association, is a mini-botany course.

The arboretum began in 1928 when the Lake Arrowhead Women's Club began planting trees. A 1922 fire had devastated Heaps Peak, so the club's efforts were welcomed by both professional foresters and the public. A 1956 fire swept through the area, but most of the larger trees survived.

In the early days of this century it was not beauty but timber that lured Southern Californians to Heaps Peak and the surrounding high country. One of the largest San Bernardino Mountains logging operations was conducted by the Brookings Box and Lumber Company from 1898 to 1910. Robert Brookings and company built a sawmill just outside present-day Running Springs in a hamlet known as Fredalba.

In order to haul out the thick stands of pine and fir that stretched from Heaps Peak to Arrowbear Lake, the company laid an astonishing 30 miles of railroad track through rugged terrain. A tiny Shay locomotive with a

210

balloon-like smokestack hauled the felled trees down the narrow-gauge tracks to the mill. About 8,000 acres were clear-cut. Most of the lumber went into orange crates to meet the demand of Southland's citrus growers.

Nature lovers of all hiking abilities will learn something from the interpretive displays along Heaps Peak Trail. Did you know that the willow contains salicylic acid, the active ingredient in asprin? Did you know that the Coulter pine's 8-pound pine cones are the world's largest?

It's hard not to like a nature trail that begins with the forest philosophy of Buddha and ends with the natural history of the gooseberry.

Interpretive displays reveal secrets of the piney woods. Budding naturalists will learn how to tell one pine from another. One slightly bizarre sight along the trail: the various pine cones are enshrined in elevated display cases that in the misty distance resemble objects of worship.

The pines of the San Bernardino Mountains—Coulter, sugar, ponderosa, Jeffrey and knobcone—have survived fires, loggers, and have battled and continue to battle no less than 108 species of insects. Now they face another great challenge: Smog. While the pines growing on the shoulders of 6,421-foot Heaps Peak are just above the smog line and seem to be faring well, their lower- elevation conifer cousins face an uncertain future.

After you've enjoyed Heaps Peak Trail, head down Highway 18 about 1 1/2 miles to Switzer Park Picnic Area or drive over to nearby Lake Arrowhead.

Directions to trailhead: From Interstate 10 in Redlands, exit on Highway 30 and doggedly follow the highway signs through minor detours and suburbs-in-the-making. As Highway 30 begins to climb into the San Bernardino Mountains, it becomes Highway 330. Eighteen miles from Redlands, you'll reach a highway junction on the outskirts of Running Springs. You'll bear northwest on Highway 18 (following signs toward Lake Arrowhead). Four miles of driving along this winding mountain road brings you to Heaps Peak Arboretum. There's plenty of parking just off the road.

Lake Arrowhead

SAN BERNARDINO
NATIONAL FOREST

Heaps Peak
Arboretum Trail

to Hwy. 10

Switzer Park
Picnic Area

Rim of the World Dr.

to Hwy 330

60

Cougar Crest Trail

Highway 38 to Bertha Peak
   6 miles round trip; 1,100-foot elevation gain

   Cougar Crest, the forested ridge between Big Bear Lake and Holcomb Valley is a treat for hikers. From the ridge, as well as from the ridge's two prominent peaks—Bertha and Delamar—you get great views of the lake, towering Mount San Gorgonio and tranquil Holcomb Valley.

   Holcomb Valley wasn't always so tranquil. In 1860, Billy Holcomb was out bear hunting and wandered over the ridge of hills that separates Bear Valley from the smaller, parallel valley to the north. He found gold. Prospectors swarmed into the valley from all over the West.

   This day hike climbs the forested slopes above Big Bear Lake to a junction with the Pacific Crest Trail. From the PCT, you can ascend to Bertha Peak or to more distant Delamar Mountain for grand views of the middle of the San Bernardino Mountains.

   Directions to trailhead: From Highway 18 in the town of Big Bear Lake, turn north on Stanfield cut off, crossing to the north shore of the lake

and a junction with Highway 38. Turn left, drive a mile to the Big Bear San Bernardino National Forest Ranger Station, then a short distance beyond to the signed Cougar Crest trailhead and parking area off the north side of the highway. If you're approaching from the east on Highway 38, the trailhead is a bit more than two miles beyond the hamlet of Fawnskin.

Prospector
Billy Holcomb

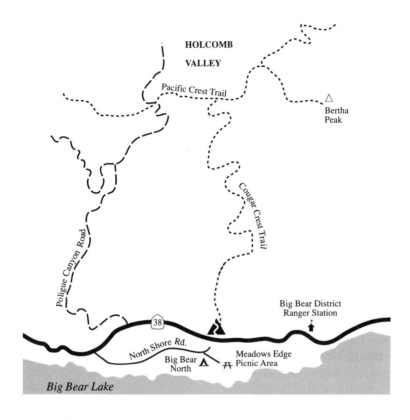

The Hike: From the signed trailhead, join wide Cougar Crest Trail, a retiring dirt road. You climb through a pine and juniper woodland and pass a couple of old mining roads. After a mile, the trail narrows and begins ascending forested Cougar Crest via a series of well-constructed switchbacks.

Soon you'll begin enjoying over-the-shoulder views of Big Bear Lake and its dramatic backdrop—the two-mile-high peaks of the San Gorgonio Wilderness.

A bit more than two miles from the trailhead, Cougar Crest Trail reaches a signed junction with the Pacific Crest Trail. To reach Bertha Peak you'll bear right (east) and continue along the ridge crest for 1/2 mile to an intersection with an old dirt road. The Pacific Crest Trail continues straight at this junction, but you bear right on the dirt road and ascend a half-mile through pinyon pine and juniper woodland to the small relay station atop Bertha Peak. Best views are a bit below the peak.

61

Pine Knot Trail

Aspen Glen Picnic Area to Grand View Point
6 1/2 miles round trip; 1,200-foot elevation gain

Rim of the World Highway offers the traveler a fine view of Big Bear Lake. A better view—a hiker's view—is available from Pine Knot Trail, which climbs the handsome, pine-studded slopes above the lake and offers far-reaching panoramas of the San Bernardino Mountains.

Pine Knot Trail takes its name from a little community of cabins, stores and saloons that sprang up when Rim of the World Highway was completed. After World War II, the town of Pine Knot changed its name to Big Bear Lake Village.

While Pine Knot Trail offers grand views of the lake, this hike's destination—Grand View Point—does not overlook the lake. The grand view is a breathtaking panorama of the San Gorgonio Wilderness and the deep canyon cut by the Santa Ana River.

Directions to trailhead: From California 18 in Big Bear Lake Village, turn southwest on Mill Creek Road and proceed about a half-mile to Aspen Glen Picnic Area on your left. The signed trail departs from the east end of the picnic area by Mill Creek Road.

The Hike: From Aspen Glen Picnic Area, Pine Knot Trail climbs a low, lupine-sprinkled ridge. The path follows a fence line for a short distance, then dips into and out of a willow-lined creekbed. You will get great over-the-shoulder views of the south shore of Big Bear Lake.

Jeffrey Pine

Ascending through Jeffrey pine and ponderosa pine forests, the trail meets and joins a fire road; after a short distance, it again becomes a footpath. Now your over-the-shoulder view is of the north shore of Big Bear Lake.

Pine Knot Trail passes near one of the runs of the Snow Forest Ski Area, then meanders through an enchanted area of castellated rocks. About 2 miles from the trailhead the trail intersects dirt Forest Service Road 2N17. Before you is a meadow, a rather amusing-looking landscape decorated with boulders, ponderosa pine, Indian paintbrush and skunk cabbage. Bear left on the dirt road for just 50 feet or so, then pick up the signed footpath again.

Passing black oak and willow, Pine Knot Trail skirts the moist meadow and soon arrives at Deer Group Camp. Benches and tables suggest a picnic or rest stop.

From the camp, continue on Pine Knot Trail, which crosses and then parallels another dirt Forest Service road. Ahead of you are tantalizing views of San Gorgonio Wilderness peaks—just a hint of things to come when you reach trail's end.

About a mile from Deer Group Camp, the trail intersects dirt Forest Service Road 2N11. Cross the road and follow the signed trail on a quarter-mile ascent to the top of a ridgeline.

From Grand View Point, enjoy the views of San Gorgonio Wilderness, a panorama of Southern California's highest peaks.

62

Santa Ana River Trail

South Fork Campground to Heart Bar Campground
9 miles round trip; 800-foot elevation gain

For most of its length, Southern California's largest river is not a thing of beauty. Concrete-lined and channelized, the Santa Ana River that crosses Orange County is a thoroughly domesticated watercourse. Its once-extensive riverbed has been covered with subdivisions, its natural course altered for human convenience. Glimpsing the river as it passes Costa Mesa backyards, Anaheim Stadium or the I-10/I-15 interchange does not, in truth, inspire further exploration.

Fortunately for hikers and nature lovers, there's another Santa Ana River, unfettered and unchanneled. At its headwaters high in the San Bernardino Mountains, the river waters a beautiful meadow and cuts through a deep canyon that separates the high peaks of the San Gorgonio Wilderness from the mountains of the Big Bear Lake area. The river, born of natural springs and snowmelt, is in its upper reaches an important wildlife habitat.

A 4 1/2-mile length of the Santa Ana River Trail explores the river's headwaters. Ambitious plans are afoot for the trail, which one day may descend all the way from the San Bernardino Mountains to the sea. The idea is to connect the famed Pacific Crest Trail with Southern California's coastline.

Equestrians have been especially vocal in boosting a "crest to coast" route. The lower part of the trail, which follows the concrete channel from the river mouth inland to Yorba Linda at the base of the Chino Hills, is popular with cyclists and equestrians; it's not exactly a thrill a minute for walkers.

For hikers, the true Santa Ana River Trail begins in an area of the San Bernardino National Forest called Heart Bar, first settled by Mormon pioneers in the 1850s. During the latter part of the 19th Century and the first half of this one, cattlemen sent their herds to graze the lush Santa Ana River meadows. It was one cattleman's brand, a heart with a bar beneath it that gave the land its name about a century ago.

Santa Ana River Trail parallels the river as it winds from South Fork Campground to Heart Bar Campground. The path stays in piney woods for most of its length. A few side trails allow passage to the river.

Directions to trailhead: From Interstate 10 in Redlands, take the Highway 38 exit and proceed north 32 miles to South Fork Campground.

Almost opposite the entrance to the campground, on the north side of the highway, you'll find the Santa Ana River trailhead parking lot and the signed trail.

Santa Ana River Trail ends at Forest Road IN02, near Heart Bar Campground. If you want to make a one-way hike, you can arrange to have transportation waiting at the Forest Road IN02 trailhead. To reach this trailhead from the South Fork Campground trailhead, you would continue east on Highway 38 to the signed Heart Bar Campground turnoff, then drive a mile past the campground on the dirt Forest Road IN02 to the second signed Santa Ana River trailhead.

The Hike: From the parking area opposite South Fork Campground, Santa Ana River Trail meanders by its namesake, then veers under the Santa Ana River Bridge. Notice the rugged construction of the bridge and the wide bed of the river, two indications of the Santa Ana's size and strength after a storm.

The trail makes a short circle, reaches a second signed trailhead at the entrance to South Fork Campground and heads west. Switchbacking up a slope, the trail soon turns east—your direction for the rest of this hike.

During the first mile you will intersect a number of dirt roads, but strategically placed signs keep you on the path. Most of the climbing is in the first mile.

The trail travels through a mixed forest of ponderosa and Jeffrey pine, white fir and black oak. Ground squirrels are abundant, and deer are seen occasionally. Steller's jays, Western bluebirds, pygmy nuthatches, robins and juncoes are among the birds you may see.

Above you to the southwest is the San Gorgonio Wilderness, dominated by its 11,499-foot signature peak, highest point in Southern California. To the north, above the forested canyon of the Santa Ana River, is Sugarloaf Mountain (9,952 feet), highest peak in the San Bernardinos outside the wilderness.

About the trail's midpoint you'll spot Heart Bar Station, headquarters for a Forest Service fire crew. Continuing east, the trail offers great views of well-named Big Meadow. Watering the meadow are Heart Bar Creek, Coon Creek, Cienega Seca Creek and the headwaters of the Santa Ana. Big Meadow is especially pretty when a breeze sways the willows and tall grasses. During late spring and summer the meadow is splashed with colorful Indian paintbrush, purple sage, columbine, monkeyflower and lupine.

The meadows where cattle once grazed are now a valuable habitat for rabbits, foxes, skunks and raccoons. California golden beaver were brought into the area, and several pairs of them maintain dams on the Santa Ana River.

About a mile from trail's end you will intersect an unsigned side trail leading left down to Big Meadow and over to Heart Bar Campground. Continue straight at this junction to the end of the trail at Forest Road.

View of Santa Ana River country, San Gorgonio
Wilderness, from Grandview Point

218

63

Aspen Grove Trail

Forest Road 1N05 to Fish Creek Meadows
5 miles round trip; 600-foot elevation gain
Wilderness permit required

One of the prettiest sights of autumn is the fluttering of the aspen's golden-yellow leaves. From a distance, the trees stand apart from the surrounding dark forest. In the right light, the aspens seem to burn, like fire in the wind.

Botanists say the aspen is the most widely distributed tree on the North American continent. Even not-so-lyrical American fur trappers and mountain men of the last century were impressed by the tree's range and beauty.

The water-loving aspen is a rarity in Southern California, but there is a handsome little grove in the San Bernardino Mountains. Aspen Grove, reached by a trail with the same name, is an ideal autumn excursion.

One of the most ecologically diverse ranges in the state, the San Bernardino Mountains host the world's largest Joshua tree and the tallest known lodgepole pine, so it's not too surprising to find an aspen grove. Coastal, desert and even alpine plant species are found in these mountains.

The hike to Aspen Grove is particularly inviting after Jack Frost has touched the trees. After the first cold snap, the aspens display their fall finery, a display of color unrivaled in Southern California.

It's only a short quarter-mile saunter to the aspens that line Fish Creek, but the trail continues beyond the grove, traveling through a pine and fir forest and a lovely meadow.

Directions to trailhead: From Interstate 10 in Redlands, exit on Highway 38 and proceed 32 miles east to the signed turnoff for Heart Bar Campground. (As you head up 38 into the San Bernardino National Forest, remember to stop at Mill Creek Ranger Station just beyond the hamlet of Mentone and pick up a wilderness permit.) Turn south (right) on dirt Forest Road 1N02, and drive 1 1/4 miles to a fork in the road. Stay right at the fork and follow it on a 1 1/2-mile climb to a small parking area and signed Aspen Grove Trail on your right.

Fish Creek, where the aspens grow, is the boundary of the San Gorgonio Wilderness. Mill Creek Ranger Station can supply a permit, map and trail information.

The Hike: The trail, for its first quarter-mile an abandoned dirt road, descends toward Fish Creek. The very beginning of Aspen Grove Trail offers the best view of San Gorgonio Wilderness peaks—the highest in Southern California. To the west stands mighty Grinnell Mountain, named for turn-of-the-century University of California zoologist Joseph Grinnell, who studied the animals of the San Bernardino Mountains. To the south is Ten Thousand Foot Ridge, headwaters for Fish Creek, which you soon see and hear meandering below.

At Fish Creek, a sign marks the boundary of the San Gorgonio Wilderness. Cross the creek and enjoy the aspen grove that lines Fish Creek. It's a small grove, but a pretty one. No one will blame you if you picnic among the whitewashed trunks and quaking leaves and hike no farther.

The aspens have been suffering of late at the hands of— or more accurately, the jaws of— a creature that loves the trees even more than humans. The aspen-chomping California golden beaver is not a native of the San Bernardino Mountains, but since its introduction it has found the area — and the aspens to its liking. Forest Service wildlife experts are working on a plan to manage the native aspens and the nonnative beaver.

After admiring the aspens, continue on Aspen Grove Trail, which heads up-creek. The path soon wanders a bit away from Fish Creek and travels through a forest of ponderosa pine, Jeffrey pine and Douglas fir.

About a mile from Aspen Grove, the trail passes little Monkey Flower Flat. During late spring and early summer, columbine and lupine join the monkeyflowers in bedecking the flat.

Beyond Monkey Flower is a much larger flat—Fish Creek Meadow. Aspen Grove Trail skirts this meadow and ends at a signed junction with Fish Creek Trail. The left fork of Fish Creek Trails leads a bit more than half a mile to Forest Road 1N05. Take the right fork of the trail, which angles toward Upper Fish Creek. The path ascends above the creek, passes through a pine and fir forest and, a bit more than a mile from the junction with Aspen Grove Trail, reaches Fish Creek Camp. This fir-shaded camp is an ideal place to relax.

64

Vivian Creek Trail

Mill Creek Canyon to Vivian Creek Trail Camp
   2 1/2 miles round trip; 1,200-foot elevation gain
Mill Creek Canyon to Halfway Trail Camp
   5 miles round trip; 1,800-foot elevation gain
Mill Creek Canyon to High Creek Trail Camp
   8 miles round trip; 3,400-foot elevation gain
Mill Creek Canyon to Mount San Gorgonio Peak
   14 miles round trip; 5,300-foot elevation gain
Wilderness permit required

*"The mountains"—he continued, with his eyes upon the distant
heights—" are not seen by those who would visit them with a rattle and
clatter and rush and roar—as one would visit the cities of men. They
are to be seen only by those who have the grace to go quietly; who
have the understanding to go thoughtfully; the heart to go lovingly;
and the spirit to go worshipfully."*

—Harold Bell Wright
The Eyes of the World, 1914

A half-dozen major trails lead through the San Gorgonio Wilderness to
the top of Mount San Gorgonio, Southern California's highest peak.
Oldest, and often regarded as the best, is Vivian Creek Trail.

Not long after the formation of San Bernardino Forest Preserve in 1893,
pioneer foresters built Government Trail to the top of San Gorgonio. This
path was later renamed Vivian Creek Trail, because it winds along for a
few miles with its namesake watercourse before climbing the steep upper
slopes of San Gorgonio.

Most of us have marveled at the 11,499-foot mountain, which is most
striking in winter when its snow-covered peak can be seen reaching far
above the metropolis. From the top there's a 360-degree panoramic view
from the Mexican border to the southern Sierra, from the Pacific to the far
reaches of the Mojave.

Vivian Creek Trail begins in Mill Creek Canyon. The lower stretches
of the canyon, traveled by Highway 38, displays many boulders, evidence
of many floods in years past.

Upper Mill Creek Canyon is where Big Falls falls. Tumbling from the
shoulder of San Bernardino Peak, snowmelt-swollen Falls Creek rushes
headlong over a cliff near Mill Creek Road. (Use caution: many foolish

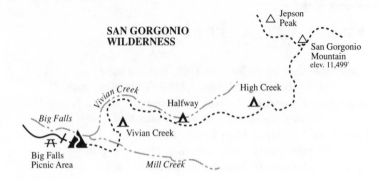

SAN GORGONIO
WILDERNESS

Jepson
Peak

San Gorgonio
Mountain
elev. 11,499'

Vivian Creek

High Creek

Halfway

Big Falls

Vivian Creek

Big Falls
Picnic Area

Mill Creek

people have been killed or injured by trying to climb Big Falls.

Mill Creek Canyon was the retreat for pastor-turned-novelist Harold Bell Wright (1872-1944). His wholesome, tremendously popular novels featured rugged individualists, as well as Southwest and Southland settings. One novel, *Eyes of the World*, uses the San Bernardino Mountains as a setting and explores the question of an artist's responsibility to society and to himself.

Leaving the head of Mill Creek Canyon, Vivian Creek Trail climbs into the valley cut by Vivian Creek, visits three inviting trail camps—Vivian Creek, Halfway and High Creek—and ascends rocky, lodgepole pine-dotted slopes to the top of Old Grayback.

Directions to trailhead: From Interstate 10 in Redlands, exit on Highway 38, and proceed 14 miles east to a junction with Forest Home Road. (Halfway to this junction, on Highway 38, is Mill Creek Ranger Station, where you must stop and obtain a wilderness permit.) Follow Forest Home Road 4 1/2 miles to its end, at Big Falls trailhead and a day use area.

The Hike: The trail, an old dirt road, travels 3/4 mile through Falls Campground (now a picnic area) to another (the former) Vivian Creek trailhead. The trail, a dirt path from this point, crosses boulder-strewn Mill Creek wash, then begins a steep ascent over an exposed, oak-dotted slope. Soon you'll reach Vivian Creek Trail Camp, where pine- and fir-shaded sites dot the creek banks.

Past the camp, Vivian Creek Trail follows its namesake, crossing from one side to the other and passing little lush meadows and stands of pine and cedar.

Halfway, a relatively new trail camp, about halfway between Vivian Creek and High Creek Camps, called Halfway Camp, is another welcome retreat. Another 2 miles of steep climbing up forested slopes brings you to High Creek Camp.

Above High Creek, located at 9,000-foot elevation, you leave behind the ponderosa pine and cedar and encounter that hearty, high-altitude survivor, the lodgepole pine. Two miles high, you start getting some great views; at 11,000 feet, the trail ascends above the timberline.

When you reach a junction with the trail coming up from Dollar Lake you'll turn right. Soon you'll pass a junction with the Sky High Trail, cross a last rise and climb to the summit of San Gorgonio.

No other Southern California mountain commands such an uninterrupted panoramic view. To the north are the deep meadowlands of the upper valley of the Santa Ana River. To the west is the murky megalopolis. To the east is the Mojave Desert. South is San Gorgonio Pass and just across it, nearly level with your feet, is Mount San Jacinto.

As Harold Bell Wright described the scene in *Eyes of the World*: "At last their wanderings carried them close under the snowy heights of San Gorgonio—the loftiest of all peaks. That night, they camped at timberline; and in the morning, made their way to the top, in time to see the sun come up from under the edge of the world."

Mt. San Gorgonio

65

Kitching Creek Trail

Kitching Creek to Kitching Peak
9 1/2 miles round trip; 2,400-foot gain
Wilderness permit required

Kitching Peak, which lies atop the headwaters of the Whitewater River in the San Gorgonio Wilderness, has a wonderful air of remoteness. High on the dry southeast end of the San Bernardino Mountains, the 6,598-foot peak offers superb views of Mount San Jacinto and Mount San Gorgonio, as well as the Mojave and Colorado Deserts.

While San Gorgonio Wilderness is Southern California's most heavily used wilderness area, the Whitewater country, added to the wilderness in 1984, is mostly trailless and rarely traveled. No doubt this rugged country could be considered among the most wild—if not the most wild—region in the Southland.

On the steep slopes of the awesome Whitewater country, the bighorn sheep have their lambing grounds, and in its waters, the legendary San Gorgonio trout is making its last stand. Deer, mountain lions and even black bears live here.

The Whitewater River, swollen by snowmelt from the shoulders of Mount San Gorgonio, rushes down the San Bernardino Mountains to meet the desert sands far below. Many pioneer water-seekers of the last century tried to capture this river and send its waters to the San Bernardino Valley and Palm Springs. Today, north-bound Pacific Crest Trail hikers leave the desert behind and enter the San Bernardino Mountains through Whitewater Canyon.

Only one trail ascends to Kitching Peak, but it's a path with three names: Kitching Creek, Kitching Peak and Millard. By whatever name, this path, which for the most part travels wooded slopes and canyons, is somewhat surprising for the "desert" end of the San Bernardinos. This hike ascends the east branch of Millard Canyon to a divide, then travels a ridgeline to the summit of Kitching Peak. Clear-day winter views are unforgettable.

Directions to trailhead: From Interstate 10, 2 miles east of Banning, exit on Fields Road; you'll head north on Fields Road to a stop sign. Ahead is Malki Indian Museum, but turn right on Morongo Road where a sign points to Millard Canyon. Follow Morongo to its end, and make a left on Millard Canyon Road, which jogs right, then left, then right again, where the pavement ends. From pavement's end, continue following

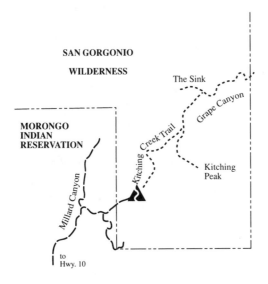

SAN GORGONIO
WILDERNESS

The Sink

Grape Canyon

MORONGO
INDIAN
RESERVATION

Kitching Creek Trail

Kitching
Peak

Millard Canyon

to
Hwy. 10

Forest Service Road 2S05 3.8 miles to a signed junction where you'll bear right on Forest Service Road 2SO3 toward Kitching Peak. Continue one-half mile to another junction where you'll stay left; from here, it's one last mile on a somewhat nasty dirt road to the trailhead. Depending on your vehicle, you might want to walk the last half-mile to the trailhead.

The Hike: The trail ascends northeast up the east branch of Millard Canyon. Oak and spruce shade the trail, which crosses and recrosses little Kitching Creek. After 2 miles, the path rises out of the shade of the canyon and switchbacks up the brushy ridge that divides Millard Canyon for the canyon cut by the Whitewater River.

Atop the ridge is a signed junction. Kitching Creek Trail (2E09) heads north another two miles to The Sink, a trail camp. You veer sharply right (south) on Trail 2E24 along the oak- and chaparral-covered ridgeline. Farther along you'll encounter a stand of white fir and a few sugar pine.

Sometimes this ridgetop trail is quite brushy, so you might have to push through the chaparral to get to the very top of Kitching Peak. From the summit, almost due south, is mighty Mount San Jacinto, and just below that great gash between the San Jacinto and San Bernardino Mountains—San Gorgonio Pass. East are the Little San Bernardino Mountains of Joshua Tree National Monument. You can trace the course of Whitewater River into the Coachella Valley and off toward Palm Springs. Above you to the north is San Gorgonio, highest peak in Southern California.

Chapter 11

SAN JACINTO MOUNTAINS

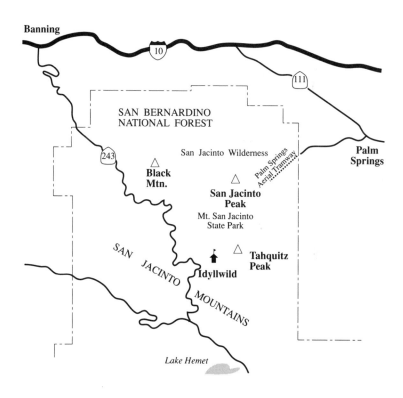

San Jacinto Mountains

Many hikers in the San Jacinto Mountains can't resist comparing this range with the High Sierra. While comparisons often leave low chaparral-covered mountains on the short end, the alpine San Jacintos fare well because the range shares many geologic similarities with the Sierra Nevada. Both ranges are bold uplifted masses of granite. Both are westward tilted blocks located near powerful earthquake faults. Both veer abruptly out of the desert without geologic fanfare of foothills preceding them.

Carey McWilliams called Southern California an "island on the land." The San Jacintos could well be described the same way. The 10,000-foot peaks of the San Jacintos and their shorter, but no less majestic, stony neighbors are completely separated from the rest of Southern California by low passes and desert valleys. The range is bounded by San Gorgonio Pass on the north, the San Jacinto Valley on the west, the Colorado Desert and the great Coachella Valley on the east, and Anza-Borrego Desert State Park to the south. The San Jacintos seem an island in the sky because of their incredibly rapid rise from the desert floor. No other place in California do alpine and desert vegetation thrive in such close proximity. Six distinct life zones, from cactus-dotted desert and palm canyons to arctic alpine summits, can be encountered within five horizontal miles of travel. On the base is Lower Sonoran vegetation of creosote and ironwood. Above this is the Upper Sonoran or manzanita and scrub oak, soon giving way with rise in elevation to dense mountain forests of pine and cedar. In narrow belts around the high summits are those hearty survivors—the lodgepole pine and limber pine. Finally some stunted species, including alpine sorrel, grow on the peaks and are classified in the Arctic-Alpine Zone. each life zone has a unique set of inhabitants. Shy and reclusive bighorn sheep patrol the desert-facing high country, mule deer browse the verdant meadows, golden eagles soar over the high peaks.

During the great logging boom of 1880-1910, timber barons sent their choppers farther and farther up the slopes of the San Jacintos. Ranchers grazed thousands of sheep and cattle in the alpine meadows. Even the most shortsighted could see the destruction of the mountain watershed, and with local settlers urging protection for the range, President Grover Cleveland established the San Jacinto Timberland Reserve in 1897. It was a huge chunk of land, extending from the San Gorgonio Pass to the Mexican border. The San Jacinto Reserve was later combined with a portion of the Santa Ana Mountains to create the Cleveland National Forest. After several devastating fires in 1924, federal foresters decided the huge tract of land was too unwieldy for fire suppression purposes, and the San Jacintos were taken from the Cleveland National Forest.

In the mid-thirties, CCC workers camped in Round and Tahquitz Valleys, and built an extensive, well-engineered trail system through the San Jacintos. Some years, as many as 15,000 hikers travel the backcountry on these trails.

The wild areas in the San Jacinto Mountains are now administered by both state park and national forest rangers. The middle of the region, including San Jacinto Peak, is included within Mount San Jacinto Wilderness State Park. On both sides of the peak, north and south, the wilderness is administered by the San Jacinto District of the San Bernardino National Forest.

Access to the San Jacintos was difficult until Highway 243, "The Banning to Idyllwild Panoramic Highway" was built. As late as World War II, it was a muffler-massacring, steep, narrow, unpaved route that forded streams. A new paved "high gear" road opened in 1948, with actress Jane Powell performing the ribbon-cutting duties as the Banning High School Band played.

Boosterism in Southern California has rarely taken a backseat to beauty, and one result of this attitude is the Palm Springs Aerial Tramway. To attract tourists, it became a Palm Springs Chamber of Commerce scheme to build a tramway up Mount San Jacinto. An organization called the San Jacinto Winter Park Authority was formed; it tried to sell the idea to the public as an attraction for skiers. Only the most naive believed there could be any possibility of skiing down the mountain's impassable middle slopes. Conservationists, who thought a mechanical contrivance would despoil the wilderness, waged a fifteen-year battle with developers. The developers won. The Palm Springs Aerial Tramway opened in 1963, and now provides eighteen-minute access to country that once required a day's strenuous hiking to reach.

The range is one of those magical places that lures hikers back year after year. The seasons are more distinct here than anywhere else in Southern California. Hikers also enjoy the contrasts this range offers—the feeling of hiking in Switzerland while gazing down on the Sahara.

66

Ernie Maxwell Trail

Humber Park to Saunders Meadow
5 miles round trip; 300-foot elevation gain

The founder of the *Idyllwild Town Crier* is honored by the Ernie Maxwell Scenic Trail, a woodsy, 2 1/2-mile path through the San Jacinto Mountains. Maxwell, long-time Idyllwild conservationist, has hiked his namesake trail many times.

"Lots of people helped build the trail, but I hogged all the credit," he often jokes.

As Maxwell explains it, his trail came into being as a result of his horse's inability to get along with automobiles. After riding through the San Jacinto Wilderness, Maxwell and his fellow equestrians were forced to follow paved roads back through town to the stables. Maxwell's barn-sour pack horses, so slow and sullen on the trail, would become suddenly frisky and unmanageable as they neared home. Equine-auto conflicts were frequent. Maxwell thought: Why not build a trail from Humber Park, at the edge of the San Jacinto Wilderness, through the forest to the stables, thus avoiding the horse-spooking congestion of downtown Idyllwild?

Maxwell got cooperation from the U.S. Forest Service and from Riverside County convicts, who provided the labor. Ernie Maxwell Trail was completed in 1959.

And a lovely trail it is. The path meanders through a mixed forest of pine and fir and offers fine views of the granite face of Marion Ridge.

Since founding the *Idyllwild Town Crier* in 1946, Maxwell has often written about what he wryly calls "the urban-wildlands interface issue. That's the one that deals with more and more people moving into the hills."

People began moving into the hills more with their axes and sheep more than a hundred years ago. Fortunately, the San Jacinto Mountains have had many conservation-minded friends, including Ernie Maxwell, who for many years served as president of the local chapter of the Izaak Walton League. Maxwell has seen the emphasis of the surrounding National Forest change from commodity production to recreation; seen isolated Idyllwild become a (sometimes too-) popular weekend getaway. Conservationists are aware that the future of the mountains depend to a large extent on the attitude of the millions of Southern Californians living 7,000 feet below and a 1 1/2-hour drive away from Idyllwild.

"Walk the trails," urges Maxwell. "Enjoy the fresh air. And get to know these mountains. The mountains need more friends."

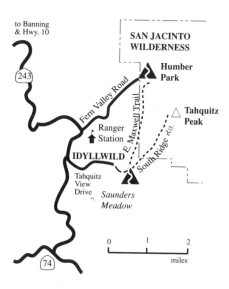

Directions to trailhead: From Interstate 10 in Banning, exit on California 243 (Banning-Idyllwild Highway) and proceed about 25 miles to Idyllwild County Park Visitor Center. A small museum interprets the history and natural history of the area.

From downtown Idyllwild, head up Fern Valley Road. Following the signs to Humber Park, drive two miles to the large parking area. Signed Ernie Maxwell Trail departs from the lower end of the parking lot.

The Hike: The trail begins at Humber Park, the main jumping-off point to the San Jacinto Wilderness for hikers and rock climbers. You'll get frequent over-the-shoulder views of the dramatic pinnacles popular with Southern California climbers.

The mostly level trail (the convicts did a great job) contours gently around wooded slopes. Ponderosa, Jeffrey and Coulter pines, fir and incense cedar grace the mountainside and carpet the path with needles.

This hike's destination, Saunders Meadow, is named for Amasa Saunders, who in 1881 operated a huge sawmill not too far down slope in Strawberry Valley. Take a moment to be thankful that not all the pine and fir became grist for Saunders' mill, then scout the tree tops for the abundant bird life. Look for Steller's jays, the white-headed woodpecker, and the colorful orange-headed, yellow-breasted western tanager.

Ernie Maxwell Scenic Trail ends somewhat abruptly and ingloriously at dirt Tahquitz View Drive. Maxwell had envisioned that his trail would continue another few miles around Idyllwild and connect to the path leading to Suicide Rock, but this trail plan ended in a bureaucratic thicket.

Contemplating the notion that half a terrific trail is better than none, return the same way.

231

◭67
South Ridge Trail

South Ridge Road to Tahquitz Peak
6 miles round trip; 2,000-foot elevation gain
Wilderness permit required

Tahquitz Peak dominates the southern San Jacinto Mountains, lording over Strawberry Valley and Idyllwild on one side, and Tahquitz Valley on the other. There's a fire lookout tower on the summit that's staffed during the long (June-November) fire season. The view from the peak is inspiring; the hiker who treks to the top is rewarded with great clear-day vistas of the San Jacintos, the desert and the distant Santa Rosas.

You may notice what appear to be insect-like creatures high on the rock walls of the mountain. Southland rock- climbers often come to practice their craft on the superb rock walls of Tahquitz. You may hear the distant shouts of "On belay," "climbing," or sometimes "Ohhhhhh nooooo."

Lily Rock, named for a surveyor's daughter, is the official name of the great rock, though most climbers prefer the more rugged-sounding Tahquitz. After taking one of the hundred routes (some quite hazardous) up the several faces of the rock, you can't blame the climbers for prefering something more dramatic-sounding than Lily.

South Ridge Trail, true to its name, ascends the steep south ridge of Tahquitz Peak. The trail climbs through stands of fine and fir and offers great views of Strawberry Valley and the storybook hamlet of Idyllwild.

If you want a longer hike than the six-mile round trip to Tahquitz Peak, there are a number of ways to extend your trek. By arranging a car shuttle, you could descend Tahquitz Peak to Humber Park at the outskirts of Idyllwild. For a very long loop hike, you could even follow the Ernie Maxwell Trail from Humber Park down to the foot of South Ridge Road, then up the road to the South Ridge trailhead.

A wilderness permit is required for South Ridge Trail, and for all other trails that enter the San Jacinto Wilderness. To obtain your permit, or to get the latest trail updates, drop by the San Bernardino National Forest's San Jacinto Ranger Station, located in Idyllwild, just off Highway 243.

Directions to trailhead: From Interstate 10 in Banning, exit on Highway 243 (Banning-Idyllwild Highway) and proceed about 25 miles to Idyllwild. After you've obtained your wilderness permit from the Forest Service Station in Idyllwild, you'll double back a wee bit to the south edge of town and make a left turn on Saunders Meadow Road. Turn left on Pine Avenue, right on Tahquitz Drive, then right on South Ridge Road. (If the gate across this road is closed (it's usually open during good weather), you'll have to park at the base of South Ridge Road. Otherwise, passenger cars with good ground clearance may continue 1 1/2 miles up part dirt/part paved, potholed South Ridge Road to its terminus at signed South Ridge trailhead.

The Hike: (See Trail 66 map) From the trailhead at the top of South Ridge Road, the well-constructed path zigzags through a forest of Jeffrey pine and white fir. You'll get fine south views of Garner Valley and Lake Hemet. Thomas Mountain and Table Mountain. Far off to the west, on a clear day, you'll be able to pick out the Santa Ana and San Gabriel Mountains.

South Ridge Trail climbs to a boulder-strewn saddle, which marks the trail's halfway point. Here you'll find a rock window-on-the-world, a great place to rest or to frame a picture of your hiking mate.

From the saddle, the trail climbs in earnest past thickets of spiny chinquapin, and past scattered lodgepole pine. You'll sight the fire lookout tower atop Tahquitz Peak many a switchback above you, but the last mile of trail goes by faster than you might expect if you maintain a slow, steady pace.

Enjoy the summit views, then either return the same way or follow your heart and Forest Service map through the San Jacinto Wilderness down to Humber Park and Idyllwild.

Admiring Tahquitz Peak from South Ridge Trail

Season: All Year

68
Desert View Trail

Mountain Station to Desert View
2 miles round trip
Mountain Station to Round Valley
6 miles round trip; 500-foot elevation gain

Palm Springs Aerial Tramway makes it easy for hikers to enter Mount San Jacinto State Wilderness. Starting in Chino Canyon near Palm Springs, a tram takes passengers from 2,643-foot Lower Tramway Terminal (Valley Station) to 8,516-foot Upper Tramway Terminal (Mountain Station) at the edge of the wilderness.

The Swiss-made gondola rapidly leaves terra firm behind. Too rapidly, you think. It carries you over one of the most abrupt mountain faces in the world, over cliffs only a bighorn sheep can scale, over several life zones, from palms to pines. The view is fantastic.

Now, most Nature-lovers enjoy witnessing flora and fauna changes equivalent to those viewed on a motor trip from the Mojave Desert to the Arctic Circle in just minutes. In pre-Tramway days, John Muir found the view "the most sublime spectacle to be found anywhere on this earth!"

For an introduction to the alpine environment of Mount San Jacinto State Park, take the short nature that begins at Mountain Station, then join Desert View Trail for a superb panorama of Palm Springs. After enjoying

Palms to pines, the easy way

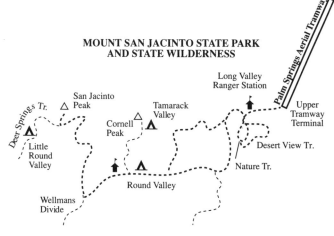

MOUNT SAN JACINTO STATE PARK
AND STATE WILDERNESS

the view of the arid lands below, you can extend your hike by looping through lush Round Valley.

Directions to trailhead: From Highway 111 at the northern outskirts of Palm Springs, turn southwest on Tramway Road and drive 3 1/2 miles to the tramway terminal.

The Hike: From Mountain Station, walk down the paved pathway to the signed beginning of the trail to Desert View. You join the Nature Trail for a short distance, cross the path used by the "mule ride," and soon get the first of a couple great desert views. The view takes in Palm Springs, Tahquitz and other palm-lined canyons of the Agua Caliente Indian Reservation, along with the basin and hills of the Coachella Valley.

Continue on Desert View Trail, which makes a full circle and junctions with the path back up to Mountain Station. For a longer hike, walk through the Long Valley Picnic Area to the state park ranger station. Obtain a wilderness permit here.

Continue west on the trail, following the signs to Round Valley. The trail parallels Long Valley Creek through a mixed forest of pine and white fir, then climbs into lodgepole pine country. Lupine, monkeyflower, scarlet bugler and Indian paintbrush are some of the wildflowers that add seasonal splashes of color.

After passing a junction with a trail leading toward Willow Creek, another 3/10 mile of hiking brings you to Round Valley. There's a trail camp and a backcountry ranger station in the valley, and splendid places to picnic in the meadow or among the lodgepole pines. The truly intrepid hiker will head for the summit of Mount San Jacinto, a 3 1/2 mile ascent from Round Valley.

An alternative to returning the same way is to retrace your steps 3/10 of a mile back to the junction with Willow Creek Trail, take this trail a mile through the pines to another signed junction, and follow the signed trail north back to Long Valley Ranger Station. This alternative adds only about 1/4 mile to your day hike and allows you to make a loop.

69

Spitler Peak Trail

Apple Canyon to Desert Divide
  10 miles round trip; 2,000-foot elevation gain
Apple Canyon to Apache Peak
  12 miles round trip; 2,600-foot elevation gain
Apple Canyon to Antsell Rock
  14 miles round trip; 2,600-foot elevation gain

Riding the Palm Springs Aerial Tramway or driving the Palms to Pines Highway are two ways to view the astonishing change in vegetation that occurs with a change in elevation in the San Jacinto Mountains. A third way to observe the startling contrast between desert and alpine environments is to hike up the back side of the San Jacinto Mountains to aptly named Desert Divide. The imposing granite divide, which reminds some mountaineers of the High Sierra, offers far-reaching views of the canyons back of Palm Springs and of the Coachella Valley.

Most visitors to the San Jacinto Mountains begin their explorations in Idyllwild or from the top of the tramway. Few hike—or even think about—Desert Divide. Too bad, because this land of pine forest, wide meadows and soaring granite peaks has much to offer.

The trail begins in Garner Valley, a long meadowland bordered by tall pine. Meandering across the valley floor is the South Fork of the San Jacinto River, whose waters are impounded at the lower end of the valley by Lake Hemet. Splashing spring color across the meadow are purple penstemon, golden yarrow, owl's clover and tidy tips. Autumn brings a showy "river" of rust-colored buckwheat winding through the valley.

Spitler Peak Trail offers a moderate-to-strenuous route up to Desert Divide. You can enjoy the great views from the divide and call it a day right there, or join Pacific Crest Trail and continue to the top of Apache Peak or Antsell Rock.

Directions to trailhead: The hamlet of Mountain Center is some 20 miles up Highway 74 from Hemet and a few miles up Highway 243 from Idyllwild. From the intersection of Highway 243 (Banning-Idyllwild Highway) and Highway 74 in Mountain Center, proceed southeast on the latter highway. After 3 miles, turn left at the signed junction for Hurkey Creek County Park. Instead of turning into the park, continue 1 3/4 mile on Apple Canyon Road to signed Spitler Peak Trail on the right. Park in the turnout just south of the trailhead.

The Hike: Spitler Peak Trail begins among oak woodland and chaparral. The mellow, well-graded path contours quite some distance to the east before beginning a more earnest northerly ascent. Enjoy over-the-shoulder views of Lake Hemet and of Garner Valley. Actually, geologists say Garner Valley is not a valley at all but a graben, a long narrow area that down-dropped between two bordering faults.

Garner Graben?

Nope, just doesn't have the right ring to it.

The trail climbs steadily into juniper-Jeffrey pine-Coulter pine-forest. Most of the time your path is under conifers or the occasional oak. There always seem to be quite a number of deadfalls to climb over, climb under or walk around along this stretch of trail.

About a mile from the divide, the going gets steeper and you rapidly gain elevation. Finally you gain the windblown divide just northwest of Spitler Peak and intersect signed Pacific Crest Trail. Enjoy the vistas of forest and desert. Picnic atop one of the divide's many rock outcroppings.

PCT, sometimes known as Desert Divide Trail in these parts, offers the energetic a range of options. PCT heads north and soon passes through a section of ghost forest—the charred result of the 1980 Palm Canyon Fire that roared up these slopes from Palm Springs. After a half-mile you'll pass a side trail that descends steeply another half-mile to Apache Springs. Another half-mile along the PCT brings you to a side trail leading up to bare 7,567-foot Apache Peak.

Another mile brings you to a point just below 7,720-foot Antsell Rock. Unless you're a very good rock-climber, stay off the unstable slopes and avoid the urge to ascend to the very top of the rock.

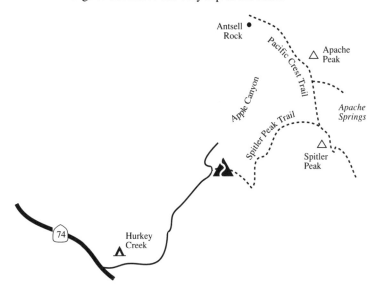

70

Ramona Trail

Highway 74 to Ramona Camp
    7 miles round trip; 1,400-foot elevation gain
Highway 74 to Thomas Mountain
    11 miles round trip; 2,100-foot elevation gain

For more than a century, the romantic novel *Ramona* has fascinated Southern Californians. Helen Hunt Jackson's 1884 saga of star-crossed Indian lovers and Spanish/Mission customs is the region's most enduring myth. Senora Moreno's Southern California rancho is the setting for the story which tells of the romance between half-Indian/half-Anglo Ramona Ortegna and her full-blooded Indian lover Alessandro. After Senora refuses Ramona permission to marry the Indian, the couple elopes, and is chased from place to place by evil, land-grabbing Americans. Poor shepherd Alessandro is killed, the rancho is sold to American capitalists and Ramona is left broken-hearted.

Ramona's name endures today on a town, an expressway, an amphitheater and many more locales, so it's not surprising to find a trail and a camp named for the beautiful Indian girl. Ramona Trail, in the San Jacinto Mountains, tours classic Ramona country—a pastoral valley opening up to the desert coupled with a dramatic backdrop of pine-covered mountains.

Ramona Trail climbs to a divide where Tool Box Spring offers water and Ramona Camp some welcome shade. Pack your copy of *Ramona* and read it under the pines.

Directions to trailhead: Drive to Mountain Center, some 20 miles up Highway 74 from Hemet, or a few miles from Idyllwild on Highway 243. From the junction of 243 and 74 proceed southeast on the latter highway 8 miles to the signed Ramona trailhead. Park in a safe manner along the highway.

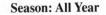

The Hike: Begin at a gate across a dirt road. Pass through the gate and walk along the dirt road a hundred yards or so to the unsigned Ramona Trail departing from the left side of the dirt road.

The well-engineered path switchbacks gently up hillside covered with sage, manzanita and red shank. The latter plant, also called ribbonwood for the way its bark peels off in long strips, is the dominant plant on the lower slopes of Thomas Mountain. Mileage posts stationed every half-mile mark your progress. Enjoy good views of Garner Valley and the Desert Divide area of the San Jacintos.

About 2 miles along, Ramona Trail enters a cool Jeffrey pine forest. Just over 3 miles from the trailhead, the trail joins a dirt road and almost immediately arrives at Tool Box Spring. Fill your canteen from the water spigot and continue on the dirt road 1/4 mile to Ramona Camp. Tables scattered amongst the pines suggest a picnic.

Ambitious hikers who wish to extend their walk will join Thomas Mountain Fire Road for the trip to Thomas Mountain. In 1861, the Charles Thomas family became the first Anglos to settle in this part of the San Jacinto Mountains.

While the dirt fire road offers pleasant, pine-shaded walking, it's open to vehicles. (Traffic is rare.) Follow the road 1 1/2 miles to a junction, then turn left another half-mile to the summit. The views of Ramona Country include a look down at Anza Valley.

*Ramona is remembered
with a pageant in Hemet
and a scenic trail*

Senator Alan Cranston admires Kelso Dunes

Chapter 12

EAST MOJAVE

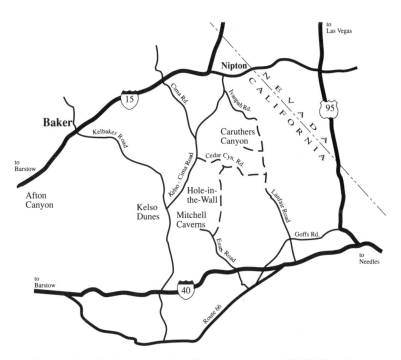

Bordered by I-15 to the north, I-40 to the south, and U.S. 95 on the east, the 1.5-million-acre "lonesome triangle" formed by the East Mojave National Scenic Area stretches from Barstow to Needles and the state line. But don't let its freeway boundaries fool you; beyond the highway lies a desert land that invites exploration.

From the cool, mysterious environs of Mitchell Caverns to the magnificent Joshua tree forest and the boulder-strewn Caruthers Canyon, the Scenic Area offers a diverse landscape that defies categorization.

The area is the first in the nation to recieve the designation "National Scenic Area." Currently managed by the U.S. Bureau of Land Management, the park has recently been considered as a cornerstone of the California Desert Protection Act, which would designate the area as a national park. Whatever its final bureaucratic label, it's a place for the hiker to discover mountains, sand dunes, volcanic formations and a rich historical record.

▲71
Afton Canyon Trail

Afton Campground to Pyramid Canyon
  3 miles round trip
Afton Campground to Side Canyons
  6 1/2 miles round trip

It's often called the Grand Canyon of the Mojave. High praise indeed, but then Afton Canyon is a very special place—a geological wonderland sculpted by the Mojave River.

The U.S. Bureau of Land Management is in the process of rehabilitating the canyon. Decades of off-road vehicle use tore up the ancient Mojave riverbed and gouged the surrounding hills. Overgrazing led to the invasion of such opportunistic plants as the tamarisk that suck up scarce water. BLM has re-routed off-road vehicles out of the canyon floor, eliminated grazing and begun to restore the native plant community.

Long ago, Afton Canyon was cut by outlet flow from a once-large body of water that geologists call Lake Manix. Some 15 to 75,000 years ago, during a cooler and much more humid climate, wildlife was abundant around the lake, which was shallow, but about 200 square miles in size. Turtles, shellfish, camels, antelope. It's almost surreal to imagine a flock of pink flamingos, each of them standing on one leg, looking over a landscape that more resembles the Great Inagua of the Bahamas than the Great American Desert.

The Mojave River, during these wetter time and climes, must have been a river of considerable size. Even in today's arid climate, the Mojave manages to flow either below ground or above for 145 miles across the desert.

The (relatively) well-watered Mojave River Valley has always served as a route of travel. During prehistoric times, Indians traveled the Mojave Trail from the California coast to the Colorado River. DeAnza's 1776 expedition passed through Afton Canyon on its way to Mission San Gabriel.

A half-century later, Jedediah Smith followed the Mojave and, after getting a bit exasperated with the river's habit of disappearing underground for long stretches, called it, most aptly, "The Inconstant River." Kit Carson took the river route, as did Charles Fremont, who gave the Mojave its name.

Today, the best view of Afton Canyon and the path of the Mojave River may belong to the crew of the Union Pacific freight train that rumbles through the canyon. An equally fine view is available to hikers. You can

Afton Canyon, a geological wonderland sculpted by the Mojave River

explore large Afton Canyon, and its many side canyons, including the largest of them, Pyramid Canyon.

Directions to trailhead: From Interstate 15, 32 miles east of Barstow, take the Afton Canyon exit. Travel 3 miles southwest on a good dirt road to Afton Campground. Park at the campground, being careful not to take campsite space.

The Hike: Before you follow the Mojave River through Afton Canyon, you might want to cross it from the campground, under the first set of railroad trestles, and head south through Pyramid Canyon. The largest and deepest of Afton's side canyons, 1 1/2-mile-long Pyramid Canyon is an easy stroll, and a good introduction to the fascinating geology of the Afton

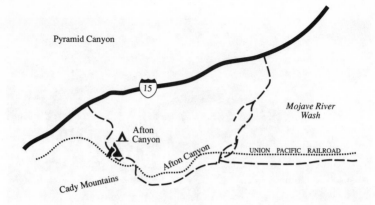

Canyon area. The grand rock walls, cut away by the once-mighty Mojave, gradually narrow until you reach what looks to be a dead end at the end of the canyon. Experienced hikers may want to scramble to the top of this "dead end" for a grand view of the surrounding desert landscape.

Return to Afton Canyon, and head upriver. You'll note a grand assemblage of desert riparian growth—native cottonwoods and willows, along with the invasive tamarisk. Among the wildlife that frequent Afton Canyon are a variety of birds, including raptors—particularly golden eagles and red-tailed hawks—and the desert bighorn sheep.

Continue hiking up-canyon on the north wall for breathtaking views of water-eroded formations, and to explore the many side canyons. These canyons are, for the most part, indicated by culverts; look for those located at numbers 192.99 and 194.65. A flashlight is useful for finding your way.

Beyond this point the canyon widens and holds less interest for the hiker. Afton Canyon extends a few more miles to a double trestle bridge near Cave Mountain. For a different perspective of the canyon, you might consider returning via the river bottom rather that than the north wall.

▲72

Kelso Dunes Trail

BLM Parking Area to top of Dunes
3 miles round trip; 400-foot elevation gain

In the heart of the heart of the East Mojave lie the Kelso Dunes, one of the tallest dune systems in America.

"They're grand, magnificent," proclaimed Senator Alan Cranston, while on a recent excursion to the Kelso Dunes. If Congress approves Cranston's proposed California Desert Protection Act, the dunes, as well as 1.5 million acres of the East Mojave now under U.S. Bureau of Land Management administration, would become Mojave National Park.

"And the dunes give off great vibrations," added Cranston as he hiked along the Kelso Dunes Trail. The good vibrations that so enthused California's senior senator are not the desert's spiritual emanations—which many visitors find considerable—but to the Kelso Dunes' rare ability to make a low rumbling sound when sand slides down the steep slopes. This sound has been variously described as that of a kettle drum, low-flying airplane or Tibetan gong.

The dunes are one of the many wonders the traveler encounters in the East Mojave, which is actually a mixture of three deserts: the low or Colorado Desert, the high or Mojave Desert, and the Great Basin. This convergence of ecosystems is bounded by Interstate 40, Interstate 15 and the Nevada state line. Sometimes referred to as the "lonesome triangle," this land is a microcosm of the whole 25-million-acre California desert.

Directions to trailhead: From Interstate 15 in Baker, some 60 miles northeast of Barstow, turn south on Kelbaker Road and proceed about 35 miles to the town of Kelso. Pause to admire the classic neo-Spanish-style Kelso Railroad Depot next to the Union Pacific tracks.

From Kelso, continue on Kelbaker Road for another 7 miles to a signed dirt road and turn west (right). Drive slowly along this road (navigable for all but very low-slung passenger cars), 3 miles to a Bureau of Land Management parking area. The trail to Kelso Dunes begins just up the dirt road from the parking area.

The Hike: Only the first quarter-mile or so of the walk to the dunes is on established trail. Once the trail peters out, angle toward the low saddle atop the dunes, just to the right of the highest point. The old saying, "One step forward, two steps back," will take on new meaning if you attempt to take the most direct route to the top of the dunes by walking straight up the tallest sand hill.

As you cross the lower dunes, you'll pass some mesquite and creosote bushes. During spring of a good wildflower year, the lower dunes are bedecked with yellow and white desert primrose, pink sand verbena and yellow sunflowers.

The sand that forms Kelso Dunes blows in from the Mojave River basin. After traveling east 35 miles across a stark plain known as the Devil's Playground, it's deposited in hills nearly 600 feet high. The westerlies carrying the sand rush headlong into winds from other directions, which is why the sand is dropped here, and why it stays here.

For further confirmation of the circular pattern of winds that formed the dunes, examine the bunches of grass on the lower slopes. You'll notice that the tips of the tall grasses have etched 360-degree circles on the sand.

Other patterns on the sand are made by the desert's abundant, but rarely seen, wildlife. You might see the tracks of a coyote, kit fox, antelope ground squirrel, pack rat, raven or sidewinder. Footprints of lizards and mice can be seen tacking this way and that over the sand. The dune's surface records the lightest pressure of the smallest feet. Sometimes one set of animal tracks intersect another in a way suggesting the demise of one animal and dinner for another.

When you reach the saddle located to the right of the high point, turn left and trek another hundred yards or so to the top. The black material crowning the top of the dunes is magnetite, an iron oxide, and one of about two dozen minerals found within the dune system.

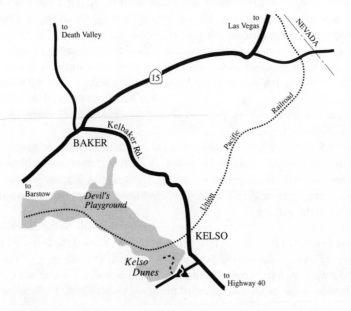

Enjoy the view from the top: the Kelso Mountains to the north, the Bristol Mountains to the southwest, the Granite Mountains to the south, the Providence Mountains to the east. Everywhere you look there are mountain ranges, small and large.

In fact, despite evidence to the contrary—most notably the stunning dunes beneath your feet—the East Mojave is really a desert of mountains, not sand.

While atop the dunes, perhaps your footsteps will cause mini-avalanches and the dunes will sha-boom-sha-boom for you. There's speculation that the extreme dryness of the East Mojave, combined with the wind-polished, rounded nature of the individual sand grains, has something to do with their musical ability. After picking up good vibrations, descend the steep dune face (much easier on the way down!) and return to the trailhead.

Hiking the dunes — two steps forward, one step back

73

Mitchell Caverns Trail

1 1/2 miles round trip
Mary Beal Nature Trail
    1/2 mile round trip
Crystal Springs Trail
    2 miles round trip

Here's a trail trivia question for you to ponder: Where in Southern California can you explore some stunning scenery, be assured that it won't rain, and know that the temperature for your hike will always be a comfortable 65 degrees?

Hint: One of the overlooked gems of the California State Park system.

If you're in the dark, then you're on the right path—the trail through Mitchell Caverns State Reserve, part of Providence Mountains State Recreation Area. Ranger-led walks through the dramatic limestone caves offer a fascinating geology lesson, one the whole family can enjoy.

In 1932, Jack Mitchell abandoned his Depression-shattered business in Los Angeles and moved to the desert. For a time he prospected for silver, but his real fascination was with what he called the "Providence" or "Crystal Caves" and their potential as a tourist attraction. He constructed several stone buildings to use for lodging. (Today's park visitors center is

The Providence Mountains

one of these buildings.) Mitchell and his wife, Ida, provided food and lodging for visitors, and guided them on tours of the caverns until 1954. By all accounts, Jack Mitchell was quite a yarn-spinner. Southern California old-timers still remember his tall tales of ghosts, lost treasure and bottomless pits.

Now that the caverns are part of the State Park system, rangers lead the tours. They're an enthusiastic lot and quite informative. Visitors walk through the two main caves, which Mitchell named El Pakiva (The Devil's House) and Tecopa (after a Shoshonean chieftain). You'll get a close-up view of stalactites and stalagmites, cave ribbon, cave spaghetti and flowstone. And you'll learn about some of the caverns' former inhabitants—the Chemehuevi Indians and a Pleistocene ground sloth that stumbled into the darkness some 15,000 years ago.

During Jack Mitchell's day, visitors had to be nimble rockclimbers, and wait for their tour leader to toss flares into the darkness. Nowadays, the caverns have been equipped with stairs and special lighting.

Guided tours are conducted once daily Monday through Friday, and three times daily on weekends September through June. There is an admission fee. A tour takes 1 1/2 to 2 hours depending on your group's enthusiasm and collective curiosity.

Directions to trailhead: From Interstate Highway 40, about eighty miles east of Barstow, exit on Essex Road and drive 16 miles to road's end at the Providence Mountains State Recreation Area parking lot. Sign up at the Visitors Center for tours.

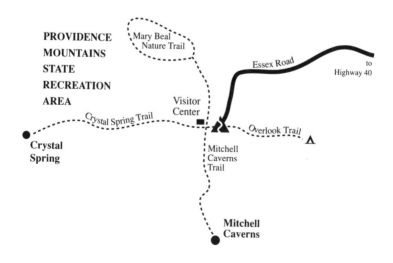

The drive to the caverns is lengthy, so you might want to consider taking a whole weekend—or more—to visit this part of the desert. There's plenty to see! The park is surrounded by the U.S. Bureau of Land Management's East Mojave Scenic Area, an awesome land of dunes, badlands and Joshua tree forests.

Because you can only tour the caverns with a park ranger and because you wouldn't want me to spoil the many surprises of the cave walk with a step-by-step description, I won't further detail the Mitchell Caverns Trail.

Ranger John Kelso-Shelton explains the mysteries of Mitchell Caverns

However, after exploring "the great indoors" allow some time to explore the park's outdoors pathways.

Pick up an interpretive booklet from the park visitors center and walk the half-mile long Mary Beal Nature Trail, which offers a great introduction to high desert flora. Cliff rose and blue sage share the hillsides with cholla, catsclaw and creosote.

The trail honors Mary Beal, a Riverside librarian who at the turn of the century, was "exiled" to the desert by her doctor for health reasons. For a half-century this remarkable woman wandered through the Providence Mountains and other remote Mojave Desert locales in order to gather and classify hundreds of varieties of plants and wildflowers. The trail was dedicated in 1952 on Beal's 75th birthday.

The short Overlook Trail leads from the park's tiny campground to a viewpoint, which offers vistas of Clipper Valley, the Marble Mountains, and hundreds of square miles of basin and range.

The one-mile long Crystal Springs Trail leads into the pinyon pine and juniper-dotted Providence Mountains by way of Crystal Canyon. Bighorn sheep often travel through this canyon.

74

Hole-in-the-Wall Trail

Hole-in-the-Wall Campground to Banshee Canyon
3/4-mile round trip
Hole-in-the-Wall Campground to Wildhorse Canyon
5 miles round trip; 400-foot gain

Hole-in-the Wall is the kind of place Butch Cassidy and the Sundance Kid might have chosen as their hideout. The famous outlaws of a century ago gave the sheriff the slip in Utah's Hole-in-the-Wall, but California's red-rock country of the same name would also have aided the outlaws' escape.

The Hole-in-the-Wall region of the East Mojave Desert is a great place to take friends and family to hide out from the stresses of urban life. The tranquil locale is an ideal site for camping, hiking, and bird-watching. Hole-in-the-Wall, now under the administration of the Bureau of Land Management, is one of the centerpieces of the East Mojave National Scenic Area.

Hole-in-the-Wall is a twisted maze of red rock. Geologists call this rhyolite, a kind of lava that existed as hot liquid far below the earth's surface, then crystallized.

A word of caution about the descent into Banshee Campground from Hole-in-the-Wall Campground: One must negotiate two sets of iron rings that have been affixed to the rocks. Descending with these rings is not particularly difficult for those who are reasonably agile and take their time. Acrophobes or claustrophobes may want to pass on this trail or join the hike in Wildhorse Canyon.

Directions to trailhead: From Interstate 40, approximately 42 miles west of Needles and nearly 100 miles east of Barstow, exit on Essex Road. Head north 9 1/2 miles to the junction of Essex Road and Black Canyon Road. Bear right on the latter road, which soon turns to dirt. (Well-graded Black Canyon Road is suitable for passenger cars.) After 8 1/2 miles of travel you'll spot Hole-in-the-Wall Campground on your left. Turn into the campground and park at the lip of Banshee Canyon on the upper loop of the camp road. The unsigned trail plunges right into the canyon.

If it's desert information you're after, stop by the California Desert Information Center located at 831 Barstow Road in Barstow. Take the Central Barstow exit.

The Hike: From the trailhead, enjoy the view of the wide Clipper Valley, the Providence Mountains to the west, and Wildhorse Canyon and Wildhorse Mesa.

Begin your descent by squeezing through the tight jumble of volcanic rock formation. Soon you'll encounter the two sets of iron rings that aid your descent. Remember the old climber's adage: Secure three limbs and move the fourth.

Past the rings, a few minutes of travel brings you to the mouth of Banshee Canyon. Look behind you at the rose-colored rock which forms a classic desert box canyon. You probably won't spot any banshees, those shrieking little elves that pop up in the Scottish Highlands, but you'll likely observe a multitude of lizards and jackrabbits. The keen-eyed may spot a golden eagle soaring overhead.

At the mouth of the canyon you'll bear left on a faint dirt road that follows a shallow wash that spreads south. The track becomes more distinct as it approaches Wildhorse Canyon Road. Trailside flora includes creosote, cholla and prickly pear cactus.

The path intersects Wildhorse Canyon Road at a cattleguard. Bear right and walk 4/10 mile on the infrequently traveled dirt road to a small parking area bordered by rocks on the north side of the road. Here you'll find the unsigned path that leads toward Wildhorse Canyon.

For a mile the trail heads north on a straight-line course, dodging cholla and yucca. The wild horses that gave the canyon its name are not in evidence, but you may encounter some horses that belong to nearby ranchers. One little filly is particularly sociable, and if you offer her the apple you have in your day pack, you'll make a fast friend, one who may just decide to tag along for the rest of the hike.

The trail climbs gently onto a low mesa that offers good views of Wildhorse Canyon to your left and some handsome rock formations on your right. The rock wears a brown/black cap of iron and manganese known as desert varnish. Like a new coat of paint on a very old house, desert varnish, perhaps only a few thousand years old, can cover rocks and ridges that are hundreds of millions of years old.

The path is a bit indistinct as it nears the pass, but the pass itself is quite obvious and you should have no trouble reaching it. From atop the pass, enjoy the view of basin and range, mountains and mesas.

Unpack your lunch at the top of the pass or descend northward to a juniper-filled canyon. The juniper is among the most drought-resistant of our cone-bearing trees and here, sheltered from the full force of the desert sun, it not only survives, but flourishes.

Return the same way or if you wish, after you retrace your steps to Wildhorse Canyon Road, you can follow this dirt road to Black Canyon Road, where a left turn brings you back to Hole-in-the-Wall Campground.

Rings help hikers reach Hole-in-the-Wall

75

Caruthers Canyon Trail

Caruthers Canyon to Gold Mine
3 miles round trip; 400-foot elevation gain

Botanists call them disjuncts. Bureaucrats call them UPAs (Unusual Plant Assemblages). The more lyrical naturalists among us call them islands on the land.

By whatever name, the isolated communities of pinyon pine and white fir in the New York Mountains of the East Mojave Desert are very special places. Nearly three hundred plant species have been counted on the slopes of this range and in its colorfully named canyons—Cottonwood and Caruthers, Butcher Knife and Fourth of July.

Perhaps the most botanically unique area in the mountains, indeed in the whole 1.5-million-acre East Mojave National Scenic Area, is Caruthers Canyon. A cool, inviting pinyon pine-juniper woodland stands in marked contrast to the sparsely vegetated sandscape common in other parts of the desert. The conifers are joined by oaks and a variety of coastal chaparral plants including manzanita, yerba santa, ceanothus and coffee berry.

What is a coastal ecosystem doing in the middle of the desert?

Botanists believe that during wetter times, such coastal scrub vegetation was quite widespread. As the climate became more arid, coastal ecosystems were "stranded" atop high and moist slopes. The botanical islands high in the New York Mountains are outposts of Rocky Mountains and coastal California flora.

Caruthers Canyon is a treat for the hiker. An abandoned dirt road leads through a rocky basin and into a historic gold mining region. Prospectors began digging in the New York Mountains in the 1860s and continued well into the 20th Century. At trail's-end are a a couple of gold mine shafts.

The canyon's woodland offers great bird-watching. The western tanager, gray-headed junco, yellow-breasted chat and many more species are found here. Circling high in the sky are the raptors—golden eagles, prairie falcons and red-tailed hawks.

Directions to trailhead: From I-40, 28 miles west of Needles and some 117 miles east of Barstow, exit on Mountain Springs Road. You'll pass the tiny town of Goffs (last chance for provisions) and head north 27 1/2 miles on the main road, known variously as Ivanpah-Goffs Road or Ivanpah Road, to New York Mountains Road. (Part of Ivanpah Road and New York Mountains Road are dirt; they are suitable for passenger cars with good ground clearance.) Turn left, west, on New York Mountains Road. A couple OX Cattle Ranch buildings stand near this road's intersection with Ivanpah Road. Drive 5 1/2 miles to an unsigned junction with a dirt road and turn north. Proceed 2 miles to a woodland laced with turnouts that serve as unofficial campsites. Leave your car here; farther along the road dips into a wash and gets very rough.

The Hike: From the Caruthers Canyon "Campground" follow the main dirt road up the canyon. As you ascend, look behind you for a great view of Table Mountain, the most dominant peak of the central East Mojave.

Handsome boulders line the trail and frame views of the tall peak before you, New York Mountain. The range's 7,532-foot signature peak is crowned with a botanical island of its own—a relict stand of Rocky Mountain white fir.

A half-mile along, you'll come to a fork in the road. The rightward road climbs a quarter-mile to an old mining shack. Take the left fork, dipping in and out of a wash and gaining a great view of the canyon and its castellated walls.

If it's rained recently, you might find some water collected in pools on the rocky canyon bottom. Enjoy the tranquility of the gold mine area, but don't stray into the dark and dangerous shafts.

Chapter 15

PALM SPRINGS

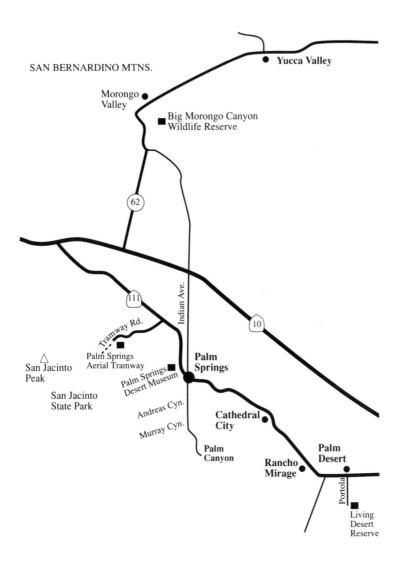

SAN BERNARDINO MTNS.

Yucca Valley

Morongo Valley

Big Morongo Canyon
Wildlife Reserve

62

Indian Ave.

111

Tramway Rd.

10

San Jacinto
Peak

Palm Springs
Aerial Tramway

Palm Springs
Desert Museum

Palm
Springs

San Jacinto
State Park

Andreas Cyn.

Murray Cyn.

Cathedral
City

Palm
Canyon

Rancho
Mirage

Palm
Desert

Portola

Living
Desert
Reserve

Big Morongo Canyon Trail

Parking Lot to Waterfall
    2 1/2 miles round trip
Parking Lot to Canyon Mouth
    12 miles round trip; 1,900-foot elevation gain

We Southern Californians are fortunate to have two deserts—the Mojave and the Colorado—at our feet. Big Morongo Canyon, tucked in the Little San Bernardino Mountains on the San Bernardino/Riverside County line, bridges these two desert worlds and offers the hiker a chance to explore one of the state's largest natural oases. Big Morongo Canyon is managed and protected by the Nature Conservancy and the U.S. Bureau of Land Management.

The relative abundance of water is the key to both Big Morongo's long human history and its botanical uniqueness. Several springs bubble up in the reserve, and one of the California desert's very few year-round creeks flows through the canyon. Dense thickets of cottonwood and willow, as well as numerous water-loving shrubs line Big Morongo Creek. This lush, crowded riparian vegetation sharply contrasts with the well-spaced creosote community typical of the high and dry slopes of the reserve and of the open desert beyond.

Big Morongo Canyon is best-known for its wide variety of birds, which are numerous because the canyon is not only at the intersection of two deserts, but also at the merging of two climate zones—arid and coastal. These climates, coupled with the wet world of the oasis, means the preserve is an attractive stopover for birds on their spring and fall migrations.

More than two hundred bird species have been sighted, including the rare vermilion flycatcher and the least Bell's vireo. Commonly seen all-year residents include starlings, house finches and varieties of quail and hummingbirds.

For the hiker, the preserve offers several short loop-trails ranging from a quarter- to one-mile-long. Some of the wetter canyon bottom sections of trail are crossed by wooden boardwalks, which keep hikers dry, and fragile creekside flora from being trampled. Desert Wash, Cottonwood, Willow, Yucca Ridge and Mesquite Trails explore the environments suggested by their names.

A longer path, Canyon Trail, travels the 6-mile length of Big Morongo Canyon. You could make this a one-way, all downhill journey by arranging a car shuttle, or by having someone pick you up on Indian Avenue.

Directions to trailhead: From Interstate 10, 15 miles east of Banning and a bit past the Highway 111 turnoff to Palm Springs, exit on Highway 62. Drive 10 miles north to the signed turnoff on your right for Big Morongo Wildlife Preserve. Turn east, and after 1/10 mile you'll see the Preserve's service road leading to a parking area.

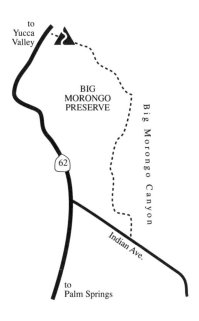

To reach the end of the trail at the mouth of Big Morongo Canyon, you'll exit on Highway 62 on Indian Avenue and drive exactly a mile to a dirt road on your left. A "Dip" sign precedes the turnoff and a pump enclosed by a chain link fence suggests your parking space.

The Hike: From the parking lot, you may pick up the trail by the Preserve's interpretive displays or join the dirt road that leads past the caretaker's residence. Pick up a copy of the Big Morongo Bird List from a roadside dispenser.

Off to the right of the old ranch road, you'll see a pasture lined with cottonwood and a barn built in the 1880s. Often the road is muddy, so detour with the signed and aptly-named Mesquite Trail which utilizes a wooden boardwalk to get over the wet spots. As you stand on the boardwalk in the midst of Big Morongo Creek, take a moment to listen to the sound of running water, the many chirping birds and croaking frogs.

Canyon Trail meanders with the creek for a gentle mile or so, and arrives at a corrugated metal check dam that has created a small waterfall. For the less-energetic, this is a good turnaround point.

The trail continues descending through the canyon with Big Morongo Creek until a bit more than three miles from the trailhead, when the creek suddenly disappears. Actually, the water continues flowing underground through layers of sand.

The canyon widens and so does the trail. About 5 miles from the trailhead is the south gate of the Preserve. The canyon mouth, and every inanimate object in the vicinity has been shot to hell by off-the-mark marksmen. Compensating for Big Morongo's somewhat inglorious end is a stirring view of snow-capped Mount San Jacinto, which lies straight ahead. Stick to your right at every opportunity as you exit the canyon and a dirt road will soon deliver you to Indian Avenue.

Lykken Trail

Palm Springs Desert Museum to Desert Riders Overlook
   2 miles round trip; 800-foot elevation gain
Palm Springs Desert Museum to Ramon Drive
   4 miles round trip; 800-foot elevation gain

Palm Springs today is a curious sight—a chain of sparkling green islands on the desert sand. For a good overview of the resort hikers can join Museum and Lykken Trails.

This hike in the hills begins at Palm Springs Desert Museum, where natural science exhibits recreate the unique ecology of Palm Springs and the surrounding Colorado Desert. Displays interpret the astonishing variety of plant and animal life as well as the powerful geological forces that shaped this desert land. The museum also has exhibits portraying the original inhabitants of the Coachella Valley, who managed to live in what seems to be a harsh and unforgiving land.

Steep Museum Trail ascends the western base of Mount San Jacinto. Letters painted on the rocks suggest that Museum was once a nature trail. After a mile's climb, Museum Trail junctions with Lykken Trail. This trail, formerly known as Skyline Trail, winds through the Palm Springs hills north to Tramway Road and south to Ramon Road.

Skyline Trail was renamed Lykken Trail in 1972 in honor of Carl Lykken, Palm Springs pioneer and the town's first postmaster. Lykken, who arrived in 1913, owned a general merchandise store, and later a

Desert Riders Overlook

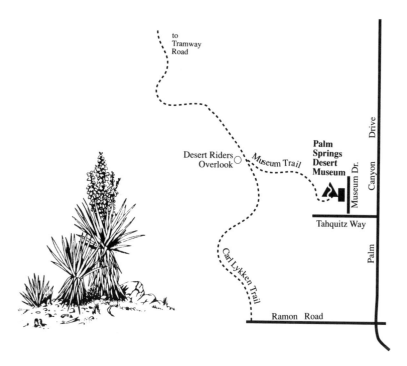

department/hardware store. Early Palm Springs social life consisted of stopping at the Desert Inn to check if any new and interesting guests had arrived, then dropping by Carl Lykken's store to pick up the mail, make a phone call (Lykken had the first telephone) and catch up on all the gossip.

Directions to trailhead: From Highway 111 (Palm Canyon Drive) in the middle of downtown Palm Springs, turn west on Tahquitz Drive, then a right on Museum Drive. Park in Palm Springs Desert Museum's north lot.

The trail begins back of the museum, between the museum and an administration building, by a plaque honoring Carl Lykken. The trail is closed during the hot summer months for health reasons (yours).

The Hike: The trail ascends the rocky slope above the museum. Soon you'll intersect a private road, jog left, then resume trail walking up the mountainside. As you rapidly gain elevation, the view widens from the Desert Fashion Plaza to the outskirts of Palm Springs to the wide-open spaces of the Coachella Valley.

A mile's ascent brings you to a picnic area, built by the Desert Riders, local equestrians whose membership included Carl Lykken. One Desert Rider, former Palm Springs Mayor Frank Bogert, is a real trail enthusiast whose efforts have contributed much to the state's trail system.

Bear left (south) on Lykken Trail, which travels the hills above town before descending to Ramon Road near the mouth of Tahquitz Canyon. You can follow Ramon Road to downtown Palm Springs or return the way you came.

78

Palm Canyon Trail

Hermit's Bench to turnaround
4 miles round trip; 200-foot elevation gain

"During the last few years much has been written in newspapers and magazine articles about Palm Canyon. Briefly stated, its charm consists in the startling combination of rocky gorges and canyons, essentially savage and desert-like, with the arboreal grace of tall, tropic-seeming palms growing in native loveliness beside a snow-fed, gushing stream. If the effect of the whole were to be summed up in one word, I think the word would be, not grandeur, nor even beauty, but strangeness to a notable degree."

—Joseph Smeaton Chase, 1922
*Our Araby: Palm Springs
and the Garden of the Sun*

Long-forgotten trail rider/nature writer Joseph Smeaton Chase wrote the book on Palm Springs — *Our Araby*, a delightful account about the early days of the then-remote oasis.

Chase, who died in 1922, lived the last few years of his life in Palm Springs. He championed the creation of Palm Canyon National Monument, in order to preserve the canyons located on the outskirts of Palm Springs, known collectively as the Indian Canyons—Palm, Murray, and Andreas.

The palm canyons never did achieve National Park Service protection, and today their sanctity is threatened by a developer, who wishes to build a golf course and resort in the lower reaches of the canyons. The canyons would, however, receive some federal protection if Congress approves the California Desert Conservation bill.

The hills and canyons bordering Palm Springs have the greatest concentration of palm trees in the United States, and in number of trees, Palm Canyon is the uncrowned king of America's desert oases. A meandering stream and lush undergrowth complement more than three thousand palms, creating a jungle-like atmosphere in some places.

Palm fans will enjoy viewing the largest concentration of California fan palms, located on the Aqua Caliente Indian Reservation. *Washingtonia filifera*, the palm's botanical name honors our first president, who is more commonly associated with chopping down cherry trees. President's Day—or any other clear winter day—is a fine time to visit the palms, some of them estimated to be 2,000 years old.

Directions to trailhead: From Interstate 10, exit on Highway 111 and proceed to downtown Palm Springs. Highway 111 is also known as Palm Canyon Drive.

Anyone with an interest in the early days of Palm Springs should stop at Village Green Heritage Center, located at 221 S. Palm Canyon Drive. The McCallum Adobe houses a museum operated by the Palm Springs Historical Society. Next door, Cornelia White's house (Cornelia was Joseph Smeaton Chase's sister-in-law) offers a glimpse into the lives of the three intrepid White sisters, hearty Palm Springs pioneers.

Continue through town on Palm Canyon Drive. At a fork, Highway 111 veers east and becomes known as East Palm Canyon Drive. You head straight ahead (south) on South Palm Canyon Drive, following the signs to "Indian Canyons." You'll reach the Aqua Caliente Indians tollgate, where you must pay a fee to enter tribal lands. The reservation is open daily 8:30 a.m. to 5:00 p.m. Parking is a short distance beyond the tollgate at the head of Palm Canyon at Hermit's Bench, where there is a trading post and a good view north into Palm Springs. Many signs remind visitors that they must be off the reservation before 5:00 p.m.

The Hike: From the trading post, the trail descends into the canyon.

Some of the palms stand 60 feet tall, with three-foot trunk diameters. In 1980, a fire burned some of the palms just below Hermit's Bench. The trees lived, but today their trunks are black and their skirts short.

The trail follows the canyon for two miles to a tiny grotto that is an ideal turnaround point.

Hearty adventurers will relish the challenge of proceeding up Palm Canyon seven more miles, gaining 3,000 feet, to a junction with Highway 74, the Palms-to-Pines Highway. Note: This strenuous hike is best done by beginning at the Highway 74 trailhead, hiking down Palm Canyon, and convincing a friend to pick you up at Hermit's Bench.

79

Season: October - June

Murray Canyon Trail

Andreas Canyon to Murray Canyon
2 miles round trip; 200-foot elevation gain

"The canyon is notable for a fine rank of "palisade" cliffs,
which with their massive sculpturing and dark Egyptian
hue make a wonderful foil for the beauty of the palms."

—Andreas Canyon, as described by
nature writer Joseph Smeaton Chase
California Desert Trails, 1919

In the foothills above Palm Springs are two lovely palm-lined canyons—Andreas and Murray. Both have hundreds of palms, crystalline streams and dramatic rock walls. Andreas, with about 700 native California fan palms and Murray with about 1,000 palms, are among the most populous palm groves in the state. Both canyons are tributaries of nearby Palm Canyon, undisputed king of California's palm oases.

Both canyons honor Palm Springs pioneers. Andreas is named after a Cahuilla Indian chieftan of the late 1800s. Irascible Scotsman and dedicated botanist Dr. Welwood Murray built a hotel/health resort in the very early days of Palm Springs. Many of those making their way to the Murray Hotel came for the curative climate and the rejuvenation of their health, but a number of literary figures also visited and these scribes soon spread the word that Palm Springs was a very special place indeed.

Andreas Canyon was once a summer retreat for the Agua Caliente band of the Cahuilla. The Indians spent the winter months in the warm Coachella Valley then sought the relative coolness of Andreas and other palm canyons during the warmer months.

Unlike most palm oases, which are fed by underground springs or sluggish seeps, Andreas is watered by a running stream. Fortunately for the palms and other canyon life, white settlers were legally prevented from diverting this stream to the emerging village of Palm Springs. Ranchers and townspeople had to turn to the larger, but notoriously undependable Whitewater River.

Meandering through the tall *Washingtonias*, hikers can travel a ways upstream through Andreas Canyon. Adding to the lush scene are alders and willows, cottonwoods and sycamores.

The trail between Andreas Canyon and Murray Canyon is only a mile long, but you can travel a few more miles up the canyons themselves.

Directions to trailhead: From the junction of State Highway 111 and South Palm Canyon Drive in Palm Springs, proceed south on the latter road for 1 1/2 miles, bearing right at a signed fork. After another mile you'll reach the Agua Caliente Indians Reservation tollgate; there is an entrance fee. Just after the tollgate, bear right at a signed fork and travel 3/4 mile to Andreas Canyon picnic ground. The trail begins at the east end of the splendid picnic area. A sign suggests that Murray Canyon is "20 min" away.

The Hike: (See Trail 78 map.) Notice the soaring, reddish-brown rocks near the trailhead. At the base of these rocks are grinding holes once used by the Cahuilla.

The trail runs south along the base of the mountains. A dramatic backdrop to the path is the desert-facing side of the San Jacinto Mountains.

It's an easy walk, occasionally following a dry streambed. Here, away from water, you encounter more typical desert flora: cholla, hedgehog cacti, burrobush.

When you reach Murray Canyon, you can follow the palms and stream quite a ways up-canyon. Joining the palms are willows, cottonwoods, mesquite, arrowweed and desert lavender. Mistletoe is sometimes draped atop the mesquite and it seems to attract a number of birds.

As you take the trail back to Andreas Canyon you can't help noticing the luxury housing and resort life reaching toward the palm canyons. And you can't help being thankful that these tranquil palm oases are still ours to enjoy.

Califonia fan palms gave Palm Springs its name

80

Jaeger Nature Trail

**2-mile loop through Living Desert Reserve
Return via Eisenhower Trail, Eisenhower Mountain
5 miles round trip; 500-foot elevation gain**

A superb introduction to desert plant life and wildlife, the Living Desert Reserve is a combination zoo, botanic garden and hiking area. The 1,200-acre, nonprofit facility is dedicated to conservation, education and research.

The Reserve's gardens represent major desert regions including California's Mojave, Arizona's Sonoran and Mexico's Chihuahuan. Wildlife-watchers will enjoy observing coyotes in their burrows and bighorn sheep atop their mountain peak. The Reserve also has a walk-through aviary and a pond inhabited by the rare desert pupfish.

Nature and hiking trails provide an opportunity to form an even closer acquaintance with an uncrowded, undeveloped sandscape. Easy trails lead past the Arabian oryx and bighorn sheep, past desert flora with name tags and eco-systems with interpretive displays, and over to areas that resemble the open desert of yester-year.

Presidents Eisenhower, Nixon, Ford and Reagan relaxed in Palm Springs. Eisenhower spent many winters at the El Dorado Country Club at the base of the mountain that now bears his name. Palm Desert boosters petitioned the Federal Board of Geographic Names to name the 1,952 (coincidentally, 1952 was the year of his election)-foot peak for part-time Palm Springs resident Dwight D. Eisenhower.

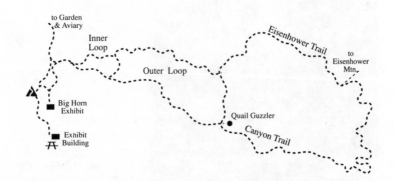

The first part of the walk through the Living Desert Reserve uses a nature trail named after the great desert naturalist Edmund Jaeger. It's keyed to a booklet available from the entrance station. An inner loop of 2/3 mile and an outer loop of 1 1/2 miles lead past a wide array of desert flora and 60 interpretive stops. A longer loop can be made using Canyon Trail and Eisenhower Trail. The hike to Ike's peak ascends about halfway up the bald mountain and offers great views of the Coachella Valley.

Directions to trailhead: From Highway 111 in Palm Desert, turn south on Portola Avenue and drive 1 1/2 miles south to the park. The park is closed mid-June to the end of August. There is an admission fee.

The Hike: The trail begins from the Reserve's exhibit buildings. Follow either the numbered nature trail, beginning at number one, or make a short rightward detour to the bighorn sheep enclosure. The trail junctions once more and you begin heading up the alluvial plain of Deep Canyon. Walking up the wash, you'll observe the many moisture-loving plants that thrive in such environments, including smoke trees, desert willows and palo verde. Stay right at the next junction and begin the outer loop of the Jaeger Nature Trail. You'll pass plenty of that common desert dweller, the creosote bush, and wind along the base of some sand dunes.

The trail climbs out of the wash and into a kind of plain that true desert rats call a "bajada." Here you'll find a quail guzzler which stores rainwater to aid California's state bird in the hot summer months. And here you'll find a junction with Canyon Trail (the south loop of the Eisenhower Trail).

Canyon Trail heads up the bajada. After climbing through a little canyon, the trail winds up the south slope of Eisenhower Mountain to a picnic area and a plaque describing the region's date industry. From the picnic area, you'll descend Eisenhower Mountain, getting good views of the mountains and the Coachella Valley. After passing the signed Eisenhower trailhead, you'll reach the north loop of the Nature Trail and begin heading west down the brittlebush-dotted floodplain back to the exhibit buildings and the central part of the Reserve.

Information Sources:

Angeles National Forest
Headquarters:
701 N. Santa Anita Ave.
Arcadia, CA 91006
(818) 574-5200
Chilao Visitors Center:
Star Route, La Canada 91111
(818) 796-5541
Arroyo Seco Ranger District:
Oak Grove Park
Flintridge, CA 91011
(818) 790-1151

Avalon Visitors Center
423 Crescent Ave.
Avalon, CA 90704
(800) 428-2566

Big Morongo Preserve
P.O. Box 780
Morongo Valley, CA 92256
(619) 363-7190

Bonelli County Park
120 Via Verde
San Dimas, CA 91773
(714) 8411

Carbon Canyon Regional Park
4422 Carbon Canyon Road
Brea, CA 92621
(714) 996-5252

Caspers Wilderness Park
33401 Ortega Highway
San Juan Capistrano, CA 92675
(714) 728-0235

Conejo Parks and Recreation
401 W. Hillcrest Drive
Thousand Oaks, CA 93160
(805) 495-6471

Crystal Cove State Park
c/o Orange Coast District
18331 Enterprise Lane
Huntington Beach, CA 92648
(714) 494-3539

Desert Information Center
831 Barstow Road
Barstow, CA 92311
(619) 256-8617

East Mojave National Scenic Area
U.S. Bureau of Land Management
Needles Resource Area
101 West Spike's Road
P.O. Box 888
Needles, CA 92363
(619) 326-3896

Eaton Canyon Nature Center
1750 N. Altadena Drive
Pasadena, CA 91107
(818) 794-1866

El Dorado Park Nature Center
7550 E. Spring Street
Long Beach, CA 90815
(213) 421-9431 ext. 3415

Griffith Park
3401 Riverside Drive
Los Angeles, CA 90039
(213) 665-5188

Living Desert Reserve
47900 Portola Avenue
Palm Desert, CA 92260
(619) 346-5694

Los Padres National Forest
6144 Calle Real
Goleta, CA 93117
(805) 683-6711
Ojai District Office:
1190 E. Ojai Avenue
Ojai, CA 93023
(805) 646-4348

McGrath State Beach
c/o Channel Coast District
24 E. Main Street
Ventura, CA 93001
(805) 483-8034/654-4611

Mount San Jacinto State Park
25905 Highway 243
P.O. Box 308
Idyllwild, CA 92349
(714) 659-2607

O'Neill Regional Park
30892 Trabuco Canyon Road
Trabuco Canyon, CA 92678
(714) 858-9366

Palm Springs Desert Museum
(619) 325-7186

Providence Mountains State
Recreation Area
P.O. Box 1
Essex, CA 92332

San Bernardino National Forest
Big Bear District:
P.O. Box 290
Fawnskin, CA 92333
(714) 866-3437
San Gorgonio District:
34701 Mill Creek Road
Mentone, CA 92359
(714) 794-1123
San Jacinto District:
P.O. Box 518
Idyllwild, CA 92349
(714) 659-2117

Point Sal State Beach
c/o La Purisima Mission SHP
RRFD 102
Lompoc, CA 93436
(805) 733-3713

Santa Monica Mountains
Conservancy
3800 Solstice Canyon #1
Malibu, CA 90265
(213) 456-7154

Santa Monica Mountains District
Headquarters
California Department of Parks and
Recreation
2860-A Camino Dos Rios
Newbury Park, CA 91320
(818) 706-1310

Santa Monica Mountains National
Recreation Area
22900 Ventura Blvd., Suite 140
Woodland Hills, CA 91364
(818) 888-3770

Santiago Oaks Regional Park
2145 North Windes Drive
Orange, CA 92669
(714) 538-4400

Topanga State Park
20829 Entrada Road
Topanga, CA 90290
(213) 455-2465

Torrey Pines State Reserve
12000 N. Torrey Pines Park Road
San Diego, CA 92008
(619) 755-2063

Tucker Wildlife Sanctuary
Star Route, Box 85A
Modjeska, Canyon
Orange, CA 92667
(714) 649-2760

Index /

Great Guides
to the Great Outdoors
from Olympus Press

- *California State Parks Guide*

- *Coast Walks: One Hundred Adventures Along the California Coast*

- *Day Hiker's Guide to Southern California*

- *Day Hiker's Guide to Southern California Volume II*

- *East Mojave Desert: A Visitor's Guide*